Fluorescent Antibody Techniques
and Their Applications

FLUORESCENT ANTIBODY TECHNIQUES
AND
THEIR APPLICATIONS

Edited by
AKIYOSHI KAWAMURA, Jr.
Institute of Medical Science, University of Tokyo

UNIVERSITY OF TOKYO PRESS
Tokyo
UNIVERSITY PARK PRESS

Baltimore, Maryland
&
Manchester, England

Published jointly by
University of Tokyo Press
Tokyo
and
University Park Press
Baltimore and Manchester
LIBRARY OF CONGRESS CATALOG CARD NUMBER 68–58277

269064

FOREWORD

First developed by Professor A. H. Coons, fluorescent antibody techniques and applications have now reached their highest level of achievement. In the Institute of Medical Science at the University of Tokyo, under the leadership of Associate Professor Akiyoshi Kawamura, Jr., the authors of this volume began about sixteen years ago to study the basic fluorescent antibody techniques in their respective fields, maintaining close contact with each other concerning the results of their work.

A number of monographs and reviews have been published introducing the principles and methods, but they have been too concise to give a complete picture of the technique. The authors of this book had only published their results in Japanese where they first had the opportunity to demonstrate their method in the West at a symposium for standardization of fluorescent technique in London under the sponsorship of the IAMS and at a training course for fluorescent antibody techniques in Copenhagen, sponsored by WHO. It was at these two conferences that they received recognition for the superior level of their techniques and were encouraged to publish a fuller explanation in English in book form.

Each section of FLUORESCENT ANTIBODY TECHNIQUES AND THEIR APPLICATIONS is written by the specific scientists involved in the mastery of the technique discussed, thus ensuring the most comprehensive explanation.

This book is not a general introduction but describes rather the specific applications of the fluorescent antibody method. It is hoped that the numerous color pictures will assure the readers that the same results will be obtained if the procedures outlined are followed.

We hope that this volume will contribute significantly to the existing literature on fluorescent antibody techniques and application.

Ayao Yamamoto
Institute of Medical Science
University of Tokyo

PREFACE

Almost two decades have passed since Dr. Albert H. Coons and his co-workers first established the principles of the fluorescent antibody technique. This revolutionary technique, based on more than ten years of investigation, made it possible, by using the specific reactivity of labeled antibody, to locate precisely the corresponding antigen in tissue. Subsequently a number of improvements and refinements were devised, giving this simple and reproducible technique a degree of specificity and sensitivity which has led to its increasing application in a variety of fields, including immunology, microbiology, pathology, histology and clinical diagnostics.

A number of monographs and articles dealing with the theoretical and practical aspects of this technique have been published to date, but most of these have dealt with specific applications rather than the general methodology of the technique itself. Our fluorescent antibody (FA) study group at the Institute of Medical Science began work on synthesizing a fluorescent dye, fluorescein isocyanate, more than ten years ago. When Riggs and others succeeded in synthesizing the dye and it had become readily available to us, we directed our efforts to eliminating nonspecific fluorescence—the most troublesome problem encountered in using the fluorescent antibody technique. The problem, both in terms of antigen and antibody, could be approached only on the basis of the extensive knowledge accumulated over the years by the members of the Institute and through their multi-disciplinary cooperation. A number of important improvements in the optical system were also achieved by the physicists of our staff. The total number of contributors to these studies was well over 180. The improved technique which resulted from these investigations can now be used to achieve fluorescent antibody staining with a minimum of nonspecific fluorescence and a maximum of clarity and excellence.

The details of our method were presented at a meeting of the Training Course of the FA Technique, organized by WHO in Copenhagen in 1965, and have subsequently been discussed with many investigators here and abroad. We have at present determined to publish them in the hope that they will be of value to other workers and that they will stimulate further research on methodology.

The present book is divided into two sections: the first includes theories and the general method, the second describes specific applications. The first section was written by the core of our study group, namely the editor, Assoc. Prof. Kawamura and Prof. Matsuhashi, Drs. Kawashima (immunology) and Nakamura (immunochemistry), Prof. Kusano, Assoc. Prof. Aoyama and Dr. Hayashi (pathology), and Mr. Wada (optics). The second section was also written by members of our group, all leading authorities in their fields in Japan, and is based on actual experiments and methods which we devised. We have used as many color photographs as possible to illustrate particular points in these chapters.

Some sections of the book were originally written in Japanese and were translated by Assoc. Prof. Watanabe with the cooperation of Dr. Ebisawa. The entire manuscript has been revised by Mrs. Annik L. Chamberlain, the second section by Prof. Ishikawa, and part of the first by Dr. Colin. Their dedicated labor is greatly appreciated. Much valuable advice and a number of useful suggestions were obtained on the general plan and various aspects of this book from Profs. Yamamoto and Tsunematsu; Mr. Noda kindly provided assistance with the photographic techniques. I would also like to express my cordial thanks to Mr. Shigeo Minowa for his help in furthering the publication of this book.

Institute of Medical Science
University of Tokyo
March, 1969

A. Kawamura, Jr.
Editor

LIST OF PARTICIPANTS

PART I

Y. AOYAMA — Department of Pathology, Institute of Medical Science, University of Tokyo

K. HAYASHI — Department of Pathology, Institute of Medical Science, University of Tokyo

A. KAWAMURA, Jr. — Department of Immunology, Institute of Medical Science, University of Tokyo

H. KAWASHIMA — Immunological Section, Research Laboratory, Eiken Chemical Co. Ltd., Tokyo

N. KUSANO — Department of Pathology, Institute of Medical Science, University of Tokyo

T. MATSUHASHI — Department of Allergology, Institute of Medical Science, University of Tokyo

H. NAKAMURA — Department of Physical Biochemistry, Institute of Medical Science, University of Tokyo

K. WADA — Tiyoda Optical Company Ltd., Tokyo

PART II

Y. AOYAMA — Department of Pathology, Institute of Medical Science, University of Tokyo

I. EBISAWA — Department of Internal Medicine, Institute of Medical Science, University of Tokyo

K. FUJIWARA — Department of Veterinary Medicine, Institute of Medical Science, University of Tokyo

K. HAYASHI — Department of Pathology, Institute of Medical Science, University of Tokyo

M. HOTCHI — Department of Pathology, Faculty of Medicine, Shinsyu University

T. IIDA — Central Research Laboratories, Sankyo Company Ltd., Tokyo

M. KANAMITSU — Department of Hygiene, Sapporo Medical College

A. KASAMAKI — Department of Hygiene, Sapporo Medical College

Y. KATSUTA — Department of Physical Therapy and Medicine, Faculty of Medicine, University of Tokyo

N. KUSANO — Department of Pathology, Institute of Medical Science, University of Tokyo

T. MATSUHASHI	Department of Allergology, Institute of Medical Science, University of Tokyo
K. MIZUOKA	Serological Section of Central Clinical Laboratory, University of Tokyo Hospital
T. MOTOHASHI	Nippon Institute for Biological Science, Tachikawa
Y. MURATA	Central Research Laboratories, Sankyo Company Ltd., Tokyo
H. NAGAHAMA	Department of Pediatrics, Tokyo University Branch Hospital
T. NAGASAWA	The Third Department of Internal Medicine, Faculty of Medicine, University of Tokyo
H. NAKAGAWA	National Veterinary Assay Laboratory, Kokubunji
S. NAKAMURA	Department of Internal Medicine, Institute of Medical Science, University of Tokyo
K. S. NAKANO	Department of Bacterial Infection, Institute of Medical Science, University of Tokyo
H. OGAWA	Division of Pathology of Infectious Disease, Department of Pathology, N.I.H.
M. OGAWA	Department of Hygiene, Sapporo Medical College
S. OTANI	Department of Internal Medicine, Institute of Medical Science, University of Tokyo
K. OTSUBO	Department of Carcinogenesis and Cancer Susceptibility, Institute of Medical Science, University of Tokyo
I. SAITO	Department of Neurosurgery, Faculty of Medicine, University of Tokyo
M. SAWADA	National Veterinary Assay Laboratory, Kokubunji
S. SHIBATA	The Third Department of Internal Medicine, Faculty of Medicine, University of Tokyo
H. SHIMOJO	Department of Tumor Viruses, Institute of Medical Science, University of Tokyo
I. TADOKORO	Department of Bacteriology, Yokohama City University
Y. TSUNEMATSU	Department of Bacterial Infection, Institute of Medical Science, University of Tokyo
T. USHIZIMA	Nippon Institute for Biological Science, Tachikawa (Died)
M. USUI	Department of Allergology, Institute of Medical Science, University of Tokyo
H. YAMAMOTO	Department of Enteroviruses, N.I.H.
T. YOKOYAMA	Institute for Fermentation, Osaka

CONTENTS

Foreword   v

Preface   vii

List of participants   ix

Part I

Chapter I   Introduction 3

Chapter II   Synopsis of the Fluorescent Antibody Technique 5

  1 Historical Review 5

  2 Principle 5

  3 Characteristics of the Fluorescent Antibody Technique 6

    A Specificity 6

    B Rapidity 7

    C Sensitivity 7

  4 Prerequisites 7

    A Antigen 7

    B Antibody 8

    C Fluorochrome 8

    D Conditions of Reaction 8

    E Control Specimens 8

    F Observation 9

  5 Problems 9

    A Autofluorescence 9

    B Extraneous Specific Fluorescence 9

    C Nonspecific Fluorescence 9

  6 Application 10

    A Outline of the Technique 10

Chapter III Preparation of Materials 11

  1 Preparation of Immune Serum 11

    A Immunogen 11

    B Method of Immunization 17

    C Examination of Antibodies 19

  2 Purification of Antibody 22

    A The Purification of γG-globulin 23

    B Zone Electrophoresis 25

    C Chromatographic Purification with Cellulose Ion-exchangers 26

    D Gel Filtration 29

  3 Preparation of Labeled Antibody 33

    A Fluorescent Dyes 33

    B Method of Labeling 38

    C The Properties of Fluorescent Antibody 47

    D Absorption with Tissue Powder 50

    E Storage of the Labeled Antibody 52

  4 Preparation of Substrates and Fixation 53

xii

   A   Slides and Cover Slips 53
   B   Tissue Sections 54
   C   Smear and Impression Preparations 59
   D   Preparation of Tissue Culture Cells 60
   E   Fixation (Pretreatment) 60

√ Chapter IV   Staining Methods 66
   1   Conditions 66
   2   Direct Method 66
     A   Procedure 66
     B   The Mounting Medium 69
   3   Indirect Method 70
   4   Complement Method 72
   5   Specific Staining Procedures 72
     A   Double Staining 72
     B   Counterstaining 72
     C   Combination with Routine Staining 73
   6   Controls 73
   7   Preservation of Stained Specimens 74
   8   Evaluation of Results 74

√ Chapter V   Fluorescence Microscopy 75
   1   Optical Principles : Dark-field Fluorescence Microscopy 75
   2   Immersion and Dry Dark-field Systems 76
   3   Background Contrast 76
   4   The Fluorescence Microscope 77
     A   Excitation Systems 77
     B   Light Source 78
     C   Lamp Housing 80
     D   Dark-field Condenser 81
     E   Microscope Stage 83
     F   Objectives 84
     G   Eyepieces 85
     H   Barrier Filter Holder 85
   5   Fluorescence Photomicrography 85
     A   Selection of Films 86
     B   Photomicrographic Apparatus 86
     C   Magnification 86
     D   Exposure Time 86
     E   Stability 87
General References 88
Reference 89

Part II

Chapter VI   Application of the Fluorescent Antibody Techniques 93
   1   Pox Virus 93
   2   Adeno Virus 94
   3   Herpes Group Viruses 95
     A   Herpes Simplex Virus 95
     B   Varicella-Zoster Virus 98
     C   Cytomegalovirus 100

4   Influenza Virus 104
5   HVJ 109
6   Mumps Virus 114
7   Measles Virus 115
8   Canine Distemper Virus 119
9   Rinderpest Virus 120
10 Hog Cholera Virus 122
11 Rabies Virus 123
12 Coxsackie Viruses 126
13 Poliomyelitis Virus 129
14 Japanese Encephalitis Virus 132
15 Tumor Antigen 137
16 Tobacco Mosaic Virus 146
17 Tsutsugamushi Disease Rickettsia 151
18 Staphylococci : An Approach to Analysis of Microbial Structure, Invasion
    of α-Toxin into Ehrlich Ascites Tumor Cells and Formation of Kidney Abs-
    cesses in Mice 154
19 Gonorrhea 156
20 Shigella 160
21 Bordetella Pertussis 162
22 Mycoplasma 164
23 Syphilis Treponema 166
24 Tyzzer's Disease 174
25 Mycotic Infections 176
26 Toxoplasma 181
27 Systemic Lupus Erythematosus 186
28 Nephrotoxic Serum Nephritis 190
29 Pulseless Disease 195
30 " Unwanted " Specific Fluorescence 196

PART I

CHAPTER I

INTRODUCTION

For a long time, it was a far reaching dream for many workers engaging in biomedical research to visualize the distribution and localization of antigen in tissue and cells directly under the microscope. Although the presence of antigenic material in tissue can be deduced, with more or less certainty, by histochemical or physical methods depending upon the nature of the antigen, it was indispensable to develop a new method which could trace antigen by the specific combination of the corresponding labeled antibody, in order to identify the specific antigen and to learn about its distribution *in situ*.

The dream came true with the development of techniques for using several kinds of labeled antibodies, such as fluorescent antibody and antibody labeled with ^{131}I or with ferritin. Although the latter two methods have certain advantages, autoradiography is necessary with ^{131}I-antibody and the ferritin-labeled antibody along with electron microscopy. For general use, therefore, the fluorescent antibody technique has the advantage of being a relatively simple and rapid procedure.

Within a very short period after its discovery by Coons and his co-workers, the fluorescent antibody (FA) technique was being applied to a variety of biomedical problems. The technique is based on the successful conjugation of antibody with a dye of high quantum yield without denaturation. In the original method a new dye, fluorescein, with an intense greenish yellow fluorescence, was used instead of azo-dyes and conjugated with antibody through carbamide bonding in place of diazo-bonding in order to minimize the denaturation of antibody. Fluorescein isocyanate, however, is so labile that its synthesis is difficult. Hence, attention was focused on the synthesis of some other dye which would be less problematical.

Meanwhile, Riggs and others succeeded in devising a method for synthesizing fluorescein isothiocyanate which could largely fulfill the various demands of workers; subsequently its crystallization was achieved in the Baltimore Biological Laboratory. Popular use of the FA technique started only after the dye became available commercially. A simple and efficient method of conjugating the dye without denaturation and of purifying the conjugate was established by investigators following advances in immunochemistry. Improved methods of pretreating or fixing tissue sections also brought about further refinements in the technique.

These manifold improvements resulted in the successful elimination of nonspecific fluorescence, the most serious flaw in the technique. Together with improvements in the optical system, these developments have largely nullified the requirement for special skills in using the FA technique and have made it suitable for general use in the laboratory.

The first part of this book gives the theory and the general characteristics and critical points of the FA technique. The preparation of materials, staining methods, and microscopic observation of the stained preparations are all described in detail. All of these methods are the product of our own investigations, and we have tried to organize them so as to provide a clear and useful guide for the actual laboratory use of this technique. In the second part, some of the results which we obtained by the application of our methods to specific tissues are illustrated with photographs, many of them in color. We hope that these will provide additional information and also evidence that the FA technique can be carried out successfully by anyone with a minimum of training in cytology.

CHAPTER II

SYNOPSIS OF THE FLUORESCENT ANTIBODY TECHNIQUE

1. Historical Review

Classical histochemistry aims at visualizing and differentiating nucleic acids, enzymes, fats and microorganisms. Immunohistochemistry is an advanced technique of histochemistry which uses antigen-antibody systems with high specificity. Antibodies used as specific staining agents for antigen in tissue or cells are not, however, visible unless tagged with a tracer such as dye or isotope. This technique was attempted by Reiner (1930)[25] and Heidelberger et al. (1933)[15] more than 35 years ago with azo-dyes, but did not achieve general use because of its low sensitivity.

Hopkins et al. (1933),[17] Fieser et al. (1939)[11] and Creech et al. (1941)[10] tried using fluorescent substances as tracers, but they were too deleterious to the antibody itself to be acceptable. In 1941–42, Coons et al.[6,7] succeeded for the first time in tracing pneumococcus soluble polysaccharide antigen in tissue sections of mice infected with pneumococcus, using a fluorescein labeled antibody. In 1950 they developed a new fluorescein isocyanate to label the antibody globulin, and thus paved the way for the modern development of the fluorescent antibody technique.[8] Later refinements were contributed by Riggs et al. (1958)[26] in the synthesis of fluorescein isothiocyanate (FITC), which can easily be conjugated to globulin (Marshall et al., 1958),[19] and by Goldstein et al. (1960)[13] in the use of gel filtration and column chromatography for the purification of labeled antibody.

Other methods used in immunohistochemistry, such as autoradiography and the ferritin antibody technique,[29,30] are also now available. The former is more sensitive than the fluorescent antibody technique, but the specimen must be reacted with sensitive emulsion for a few days in order to observe distribution of radioactive grains and the location of antigen within the tissue or cells is difficult. The latter also has numerous technical disadvantages, especially non-specific binding, but it is useful for ultrastructure studies and localization of antigen. In many cases in medical and biological research, combined use of these methods can be most rewarding.

2. Principle

The fluorescent antibody technique combines histochemical and immunological methods to pinpoint specific antigen-antibody complexes present in tissue sections or cellular smears with the aid of fluorochrome substances conjugated to the antibody. Fluorochromes and ultraviolet light sources are the mainstay of the techniques. A fluorochrome is a substance which emits light of longer wavelength than the exciting radiation. This is called fluorescence when the substance emits light only while it is being excited, and phosphorescence when the light continues to be emitted even after the energy source has been cut off. Fluorescent substances can be tagged or conjugated to the antibody globulin without interfering with its immunological specificity and its ability to combine with antigen.

When tissues or cells containing a particular antigen, e.g. influenza A2 virus, are stained with its specific fluorescein-conjugated antibody and examined under a fluorescence microscope, only cells containing or infected with influenza A2 virus fluoresce. (This procedure is the direct method; see Fig. 1.) Cells infected with influenza B virus will not fluoresce at all if the fluorescent antibody has been carefully checked for specificity and is appropriately diluted. The fluorescent antibody technique is applicable to any antigenic substance, either within the cells or outside them——protozoa, bacteria, rickettsia, viruses, tissue antigens, hormones and enzymes.

Cells containing a particular antibody can also be stained with its specific fluorescein-labeled antigen; this procedure is called the fluorescent antigen technique. In practice, however, the structure and physicochemical properties of antigens are so varied that the labeling conditions must be examined in every case. If serum protein is the antigen, the same method of conjugation as that used in the fluorescent antibody technique (antibody staining method) can be applied, although technically this is known as the fluorescent antigen technique.

Another method used in the fluorescent antibody technique is the indirect method (Fig. 1). First, an unknown antibody is reacted with a known antigen (serological diagnosis) or an unlabeled antibody is reacted with a known or unknown antigen; these antibodies are called primary antibodies. In the second step, the serum globulin of the antigen-antibody complex formed is stained with specific antiglobulin conjugate (secondary antibody). If specific fluorescence is detected, we have indirect evidence of the presence of the specific antigen-antibody complex formed in the first step (application of the Coombs test).

There is still another method, the complement method, in which the antigen-antibody-complement complex is stained with specific anti-complement conjugate.

3. CHARACTERISTICS OF THE FLUORESCENT ANTIBODY TECHNIQUE

A. Specificity

The antibody globulin with which the fluorochrome substance is conjugated is a protein which has a highly specific reactivity for antigen. Fluorescent antibody staining with this globulin is, therefore, highly specific and affects only the

Principle and Procedure of Fluorescent Antibody Techniques

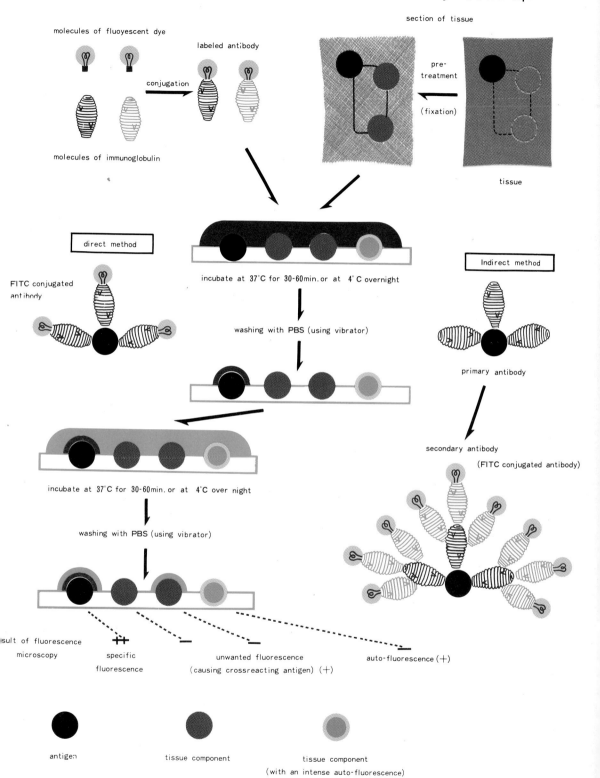

Fig.1

antigen (bacterial, viral, tissue or cellular) to which the antibody has been prepared. Hence it is possible to localize virus antigen within the cells, or to confirm the relation between the inclusion body and virus particles.

B. Rapidity

The staining procedure and microscopic examination can be completed in one to two hours. Japanese encephalitis virus antigen from human brains, rabies virus antigen from dog brains, or influenza virus antigen in nasal smears can be identified in one to two hours after the specimen is sent to the laboratory. This is much more rapid than the isolation of viruses or serological tests, which often take more than one or two weeks.

C. Sensitivity

The sensitivity of the direct fluorescent antibody technique is very similar to that of the complement fixation test, but differs from the neutralization or hemagglutination tests. The precipitin reaction B method also corresponds to that of the antibody dilution technique but not to that of the antigen dilution technique. It is impossible to determine the exact sensitivity of the method because the strength of the specific fluorescence cannot be measured quantitatively. With this technique the labeled antibody is used in excess and only two units of primary antibody can detect the antigen in sufficient amounts. Hence, the sensitivity of the technique depends on the amount of antigen. Coons (1956)[9] stated that the concentration of pneumococcal capsular polysaccharide must be at least 0.8×40^{-4} μg/mm^2 to be detected by the fluorescent antibody technique. Pressman et al. (1958)[24] suggested a similar figure of 1.4×10^{-4} μg/mm^2 for the antigen concentration in a tissue segment 5 microns thick.

The sensitivities of the indirect and complement method of the fluorescent antibody technique are about 5–10 times higher than that of the direct method.

4. PREREQUISITES

A. Antigen

The material must be prepared so that the antigen loses little or none of its reactivity and is made accessible to the antibody. The pretreatment or fixation of the material is intended to keep the antigenic material fixed firmly on the slide as well as to remove fats and other substances which interfere with the antigen-antibody reaction. Sometimes, however, fixation may enhance auto- and nonspecific fluorescence, or untreated material may be better for observation. Preparation and observation of appropriate control materials are indispensable in these cases.

The concentration of antigen in the material must be high enough to be detected by the technique, or else the most carefully prepared material will still be unsatisfactory for observation.

B. Antibody

A highly potent and specific fluorescent antibody with very weak negative charge is needed. The starting antiserum must have a high titer and should contain little or no antibody for the tissues which are to be examined. If the antiserum contains antibody for normal tissues, this must be absorbed with a preparation of the particular tissue or acetone-dried powder of other organs (see p. 50). Adequate dilution of the antibody will obviate this procedure when the antibody titer of the serum is very high. The immunizing antigen should also contain little or no normal tissue substances, and the animal should not be infected with the particular agent or any related agent.

Antibody globulin prepared from this antiserum must keep its antibody titer and be free from degenerate albumin and α-globulin, and the negative charge of the final fluorescent antibody must be as weak as possible. The negative charge of the protein molecule increases as more fluorochrome substance is conjugated with it, resulting in nonspecific adsorption to the normal tissue or increased nonspecific fluorescence. A proper ratio of fluorochrome substance to protein molecule (F/P molar ratio) is approximately 1 to 2.

Labeled and unlabeled globulins of the same antibody titer differ in that the former are more weakly charged. This is readily shown in electrophoresis by the greater mobility towards the anode of the labeled globulin and is utilized in DEAE cellulose chromatographic separation of two substances. Unlabeled globulin, on the other hand, reacts with antigen faster than labeled globulin and this characteristic is used in the one-step inhibition test.

C. Fluorochrome

Fluorochrome substances used in this technique should conjugate easily and combine firmly with antibody globulin, should not interfere with antibody reactivity on conjugation, should be stable, have a good quantum yield (fluorescence efficiency), and have as much difference as possible between the maximal absorption and maximal emission wavelengths.

D. Conditions of Reaction

Dilution of the fluorescent antibody, time and temperature of staining, pH of buffered saline and washing must be checked carefully. The staining titer must be determined beforehand with known tissue preparations containing a sufficient amount of antigen, and the working dilution should contain 2 to 4 staining untis.

E. Control Specimens

The following controls are required to ensure specificity of the staining reactions. Antigens: untreated or uninfected tissue, fixed unstained tissue, and tissue containing heterologous antigen. None of these controls should show fluorescence on microscopy. Antibody: one-step or two-step inhibition tests, staining with heterologous antibody or normal globulins labeled with fluorochrome. Removal of specific fluorescence following absorption of fluorescent antibody with homologous antigen should be confirmed.

F. Observation

A high-pressure mercury lamp, various filters and a microscope with a dark-field condenser to which photographic equipment can be readily attached are necessary for proper fluorescence microscopy and photography. The visual field must be wide, bright, and evenly illuminated and the contrast must be sharp. Correct adjustment of the ultraviolet light pathway, proper selection of filters, proper placement of condensers, and appropriate exposure times are, of course, essential.

5. PROBLEMS

Three problems complicate fluorescence microscopy at the present time.

A. Autofluorescence

The natural fluorescence due to the tissue or cell itself is called autofluorescence. It is either white or blue-violet and can be readily differentiated from specific fluorescence. Thick folded tissues are likely to show autofluorescence. It is also induced by formalin fixation and embedding in paraffin.

B. Extraneous Specific Fluorescence

This type of fluorescence occurs when the immunizing antigen is impure and contains antigenic contaminants such as protein or heterologous antigen, or when the animal is infected with some microorganisms. It cannot be removed by the usual absorption with normal tissues. Antibody to Sendai virus due to natural infection is found, for example, in sera of most stocks of mice in Japan. When anti-Japanese encephalitis serum prepared with these mice is conjugated with fluorescein isothiocyanate and used to localize the virus antigen, respiratory epithelial cells not infected with Japanese encephalitis virus will nevertheless show specific fluorescence. This merely indicates the presence of Sendai virus antigen in the respiratory epithelium and has nothing to do with the distribution of Japanese encephalitis virus in mice.

Natural infection of experimental animals with PPLO can also occur.

C. Nonspecific Fluorescence

Nonspecific fluorescence may come from the fluorochrome substance, from antibody with too strong a negative charge, from improper fixation of the tissue, or from letting the specimen dry out during the staining procedure.

It was a major problem with Coons' fluorescein isocyanate (FIC) but occurs much less frequently with fluorescein isothiocyanate (FITC).

Careful control of the concentrations of globulin and FITC, of the reaction time and temperature and of purification of the conjugate by gel filtration and

DEAE cellulose column chromatography reduces the possibility of nonspecific fluorescence. Use of a high titer antiserum, careful salting out of globulin fractions from the serum to remove non-antibody protein and to prevent degeneration of proteins, absorption with acetone-treated organ powders and proper dilution of the conjugate provide further insurance for specificity.

6. APPLICATION

The fluorescent antibody technique has applications in microbiology, immunology, pathology, histology, allergology and almost every field of medical and veterinary science for the identification and localization of etiological agents in tissues and cells. It is extremely useful for rapid diagnoses of many viral, rickettsial, bacterial and protozoan infections. It can also be used in cases of bacterial agglutination (*Neisseria*, etc.) and precipitin reaction (TMV, etc.) where it is difficult to read the reaction when carried out by normal methods. A positive reaction gives a fluorescent aggregate of bacterial cells against a dark background whereas spontaneous agglutination results in an even distribution of fluorescence.

A. Outline of the Technique

The fluorescent antibody technique can be summarized as shown in Fig. 2. A detailed discussion of the procedures is given in the following chapters.

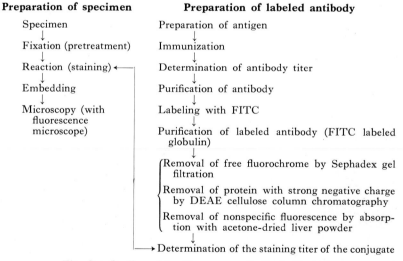

Fig. 2.   Outline of the Fluorescent Antibody Technique

CHAPTER III

PREPARATION OF MATERIALS

1. Preparation of Immune Serum

A. Immunogen

The immunogen must be free from extraneous antigens and contain as little unwanted "normal" tissue antigen as possible. However, in the preparation of labeled secondary antibody in the indirect method, both γG-globulin (see p. 23) and whole globulin fractions must be used. In the complement method, antibody to complement itself is required as the secondary antibody, and antibody to guinea pig γ-globulin should not be substituted.

To avoid the production of antibody to normal tissue, the adult animal may be immunized with antigen prepared from tissue of the same species. Influenza virus antibody prepared in adult fowls with antigen from the infected allantoic fluid of embryonated hens' eggs, or measles antibody prepared in monkeys by immunizing with virus from monkey kidney tissue culture are examples of useful antibodies relatively free from antibody to normal tissues.

(a) Preparation of whole globulin fraction for the secondary antibody in the indirect method.

Preparation of serum globulins

Salting out with neutral saturated ammonium sulfate is the usual method for preparing globulin fractions of serum.

Materials

Serum or plasma

Normal saline or phosphate buffered saline (PBS): NaCl 8g, KCl 0.2g, anhydrous Na_2HPO_4 1.15g, KH_2PO_4 0.2g, dissolved in 1 l of distilled water, pH 7.4. (A 10 times concentrated stock solution of PBS without NaCl is usually prepared and diluted and the NaCl added just before use.)

0.5 M $BaCl_2$ solution or Nessler's reagent

Saturated ammonium sulfate solution (pH 7.0)

Magnetic stirrer

High-speed centrifuge (kept in a cold room or refrigerated)

Cellophane tube

Preparation of saturated ammonium sulfate solution

As it takes several hours for the ammonium sulfate solution to become fully saturated, it must be prepared in advance. About 400 g of chemically pure or reagent grade ammonium sulfate powder is dissolved in 500 ml of water which has been heated to 70–80°C. The solution is stirred for about 20 minutes and allowed to cool down to room temperature.   Crystals of ammonium sulfate will form at the bottom of the vessel while the supernatant will be saturated ($d = 1.245$ at 25°C).   The pH should be about 5 and should be adjusted to 7.0 with 28% ammonium and a 1:2 dilution of sulfuric acid.   The solution is filtered before use.

Some lots of ammonium sulfate may contain undesirable iron which must be removed.   This is done in the following manner: Adjust the pH of the solution to 8–9 with 28% ammonium solution and heat.   The resulting red-brown precipitate is filtered off and the pH of the filtrate is brought back to 7 with sulfuric acid.   In the case of salting out, the concentration of salt is indicated by the degree of saturation (1/2 or 50% saturation, etc.).   Usually the degree of saturation expresses the ratio of total volume to saturated salt solution in the protein solution (the exact concentration of a 50% saturated solution would be about 41% salt solution in a fixed volume of water).

The salting out procedure

This procedure is best carried out in a cold room at 2–4°C.   It may be done at room temperature, however, if the material is not left for too long.   When the starting material is plasma, the fibrinogen should be removed first at 20% saturation before salting out at 50% saturation.   Serum can be salted out immediately.   All materials used in salting out should be cooled before the procedure is begun.   The detailed treatment for serum is given below as an example of the procedure.

The serum is diluted two-fold with saline (to insure a better yield), poured into a flask and stirred gently to avoid foaming.   An equal volume of saturated ammonium sulfate solution is added drop by drop using a burette.   A thick white precipitate will form following this procedure.   The mixture is allowed to stand for 30 minutes or longer (the longer the better) to obtain maximal precipitation.

The mixture is then centrifuged at 9,000 rpm for 15 minutes, the supernatant is decanted, and the sediment is dissolved in its original volume of PBS (or saline) by repeated pipetting with a Pasteur pipette (Fig. 3).   PBS is preferable to saline for this purpose as there is less protein denaturation.   The PBS should be added to the precipitate a little at a time, and care should be taken to recover as much precipitate as possible.

The precipitation with ammonium sulfate is repeated three times in all and the final globulin precipitate is dissolved in as small a volume of PBS as possible to facilitate further procedures.   The final globulin solution is dialyzed in a cellophane tube in the cold room against tap water for 2 to 10 minutes and then against saline or PBS, with constant stirring of the outer fluid.   The outer fluid is replaced 3 to 5 times daily and the dialysis is continued until all SO_4^{--} ions or NH_4^{++} ions are removed (as indicated by the addition of $BaCl_2$ solution or Nessler's reagent, respectively).   Addition of $BaCl_2$ will cause formation of a white precipitate when phosphate ions are present but the turbidity disappears on acidification with hydrochloric acid.   It is also possible to remove the ammonium

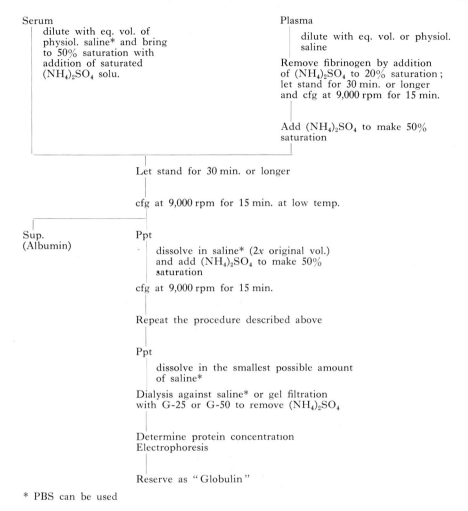

Serum
> dilute with eq. vol. of
> physiol. saline* and bring
> to 50% saturation with
> addition of saturated
> $(NH_4)_2SO_4$ solu.

Plasma
> dilute with eq. vol. or physiol.
> saline

Remove fibrinogen by addition
of $(NH_4)_2SO_4$ to 20% saturation ;
let stand for 30 min. or longer
and cfg at 9,000 rpm for 15 min.

Add $(NH_4)_2SO_4$ to make 50%
saturation

Let stand for 30 min. or longer

cfg at 9,000 rpm for 15 min. at low temp.

Sup.
(Albumin)

Ppt
> dissolve in saline* (2x original vol.)
> and add $(NH_4)_2SO_4$ to make 50%
> saturation

cfg at 9,000 rpm for 15 min.

Repeat the procedure described above

Ppt
> dissolve in the smallest possible amount
> of saline*

Dialysis against saline* or gel filtration
with G-25 or G-50 to remove $(NH_4)_2SO_4$

Determine protein concentration
Electrophoresis

Reserve as "Globulin"

* PBS can be used

Fig. 3. Fractionation of Serum Globulin

sulfate by Sephadex gel filtration instead of dialysis.

Following dialysis, any remaining precipitates in the globulin solution are centrifuged off. The resulting solution should be checked for its protein concentration (preferably by the Microkjeldahl method, Folin reaction, biurette reaction, or simply, by spectrophotometry or a protein refractometer) and for its chemical properties by immuno- or paper-electrophoresis (see p. 23, if γG-globulin fraction is required as immunogen).

The final product is stored in test tubes at 4°C or labeled immediately with fluorescein isothiocyanate.

(b) Preparation of antigen for immunization with antigen-antibody complex.

Since the light chains of γG-, γA-, and γM-globulin have common antigenic determinants, antisera against these highly purified globulin fractions cross-react with each other.   It is rather cumbersome and time-consuming to prepare non-cross-reacting antisera by the absorption technique, but the following immunization method can frequently be used instead.

In this method, a γG, γA, or γM rich fraction is first obtained by DEAE cellulose chromatography, and the antibody contained in these fractions is reacted with the corresponding antigen to form insoluble antigen-antibody complex which is used as immunizing antigen after washing to remove non-antibody proteins.   In most cases, the anti-γG-globulin serum obtained contains only anti-γ chain antibody.   An outline of this method is given below.

(b-i)   Preparation of anti-γG-globulin antiserum.

(i)   The first step is to find a human serum with a high-titer natural antibody to rabbit red cells.   Usually, in ten test sera, several will show titers higher than 64.   Aliquots of such sera are dialyzed against 0.0175 M phosphate buffer, pH 6.3–6.5.   The equilibrated sera are then applied to a DEAE cellulose column previously equilibrated with the same buffer.

The chromatographic fraction obtained is rich in γG-globulin and usually contains only a very small amount of other components, an occasional contaminant in later fractions being haptoglobin or transferrin.   This fraction is titrated against 2% rabbit red cell suspension, and the solution in a concentration 4 times the final agglutination titer is mixed and reacted with an equal volume of 2% rabbit red cell suspension.   About 0.5 ml of packed red cells per animal is required.   The reaction is allowed to proceed at 0°C for 1 hour.   The red cells are washed 3 times and finally suspended in saline to make a 50% suspension. One ml of this sensitized red cell suspension is mixed with an equal amount of Freund's complete adjuvant and injected intracutaneously into the toes in roughly equal amounts.   Three to four weeks later, subcutaneous injections without adjuvant are given.   Blood taken 1 week after this booster injection usually yields pure anti-γG-globulin antibody containing only anti-heavy chain antibody without contamination from anti-light chain antibody.

(ii)   Another method is to immunize animals with immunoprecipitates formed by the reaction of VDRL antigen with a γG-globulin antibody (reagin) prepared by DEAE cellulose column chromatography of syphilitic sera.   In this case also, about 300 μg of reaginic protein with adjuvant is injected into the animal followed by a subcutaneous booster injection without adjuvant.   Blood taken after an interval of 1 week will yield pure anti-γG-globulin antibody.   When examined by immunoelectrophoresis, an additional line is sometimes found inside the γG-globulin line; this line probably indicates the presence of an immunoglobulin, but remains as yet unidentified.

(b-ii)   Preparation of anti-γA-globulin antiserum.

The isolation of pure γA-globulin is very difficult.   Usually, this globulin is obtained by the salting out method and DEAE cellulose chromatography from the serum, rich in γA myeloma protein, of a A-multiple myeloma patient, and is used as the immunizing antigen.   Intracutaneous injection of 1 to 5 mg of γA myeloma protein mixed with Freund's complete adjuvant into laboratory animals will almost invariably produce anti-γA-globulin. The antibodies to β and γG-globulins concurrently produced can be removed by absorption with umbilical cord serum.

When myeloma protein is not available, combination immunization can be used as in the preparation of anti γG-globulin. The γA-globulin is prepared from group O, A or B human milk by the salting out method and a DEAE cellulose column at about 0.08 M, pH 7.0 (stepwise elution). Fractions with the corresponding red cell-agglutinating activity are pooled. The preparation of antigen and the immunization are carried out as described in the preceding section. In this method, however, absorption with A, B and O red cells is required because of the inevitable concurrent production of antibodies against human red cells.

It may also be possible to carry out the immunization with the immunoprecipitates from the reaction of VDRL antigen with similar chromatographic fractions of syphilitic sera.

(b-iii) Preparation of anti-γM-globulin antiserum

Since only a small amount of γM-globulin is present in serum, it is difficult to isolate in a pure state. When serum from a patient with Waldenström disease is available, γM-globulin can be prepared with relative ease by subjecting the serum to gel filtration through a Sephadex G200 column, followed by DEAE cellulose chromatography. Otherwise, combination immunization is the simplest and most convenient method.

(i) γM-globulin is eluted after the γG and γA fractions, at about 0.12 M, pH 7.0, in DEAE cellulose column chromatography. Rabbit red cells are sensitized with this γM fraction at a concentration 4 times the minimum agglutinating dose, which can be determined by the procedure described above. EDTA should be added to the sensitizing solution to prevent hemolysis. The sensitized red cells are washed twice with saline and finaly adjusted to 50% concentration. Each rabbit is inoculated with 1 ml of this antigen combined with Freund's complete adjuvant in the same way as described above. A booster injection may be given 3 to 4 weeks later. After an interval of 1 to 2 weeks, anti- γM-globulin antibody can usually be found in serum by immunoelectrophoretic analysis. An additional booster injection should be given if no anti-γM-globulin is found. With these methods, the desired antibody can be produced in almost all animals used for immunization. Occasionally anti-γG and/or anti-γA antibodies are found in the antiserum in addition to anti-γM antibody. These unwanted antibodies are in large measure directed against the common light chain antigens and can be absorbed with γG-globulin (chromatographic fraction) at the optimal ratio, thus yielding almost homogeneous anti-γM-globulin antibody.

(ii) Similar γM-globulin fractions from syphilitic patients can be used to prepare immune precipitates with VDRL antigen. Anti-γM-globulin antibody can be obtained by immunization with the precipitates. The anti-light chain antibodies produced along with the anti-μ chain antibody can also be removed by absorption with γG-globulin at the optimal ratio.

(c) Preparation of immunizing antigen in the production of antibody for complement staining.

The complement staining method developed by Goldwasser et al.[14] is a modification of the indirect method, using secondary antibody against the complement fixed to the antigen-antibody complex. Theoretically, this method is applicable to all immunologic reactions requiring complement; it is simple in that it requires only anti-complement antibody, and is quite sensitive as well.

Although few difficulties are encountered and a clear contrast is obtained with this method in relatively simple systems such as viruses in tissue culture, there are a number of problems in systems with multiple and complex components, such as tissue sections, often giving rise to a positive reaction (non-specific fluorescence) in the control staining with complement alone. This stems from the fact that the labeled anti-complement antibody which is generally used is produced by labeling anti-guinea pig γ-globulin, which is far less specific than the true anti-complement antibody. Recent efforts have been made to prepare true anti-complement antibody and to perfect the method.

Research has revealed the presence of several new C′3 components (C′ 3, 5, 6, 7, 8, 9) in addition to the classic C′1, 4 and 2 components. These components have as yet not been isolated in a chemically pure state, however, and several species of antibodies are commonly produced by immunization with any one of them even after fairly exhaustive purification. It is therefore difficult to show a definite relationship between these C′ components and their antibodies. Nevertheless, it is possible to prepare anti-complement antibodies which show several precipitin lines when examined by immunoelectrophoresis by the following procedure: Bovine serum albumin (BSA) is mixed with rabbit anti-BSA antibody in the presence of guinea pig complement. Several hundred μg protein of this antigen-antibody-complement complex is injected subcutaneously into rabbits, followed by a booster injection with an equal amount of the complex.

Although less is known about the role of the components of human complement than about those of guinea pig complement, they have an important role in immunologic reactions. It has been ascertained that β_{1C}- and β_{1E}-globulins are absorbed by the antigen-antibody complex. Muller-Eberhard and others[22] have suggested that the former is C′3 and the latter C′4. Although there is some ambiguity on this point, it is known that these antibodies are produced only on immunization with immunoprecipitates to which complement is fixed. Moreover, the properties of these complement components are modified by the antigen antibody reaction. β_{1C}-globulin is transformed into $\beta_{1A(G)}$-globulin when immunoprecipitates are added, and β_{1E}-globulin is adsorbed on the immunoprecipitates, indicating that it is a component of the complement. It may well be that C′4, C′3 and other components, which are firmly bound to the antigen-antibody complex, provide a powerful antigenic stimulus in vivo. It may be advantageous, therefore, to use the antibodies to these firmly fixed complement components in the anti-globulin technique or in fluorescent antibody staining.

A simple method of preparing antibody to human complement is as follows:

0.5 ml of washed, packed formalinized rabbit red cells are mixed with 5 ml of fresh human serum at 0°C, let stand for 1 hour, washed, and finally suspended in 0.5 ml of saline. Injection of this suspension, mixed with complete Freund's adjuvant, into laboratory animals will produce anti-β_{1C}-and β_{1E}-globulin antibodies after an interval of 2 to 3 weeks. Any anti-γG-globulin antibody which is concurrently produced can be removed by absorption with purified γG-globulin at the optimum ratio. The presence of anti-β_{1E} and β_{1C}-globulin can be detected by immunoelectrophoresis using (1) fresh serum, (2) fresh serum together with the immune precipitates, and (3) aged serum. Both β_{1C} and β_{1E} precipitin lines are formed with (1); the β_{1E} line weakens or disappears and the β_{1E} line converges with the $\beta_{1A(G)}$ line, shifting to the anode side, with (2); and the β_{1E}-line remains unaltered while the β_{1C} line converts into the $\beta_{1A(G)}$ line in (3). When anti-β_{1C} globulin alone is needed, it can be prepared by immunization with the β_{1C}-globulin eluted from zymosan, by keeping at 37°C for 1 hour pretreated with fresh human serum and washed.

In summary, no definite assessment of the antibodies for each complement component can be made until these components are available in a sufficiently pure state and quantity for identification. At present the only means of studying complement fixation with human complement is by the use of these crude anti-β_{1E}-and β_{1C}-globulin antibodies.

B. Method of Immunization

The antigen used for the production of antiserum must be as pure as possible for the fluorescent antibody technique, where the specificity of reaction is of the utmost importance; but it is often difficult to produce a high-titered antibody against such pure material. It is also essential to use animals free from infectious agents antigenically related to those present in the animals to be examined. Antiserum from infected animals meeting these criteria is most suitable because it has a high titer and is free from antibodies against tissue antigens of other animal species.

Immunization with the purified material alone usually does not work; it is necessary to combine the material with an appropriate adjuvant, such as alum or Freund's adjuvant. Freund's adjuvant* has, however, the disadvantage of producing local necrosis and/or severe aseptic inflammation and abscess. Moreover, antibodies may be produced against minute amounts (ca. 0.005 mg N) of contaminating antigens in the mixture. The antiserum obtained by this method can only be used, therefore, in critical immuno-chemical analyses after careful examination of its specificity. Alum, by contrast, does not produce severe side reactions. The proportion of protein antigen and aluminum-potassium sulfate and the immunization schedule[18] must be carefully worked out, however. It has been found that alum in an amount 128–256 times that of the protein is needed to precipitate most of the protein (more than 95%). With whole globulin,

---

* The complete adjuvant contains mycobacteria; the incomplete does not.

a high titer antiserum could easily be obtained irrespective of the ratio of alum to protein and of the schedule of immunization. With γ-globulin, however, we could only obtain antiserum giving a positive ring test at a dilution of 1: 128–256 when an intramuscular immunizing dose with a protein to alum ratio of 1: 128–256 was given, followed by booster injections at longer than 3 months' intervals.

(a)   Preparation of Freund's adjuvant

The immunogenic capacity of an antigen is markedly increased when the antigen is emulsified in liquid paraffin. Heat-killed cells of mycobacteria added to the emulsion enhance the effect even more. Mycobacteria such as *M. tuberculosis* or *M. butyricum* are used. An aliquot of cells is killed by heat, an amount corresponding to 1–2 mg/m*l* of the emulsion is weighed out and ground in a mortar, and paraffin oil (Boyal F or Drakeol No. 6) is added drop by drop to make a homogeneous suspension. A surface active emulsifier (Arlacel A) is then added little by little to the suspension to give a homogeneous emulsion, which is stored at 4°C after sterilization in an autoclave. The ratio of liquid paraffin to emulsifier should be 8.5: 1 in this case and 9: 1 in an emulsion without mycobacteria.

To prepare the final emulsion, an amount of adjuvant equal to the antigen solution is placed in a syringe with the plunger removed and the needle inserted into a cork to prevent leakage. The antigen solution is then added slowly drop by drop with vigorous stirring with a glass rod. The resulting emulsion should not separate even after standing for several hours, and a drop placed on water should not disperse. Another simple method of preparing the emulsion is to use two syringes connected by narrow polyethylene tubing. One syringe is filled with the antigen solution and the other with an equal amount of adjuvant, and their plungers are raised and depressed repeatedly for a minimum of ten minutes. A fairly good preparation can be obtained in this way.

A good antibody response is obtained by multiple injections, intramuscularly, subcutaneously, or intradermally, into laboratory animals. Injections are also frequently given intracutaneously in the pad of the foot or the toes: in the pad 3–4 cm behind the roots of the toes, in 0.1–0.2 m*l* doses; and in the undersurface of the toes in approximately 0.05 m*l* doses. In the latter case, injections are given in each toe, allowing about 1 m*l* of emulsion per animal. The emulsion should be warmed to 37°C before use.

When Freund's complete adjuvant is used only relatively small amounts of antigen are required, 0.5 to 5 mg protein usually sufficing as a single immunizing dose for a rabbit. If a subcutaneous booster injection is made about three weeks later, a high titer antiserum will result. A plain solution of antigen without adjuvant is sufficient for the booster.

(b)   Preparation of alum adjuvant

Preparation of 10% aluminum-potassium sulfate

Na_2HPO_4 ....240 mg
KH_2PO_4 ....174 mg
$CH_3COONa \cdot 3H_2O$ ......100 mg

NaCl ....11 mg   Add enough alum to give a 10%
Distilled water   75 ml   solution and make up to 100 ml
Antigen solution (protein concentration 1%......10 mg/ml) ....1 vol
10% alum solution ....25.6 vols

When alum is added little by little to the antigen solution, a precipitate is formed. If the mixture is kept at a pH of 5.5 by the addition of 30% Na_2HPO_4 or 1 N NaOH, most of the antigenic protein is recovered in the precipitate which is collected by centrifugation (4,000 rpm, 15 min). It is then resuspended in saline (pH 5.5) and 2–3 ml (30–50 mg protein) is injected intramuscularly into the animal at several sites. An antiserum of sufficiently high antibody titer is usually obtained after a booster injection with plain antigen solution given in 3 months or later.

C. Examination of Antibodies

Since the reliability of the fluorescent antibody technique depends primarily on the specific reactivity of the antisera used, a careful examination of their specificity is of the utmost importance. Determination of the antibody titer and the use of high titer antiserum are equally indispensable since the antibody is to a large extent diluted in the purification process. The following techniques are used for these purposes: (1) immunodiffusion, double diffusion, and immuno-electrophoresis; (2) the immunoprecipitin, ring, and quantitative tests; (3) complement fixation; (4) passive hemagglutination; (5) the immunohematologic technique; (6) the fluorescent treponemal antibody (FTA) test, etc. When none of these techniques is applicable, strict controls such as the negative control and inhibition tests should be included.

The following method of examination has been adopted in our laboratories. Mice are sacrificed at given intervals after injection with serum protein (e.g. human γG-globulin). Frozen sections of kidney, liver and spleen are prepared and stained with serial dilutions of corresponding fluorescent antibody. The specific fluorescence which appears in cells that have taken up the globulin makes it possible to estimate the staining potency of the fluorescent antibody. In addition, the extent of non-specific fluorescence of the treated tissue can be determined. A final check on the fluorescent antibody is best obtained by actually staining suitable tissue sections or smears in which the pure antigen is present with labeled antibody, if such material is available. The fluorescent treponemal antibody test is very useful for examining the anti-globulin serum used in the indirect method.

In general the best methods are probably immuno-diffusion and immuno-electrophoresis. Contaminants may be present even in highly purified immunizing antigen preparation and may bring about the production of unwanted antibodies. Chaplin and Cassel (1960) noted,[2] for example, that four injections of antigen in doses as small as 0.005 μg per animal produced precipitating antibody. Immunoelectrophoresis is a convenient method for detecting these extraneous antibodies. Antiserum against tissue extract can be examined, for instance, by placing the extract and the serum in the antigen well and the anti-serum in the trough between them. Antibodies to serum components are usually found together with the antibody reacting with the tissue antigen. The former can be removed by absorption with the corresponding serum components at the optimum ratio. It is impracticable, however, to carry out this type of absorption with components that can be purified only with great difficulty.

The actual absorption can be accomplished by the following procedure. First, serial dilutions of serum from the animal from which the antigen extract was prepared are mixed with the antiserum; the end point is determined when precipitin lines for the serum components are no longer formed under immunoelectrophoresis. Absorption is then carried out using a serum concentration of about 1.5 times the end point. It often takes longer than one week for the antigen-antibody complex to be completely formed. The examination should be repeated because the antibody, once completely absorbed, will reappear after several days (the so-called coming back phenomenon).

The antiserum can also be examined by the double diffusion technique but resolution of the precipitin arcs may or may not be adequate depending on the concentrations of antigen and antibody. Box titration with the ring test or the flocculation test also fails to reveal the presence of an additional antigen-antibody system when masked by the predominant system. The same is true for the complement fixation test, but the latter must be used if the antibody cannot be detected by any other reactions. With certain materials such as gonadotropin the more sensitive tanned red cell agglutination (passive hemagglutination) test may be used. Extraneous antibodies can be removed in this case by absorption with material obtained by a similar procedure from normal male urine. Completion of absorption can be ascertained by negative passive hemagglutination with red cells coated with protein material from male urine.

Absorption of extraneous antibodies against specified components of tissue in antiserum is extremely difficult unless the corresponding antigen is available in pure form. In such cases, it is best to select the antiserum with the highest titer against the target antigen and to use it at a dilution where reactions of antibodies against other antigens are no longer discernible.

The standardization of anti-globulin serum

Three classes of immunoglobulins, γG, γA, and γM, are known to be present in animal sera; two more, γD and γE, have been discovered recently in human sera. Since many of these immunoglobulins can fix complement, the anti-globulin sera used in the routine indirect method should contain antibodies against complement components as well as against the immunoglobulins themselves.

Anti-globulin sera should first be standardized by immunoelectrophoresis. The standardization of anti-human globulins is one of the best-known cases, and will serve as an example of the procedure. Immunoelectrophoretic analysis is carried out as usual, using fresh and aged human sera as antigens. Antisera showing clear precipitin arcs for γG, γM, and γA are selected for use. $\beta_{1CA}(C'3)$-globulin lines can be identified by comparing the patterns of fresh and aged sera.

Antiglobulin sera which show distinct lines for these globulins can be used as broad spectrum antisera.

The standardization of antiserum against individual immunoglobulins also uses immunoelectrophoresis with human serum as antigen. Anti-γG-globulin serum should show a single line for γG-globulin. Careful examination often reveals the presence of a γA-globulin arc superimposed on the γG-globulin arc, which has not yet been identified. In order to obtain a specific anti-γ chain antiserum, the anti-γG-globulin serum should be absorbed with purified K and L type Bence Jones proteins or with serum from a patient with a γG-globulinemia. When these sera are not available, human serum from which γ-globulin has been completely removed by DEAE or CM cellulose chromatography can be used as the absorbing antigen.

Anti-γA-and anti-γM-globulin sera should also show single arcs in immunoelectrophoresis. The anti-light chain antibodies in these sera can be absorbed with γG-globulin, which is easily obtained. γA-and γM-globulins are very difficult to purify and preparations of these globulins are frequently contaminated with other serum components. Antibodies to these contaminants found in anti-γA- or anti-γM antisera can be readily absorbed with cord serum deficient in γA- and γM-globulins, yielding a single precipitin arc after absorption.

The use of cellulose acetate membrane as the supporting medium for immunoelectrophoresis has many advantages. With this simple technique many samples can be analyzed at once and within a short time. It is very convenient for determining the appropriate amount of antigen for absorption.

Determination of the antibody titer can be made by the ring test, quantitative precipitation or hemagglutination, with purified preparations of γG-, γA-, or γM-globulin if these are available. If pure globulins are not used soluble antigen-antibody complex may be coprecipitated, giving incorrect values. The antibody titer of anti-γG-globulin is easy to estimate, however. When fairly pure preparations of γA- and γM-globulins are available (mostly from patients with A myeloma or Waldenström disease), the antibody titers of the respective antisera are determined by the passive hemagglutination test. Since only γG(anti-D) antibody is present in most cases in the cord serum of newborn babies with hemolytic disease due to anti-D antibodies, D positive O red cells sensitized with these γG- anti-D antibodies can be used for the indirect anti-globulin test. With this technique, the antibody titer of anti-γG-globulin serum can be determined.

To obtain the titer of γM antibody, naturally occurring anti-Le[a] serum can be used. Since this antibody fixes complement, Le[a] positive red cells are sensitized with the antibody in the presence of EDTA, providing red cells sensitized only with γM- anti-Le[a] antibody. The titer of anti-γM globulin serum can be determined with these sensitized red cells by the indirect antiglobulin technique. A similar indirect anti-globulin test with sensitized A or B cells can be carried out to determine the titer of anti-γA-globulin serum, since the DEAE cellulose chromatographic fraction of group O serum eluted at 0.08 M, pH 8.0 (Na phosphate buffer) contains γA- anti-A or B antibodies. In order to determine the antibody titer of anti-C′ serum components, Le^a positive cells sensitized with anti-Le^a antibody, which usually fixes C′, are used for the indirect antiglobulin test.

These immunohematologic techniques provide a sensitive and efficient method both for the determination of the antibody titers of anti-γG, -γA, -γM and anti-C′ serum components and for their standardization. The appropriate dilution of antiserum and the necessity of absorption with tissue powder, etc. must then be determined by carrying out the actual fluorescent antibody staining in a known antigen-antibody system.

2. Purification of Antibody

As has been frequently stressed, the antibody used in the fluorescent antibody technique must be highly purified and have a high specificity. It should be free from non-antibody serum proteins. Albumin, α-globulin and other proteins with a strong negative charge are apt to be adsorbed nonspecifically onto the specimen, bringing about nonspecific fluorescence. Unfortunately the physicochemical character of antibodies in serum is fairly complex, due to varying molecular weights, configurations, and electrophoretic mobilities. There are three main classes of immunoglubulins: γG(IgG), γM(IgM) and γA (IgA). With the exception of horse antiserum, most of the antibody activity in animal serum is usually associated with γG.

To purify antibody one must, first of all, isolate the globulin fractions containing antibody against certain antigen(s) with the aid of immunoelectrophoretic analysis, etc. This involves fractionation of serum proteins, which is based on differences in physicochemical properties, e.g. salting out with neutral salts, precipitation with ethanol, isoelectric precipitation, precipitation with heavy metals, chromatographic separation with ion-exchanger such as DEAE cellulose, gel-filtration with Sephadex, and fractional ultracentrifugation. In the actual fractionation, several of these methods (which are known as nonspecific methods of purification) are used in combination, depending upon the circumstances. But none of these can be used to separate globulin fractions with similar physicochemical properties from the antibody globulin.

To prepare pure antibody protein, specific methods of purification based on the specificity of antigen-antibody complexes must be used. The principle of these methods is to recover the antibody from specific antigen-antibody complexes by dissociation under suitable conditions. By acidification at low ionic strength or the addition of excess hapten, fairly pure antibody preparations with a specific activity of over 90% have been obtained. Recently an immunologically specific adsorbent for the removal of specific antibody activity in a high yield from antisera has been developed. When applied directly to whole serum, however, preparations obtained by the specific method of purification are not necessarily homogeneous. Since the affinity of each globulin fraction for the fluorescent dye varies in strength, further purification of these preparations by physicochemical means is necessary in order to prepare homogeneous fluorescent antibody. Alternatively a preparation purified nonspecifically can be further purified by a specific method. In general, however, the antigen in the fluorescent antibody technique is not purified, and the specific method of purification is only used in special cases.

The conjugation of fluorescent dye with antibody protein is mediated mainly through the ε-amino residue of lysine, resulting in reduction of the positive charge of the protein molecule as shown by changes in electrophoretic mobility or in the elution pattern in ion-exchange chromatography. Thus, the labeling of antibody protein with dye inevitably brings about an increase in nonspecific staining of tissue. This is why the best results are obtained with a conjugated antibody carrying a very small amount of dye, although this would seem inefficient at first sight. However, each serum component takes up different amounts of dye in labeling even with the same conditions and procedure. It follows, therefore, that each component would show an uneven F/P molar ratio when the whole serum or globulin fraction is conjugated with the dye. Fortunately, it is now possible to separate conjugated globulins into their individual components by DEAE cellulose column chromatography or electrophoresis. The fraction with the weakest negative charge (nearest to γG) will show an F/P molar ratio of 1 to 2 and provide a conjugated antibody with high specificity and negligible nonspecific fluorescence. This is the most common method of preparing conjugated (γG) antibody. If the antibody activity is predominantly in the γA or γM fraction, however, isolation and purification of the component and separate labeling of the individual fractions are necessary. With certain animal species and weak antigens, the antibody content of the immune serum may remain at a very low level. The separation and concentration of antibody from such a weak immune serum can be accomplished with immunologically specific adsorbent, but labeling of such low-titered serum is inevitably accompanied by technical difficulties.

For all these differences, however, isolation and purification of the appropriate globulin fraction remains the basic principle in every case. Let us now take a look at some of the nonspecific methods used for the preparation of fluorescent antibody.

A. The purification of γG-globulin

Several methods are known for the preparation of crude globulin fractions. Since the amount of immune serum dealt with is seldom large, fractionation with ammonium sulfate or sodium sulfate is usually the first step. Salting out with ammonium sulfate provides preliminary separation and concentration of the globulin fraction from the serum; the fraction obtained is subjected to further purification with zone electrophoresis and ion-exchange cellulose column chromatography. Although it is difficult to isolate a pure globulin fraction by a single precipitation, a fairly homogeneous preparation (with human and rabbit serum γ-globulin) can be obtained by repeating the procedure 3 or 4 times. The procedure is illustrated in Figs. 4 and 5.

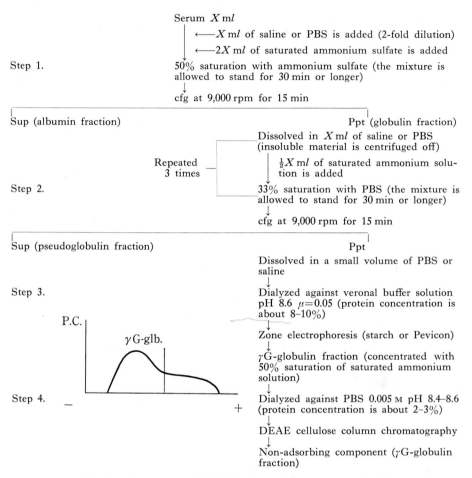

Serum X ml

    ⟵—X ml of saline or PBS is added (2-fold dilution)

    ⟵—$2X$ ml of saturated ammonium sulfate is added

Step 1.   50% saturation with ammonium sulfate (the mixture is allowed to stand for 30 min or longer)

     cfg at 9,000 rpm for 15 min

Sup (albumin fraction)   Ppt (globulin fraction)

Dissolved in X ml of saline or PBS (insoluble material is centrifuged off)

Repeated 3 times $\frac{1}{2}X$ ml of saturated ammonium solution is added

Step 2.   33% saturation with PBS (the mixture is allowed to stand for 30 min or longer)

     cfg at 9,000 rpm for 15 min

Sup (pseudoglobulin fraction)   Ppt

Dissolved in a small volume of PBS or saline

Step 3.   Dialyzed against veronal buffer solution pH 8.6 $\mu=0.05$ (protein concentration is about 8–10%)

P.C.

γG-glb.

Zone electrophoresis (starch or Pevicon)

γG-globulin fraction (concentrated with 50% saturation of saturated ammonium solution)

Step 4.   Dialyzed against PBS 0.005 M pH 8.4–8.6 (protein concentration is about 2–3%)

$-$ $+$

DEAE cellulose column chromatography

Non-adsorbing component (γG-globulin fraction)

Fig. 4. Separation of γG-Globulin with Ammonium Sulfate

Note: These procedures are carried out at low temperatures. The saturated ammonium solution is added dropwise to the serum with constant stirring, to bring the pH to about neutral. (For the preparation of a saturated solution of ammonium sulfate see p. 11)

As in the fractionation of immunoglobulin, the albumin fraction is first removed by precipitation at 50% saturation with ammonium sulfate. It should be kept in mind that more contamination results when precipitation by salting out is carried out with solutions of high protein content. In order to avoid this, the serum is first diluted two-fold with physiological saline or PBS and then an equal amount of saturated ammonium sulfate is added slowly with stirring. After letting the mixture stand for 30 to 60 minutes (step 1), the precipitates can easily be collected by centrifugation. Most of the albumin remains in the supernatant and crystalizes on gradual acidification of the solution. The precipitates are dissolved in the same volume of saline or PBS as the original serum. When a half volume of a saturated solution of ammonium sulfate is added to the first

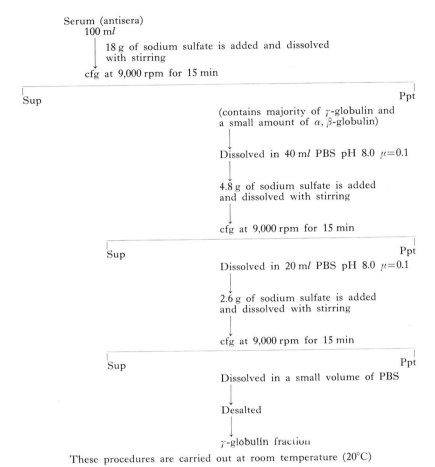

These procedures are carried out at room temperature (20°C)

Fig. 5. Separation of Serum γ-Globulin with Sodium Sulfate

fraction (33% saturation), followed by centrifugation after 30 to 60 minutes, the euglobulin fraction can be recovered as a precipitate and the pseudoglobulin fraction remains in the supernatant (step 2).   Contamination of the euglobulin fraction with fibrinogen can be avoided by centrifuging or filtering off the precipitates which form at 20% saturation with ammonium sulfate (this procedure should preferably be carried out in step 1).   As mentioned earlier fractionation by salting out must be repeated at least three times in order to obtain a relatively homogeneous fraction.   Usually the γG-globulin fraction obtained at this stage is used for the preparation of fluorescent antibody.   When necessary, further purification of the γG-globulin fraction can be achieved by electrophoresis and chromatography with ion-exchange cellulose (steps 3 and 4).

B. Zone Electrophoresis

The final precipitates in salting out are dissolved in as small an amount of saline or PBS as possible, put in cellulose tubing and dialyzed against tap water for about 1 hour.   Before the euglobulin precipitates, the tap water is replaced by the buffer solution* which is to be used in subsequent electrophoresis and the dialysis is continued overnight with stirring.   The dialyzed solution is then subjected to zone electrophoresis with starch or powdered synthetic resin such as Pevikon C-870 or Geon 420 as the supporting medium.   Either a horizontal block or vertical column apparatus may be used.   The latter type is preferable with a small amount of material as it gives better recovery.

For electrophoretic separation a solution of higher protein content should be used to ensure a good yield without significant loss of material, a concentration of 7 to 8% (70 to 80 mg protein/ml) being suitable.   After electrophoresis the protein fractions are recovered by washing or eluting the supporting medium. Precipitation with ammonium sulfate at 50% saturation may be carried out but subsequent dialysis is needed.   Concentration in vacuo or lyophilization are the procedures frequently used, but Sephadex is also quite convenient.

C. Chromatographic Purification with Cellulose Ion-exchangers.

Ion-exchange chromatography with cellulose ion-exchangers is recognized as one of the most efficient and useful methods for the separation and purification of proteins.   These cellulose ion-exchangers, especially DEAE cellulose, provide a quite efficient means for the fractionation of serum proteins as well.   It is possible to separate γG-globulin into several distinct fractions with different electrophoretic mobilities.   Although column chromatography is used in most cases, a batch method can also be used.   The adsorption and removal of serum components other than γG-globulin can be effected by a single procedure, leaving a homogeneous γG-globulin.

In the fluorescent antibody technique, this chromatographic separation is indispensable not only for the isolation of γG-globulin from immune serum but also for the purification of the conjugated protein.   Although exchangers of fairly homogeneous quality are now available commercially, differences in the ion-exchange capacity and in the quality of the cellulose material would lead to differences in the amount of serum efficiently separable and in the elution pattern; hence it is preferable to use a single lot of cellulose obtained from one manufacturer.   It must be kept in mind also that the ion-exchanger gradually loses its adsorbing capacity when kept dry for a long period of time.   Adsorbance can be regained by suspending the cellulose in 1 N NaOH at a low temperature (0 to 4°C) for 1 or 2 days, but the uniformity of the material may be lost.   It is preferable to mix the cellulose with water and store it at a low temperature, in which state it can be used for about one year.

---

* Barbital (Veronal) buffer is preferred as the buffer system for electrophoretic separation of serum globulin, as it gives a good resolution.   Normally, it is used at 0.05 M, pH 8.6.   The composition is as follows:

5,5′-diethyl barbituric acid   1.82 g
sodium 5,5′-diethyl barbiturate   10.3 g

Make up to 1 l with distilled water and heat to dissolve.

Although γG-globulin can be isolated by chromatography from whole serum, it is more efficient to isolate and concentrate the material first by salting out with ammonium or sodium sulfate as described earlier. Since different elution patterns will result depending upon the source and ion-exchange capacity of the exchanger, size of the column, amount of material applied, and the buffer system used for elution, it is difficult to give a detailed description of the optimal conditions for separation. We will only attempt here to describe the separation of γG-globulin with DEAE cellulose, which is the most common method. In actual experiments, the most suitable conditions must be determined for each case.

Whole serum or the partially purified γG-globulin fraction is dialyzed thoroughly against phosphate buffer (0.005 M, pH 7.8–8.0). Dialysis is carried out in a cold room with frequent exchanges of buffer solution. Stirring greatly shortens the time required for dialysis, which can be completed within about 24 hours. The precipitate formed during dialysis is removed by centrifugation. The concentration of the protein solution should be 3 to 4%. An amount (dry weight) of DEAE cellulose 10 to 15 times that of the protein is needed. A rough estimate of the column volume can be made from the fact that 1 g of dry DEAE cellulose corresponds to 4 to 5 ml bed volume, although there are slight differences among cellulose preparations. A column with a diameter : height

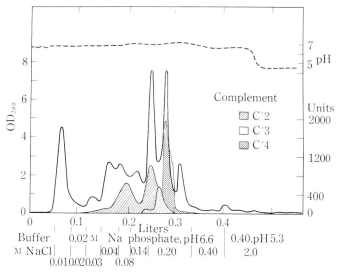

Fig. 6. Rapid Stepwise Separation of Complement Components in Guinea Pig Serum

Nineteen milliliters of serum, previously treated to destroy the C'1 component, applied to 10 g DEAE-cellulose (7.5, 3.9 cm). Adsorbent and serum separately equilibrated with 0.02 M sodium phosphate, pH 6.6. Collected 7–8 ml fractions at rate of 90 ml per hour. Temperature, 5°C. Solid line represents absorbance at 280 mμ; dashed line shows pH. From Sober and Peterson, *The Plasma Protein*, Vol. 1, p. 111.

ratio of more than 1:10 is generally more efficient. For instance, 25 m*l* of a 4% protein solution contains 1,000 mg (4 mg/m*l* × 25 m*l*) or 1 g of protein and therefore 10 to 15 g of dry cellulose is needed to prepare a column with a 2 cm diameter and 20 to 25 cm height. Commercial preparations of cellulose must be washed repeatedly with 1 N NaOH and 1 N HCl, using a glass filter and aspirator, followed by washing with distilled or deionized water and finally equilibration with buffer.

The pH and conductivity of the effluent should be checked to ensure complete equilibrium. Cellulose conditioned in this way is again suspended in an appropriate volume of buffer and used to prepare the column; a homogeneous suspension and a large volume of buffer are essential to obtain a homogeneous column. Care should be taken that some buffer is always left above the cellulose in order to prevent crack formation. The flow rate is adjusted to 10 to 20 m*l*/hour. Abrupt application of pressure to ensure an accelerated flow rate during the elution process should be avoided. Repeated regeneration of cellulose will result in a limited low flow rate because of the presence of fine fragments of cellulose fibers produced during the process. These fibers can be removed by decantation of the cloudy supernatant during regeneration.

The eluted fractions of a given volume or weight are collected using a fraction collector. The combined use of an automatic recorder with a UV spectrophoto-

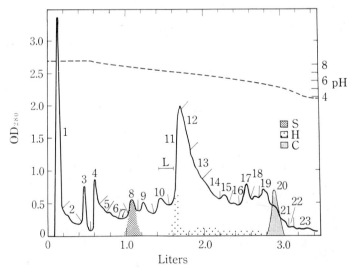

Fig. 7. Effluent Diagram of Normal Human Serum Protein
Pooled, clarified serum (30 m*l*, 2 g protein) applied to 25 g DEAE cellulose after adsorbent and serum had been separately equilibrated with Tris-phosphate at pH 8.6 (0.005M in phosphate). Collected 10 m*l* fractions at 35 m*l* per hour. Concave gradient (3400 m*l*) to 0.5 M Tris-H$_2$PO$_4$. Temperature, 5°C. Solid line represents absorbance at 280 mμ; dashed line shows pH. L represents lipoprotein; S, siderophilin (transferrin); H, absorption at 405 mμ; and C, ceruloplasmin. From Sober and Peterson, *The Plasma Protein*, Vol. 1, p. 113.

meter provides a convenient means for visualizing the elution behavior of the protein. An instrument capable of measuring absorption at a visible wavelength ($\lambda = 490$ to 495 mμ) is desirable.

With 0.005 M, pH 8.0 phosphate buffer, most of the γ-globulin will be eluted without adsorption onto the cellulose, leaving the contaminating γ_1-globulin and a small amount of β-globulin which can be eluted by either increasing the ionic strength or lowering the pH of the eluting buffer. With either a continuous or a stepwise gradient, most of the β-globulin may be eluted at 0.25 M NaH$_2$PO$_4$, but somewhat different conditions may be encountered depending upon the DEAE cellulose and the serum sample being used. The actual conditions for elution must therefore be determined empirically.

A typical elution pattern for serum proteins and the conditions required for elution are illustrated in Figs. 6 and 7.[23), 32)] For the batch method, Stanworth's description[33)] should be referred to.

D. Gel Filtration

The best media for gel filtration are Sephadex (Pharmacia, Uppsala, Sweden) and Biogel C; various samples and their properties are listed in Table 1. Formerly, preparations of three different particle sizes were manufactured. At present, except for the fine and coarse grades of G25 and G50, all Sephadex comes in a bead form enabling easier manipulation and more efficient filtration.

The principles of gel filtration have been described by a number of other researchers, and will be discussed here only briefly. Substances with molecular weights exceeding a certain limit do not diffuse into the dextran gel and come through the column without being retained, while substances with smaller molecular weights do diffuse into the dextran gel and are retained until further elution. There are two types of procedure, the batch and column methods; the former is more suitable for processing large amounts of material and the latter for smaller amounts. A higher resolving capacity can, of course, be expected with the latter procedure. Thus, gel filtration with Sephadex makes it possible to fractionate a mixture easily and efficiently on the basis of differences in molecular size, as in, for example, the separation of γG and γM. In addition, this method can be used for substituting a dialyzing solution without dialysis, desalting, removing free dye in the fluorescent antibody technique, etc.

Procedure: The amount of Sephadex to be used is determined by the size of the sample. With the column method, the volume of water contained in the gel structure (inner water) cannot be measured directly; however, the volume of the packed gel (bed volume) and the volume of outer water (void volume) can be determined and calculation therefrom gives, indirectly, the value for the inner water.

Determination of the void volume can be made by using a sample of molecular size sufficiently large to prevent it from diffusing into the gel network and by measuring the volume of water needed to elute it. For this purpose, one can use the Blue Dextran (molecular weight 2,000,000) available commercially. By

Table 1.　Characteristics of Various Types of Dextran

1.　Sephadex

Type of Dextran	Water regain W_R g.water/g.dry gel	Operating range (molecular weight)	
		for polysaccharides	for proteins
G–10	1.0±0.1	700 under	
G–15	1.5±0.1	1,500 under	
G–25	2.5±0.2	100– 5,000	
G–50	5.0±0.3	500– 10,000	
G–75	7.5±0.5	1,000– 50,000	3,000– 70,000
G–100	10.0±1.0	1,000–100,000	4,000–150,000
G–150	15.0±1.5	1,000–150,000	5,000–400,000
G–200	20.0±2.0	1,000–200,000	5,000–800,000

2.　Biogel

Type of Biogel	Water regain W_R g.water/g.dry gel	Wet mesh	Operating range molecular weight for protein
P–2	1.3	50–100	200– 2,000
P–2	1.6	100–200	200– 2,000
P–4	2.6	50–150	500– 4,000
P–6	3.2	50–150	1,000– 5,000
P–10	5.1	50–150	5,000– 17,000
P–20	5.4	50–150	10,000– 30,000
P–30	6.2	50–150	20,000– 50,000
P–60	6.8	50–150	30,000– 70,000
P–100	7.5	50–150	40,000–100,000
P–150	9.0	50–150	50,000–150,000
P–200	13.5	50–150	80,000–300,000
P–300	22.0	50–150	100,000–400,000

following the blue color down through the column, it is possible to make a direct measurement of the void volume with a graduated cylinder, giving different values according to the types of Sephadex used.　This value, once determined, can be used generally for the same gel lot.　Although ideally a sample size equal to the volume of inner water should be used, in actuality about one-tenth the volume of inner water is usually used, taking into account the influence of the rate of flow and diffusion.

The height of the column should exceed the length by about 10 times the diameter to minimize irregularity in the elution pattern.　Care should be taken to eliminate in vacuo any fine bubbles left after swelling of the Sephadex.　Gels of a large G number take a longer time to swell (over 24 hours with G-200) but the time may be shortened by raising the temperature.　No special precautions are necessary for preparing a homogeneous column with Sephadex in bead form, but a water layer must always be left on the top of the column bed after packing. Temperature changes sometimes lead to formation of bubbles in the gel, which should be avoided. An ordinary glass chromatography tube with a stopcock at the bottom is used for the column. Tubes specially designed for gel filtration are also available commercially. The flow rate is determined by the size of the column, volume of sample, type of gel and other factors. These can be adjusted so that a substance of a molecular size small enough to enter the gel pore can diffuse completely and enter into the gel within the elution period of the void volume. The time interval varies with the amount of Sephadex used. With a column of sufficiently large bed volume, nearly complete separation is possible even with a fairly high flow rate, approaching the rate of free elution with a fully opened stopcock.

When the column is ready, the sample is applied. It is carefully placed on top of the bed to form a stable layer. In order to avoid disturbing the gel surface, the sample may be added either bit by bit or onto a filter paper placed on the gel surface. With the former method, however, it may be difficult to apply the sample without disturbing the gel. With the latter, an irregular pattern may be formed due to the faster flow of sample running down the gap between the glass wall and the filter paper. A special applicator made from a plastic tube with nylon net fixed to the bottom is available commercially and has neither of these disadvantages (Fig. 8). A similar charger can easily be made in the laboratory. As soon as the liquid layer above the gel has flowed down, another bit of sample is gently applied. After letting all the sample run into the gel, a small volume of

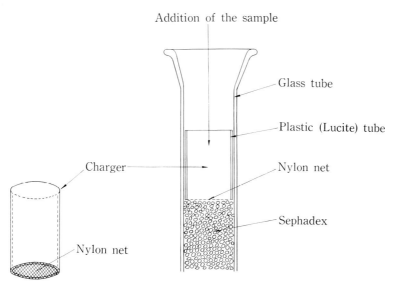

Fig. 8. Charger for Gel Filtration
Nylon net is attached to the lower edge of the Lucite tube, with the diameter equal to the inner diameter of the glass tube.

eluant or buffer is added in several portions, and finally the flow is allowed to continue at a given rate.

In the fluorescent antibody technique, gel filtration is used to remove the free dye. When 0.005 M phosphate buffer* plus 0.1 M NaCl is used as the buffer in this filtration, exchange of buffer can be made simultaneously and the solution of conjugated protein obtained is ready for use with DEAE cellulose column chromatography in the next step. DEAE Sephadex can also be used. Fractions of a given volume of eluate are collected with an automatic fraction collector; the eluate can be checked with an automatic OD analyzer (OD at 495 mμ to measure the fluorescent dye). With a small sample, the fractions appearing first can be collected manually using the fluorescent dye as a marker. Successful desalting with Sephadex of salted out material is evidenced by the distribution of protein as measured by OD at 280 mμ and of ammonium sulfate as detected by the addition of BaCl$_2$. Measurements of conductivity and pH are also used to check for effective separation.

The material recovered in the eluate is generally 1.5 times more dilute than the starting sample and frequently has to be concentrated. Concentration by salting out may be used but a desalting procedure must then follow. Other methods of concentration are more or less acceptable. Concentration with Sephadex provides a simple and time-saving means without denaturation of the material and is preferred in these experiments. Addition of dry Sephadex powder (into which the desired substance cannot enter) to the solution followed by separation of the swollen Sephadex by an appropriate means effects an immediate concentration of the solution. Centrifugation is preferred for the separation but is inevitably accompanied by a certain loss of material, which can be minimized by washing the gel with a small amount of water. For this purpose Type G-25 or G-50 Sephadex (coarse grade) is most frequently used, the amount being determined by the water regain.

With M ml of protein solution at a concentration of $x\%$, use of y grams of Sephadex with a water regain of A yields the following concentration (c) of protein solution:

$$c = x \times \frac{1}{M-Ay} \quad (M \text{ should be greater than } Ay)$$

For example, when 1 g of Sephadex with a water regain of 7 (g water/g dry gel) is mixed with 10 ml of 0.1% protein solution, 3 ml of an approximately 0.3% solution will be obtained on the assumption that free water can be recovered completely by centrifugation. On further addition of 0.3 g of Sephadex, a solution concentrated roughly ten-fold will be obtained.

The separation of free water (concentrated solution) by centrifugation is best

---

* A 20 times concentrated stock solution (0.1 M Na$_2$H$_2$PO$_4$·2H$_2$O 1 vol+0.1 M Na$_2$HPO$_4$· 12 H$_2$O 2 vols) is usually prepared and diluted, and the NaCl added just before use (pH 7.0).

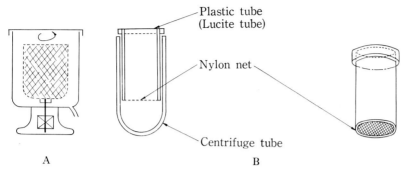

Plastic tube
(Lucite tube)

Nylon net

Centrifuge tube

A B

Fig. 9. Basket Type Centrifugation and Basket Type Adaptor
A. Basket type centrifugation
B. Basket type adaptor
Nylon net is attached to the lower edge of the plastic tube.

done by using a basket-type adaptor assembly with the centrifuge tube. The adaptor can be made in the laboratory from plastic tube and nylon net (Fig. 9).[12]

Similarly, addition of dry Sephadex to the solution after prior addition of buffer or distilled water, followed by centrifugation, results in the elimination of low molecular weight substances. This method can be repeated, and used efficiently as a batch method. The Sephadex can be recovered and after washing and drying can be used repeatedly.

3. PREPARATION OF LABELED ANTIBODY

A. Fluorescent Dyes

(a) Properties

When molecules absorb a sufficient amount of radiation energy they become excited, i.e. their electrons take on a different arrangement. This excess energy, in a labile state, is rapidly lost on collision with neighboring molecules. Some molecules, however, have covalent bonds which form a more rigid structure; in this case the energy is lost by emission of light and the molecules return to their original stable state. This emission of light is called fluorescence. The wavelength of the light emitted is longer than that of the exciting radiation in almost every case (Stock's law). Coons and other workers attempted to use fluorescent dyes, which emit visible light on excitation with UV or near UV light, as tracers or labels for antibody. Fluorescent dyes with good absorption characteristics, relative stability of excitation, and efficiency of fluorescence (i.e. quantum recovery rate or ratio of the amount of emission to the quantum absorption) are the most useful as tracers. The efficiency of a fluorescent compound is usually smaller than unity, that of most fluorescent dyes being quite a bit smaller. The efficiency value for fluorescein, for example, is 0.70, while that of rhodamine B is 0.25.

Changes in fluorescence: While fluorescent dyes are generally stable in the solid state, the fluorescence decreases rapidly in solution or when the amount of dye is very small in proportion to the energy and duration of the exciting radiation. By contrast, the fluorescence of natural (autofluorescent) materials is much more stable. These facts should be kept in mind when dealing with fluorescent dyes in the fluorescent antibody technique, especially labeling, storage of the preparation, microscopic observation, etc. In addition, it should be remembered that such factors as the nature of the solvent, viscosity, temperature, and pH can affect fluorescence. The pH is especially important because any variation can cause a change in the ionizing balance of the molecules. The fluorescence of an FITC-labeled compound at pH 6.0, for example, is about 50% that at pH 8.0, and the absorption at 495 mμ decreases in a similar fashion. The other factors mentioned above influence the fluorescence by changing the stability of the excitation state.

(b)   Fluorescent dyes used for the fluorescent antibody technique

The strength of fluorescence is determined by the absorption characteristics, extent of excitation and the efficiency of fluorescence. However, strong fluorescence is not sufficient to make a dye effective in the FA technique. Ideally, a dye should conjugate readily and firmly with the antibody, should not reduce the antibody activity perceptibly, and, in addition, should have a good efficiency of fluorescence and sufficient stability.

When the FA technique was first being developed, the attention of researchers was largely focused on discovering a dye which fulfilled these conditions. Fluorescein isocyanate (FIC), which was first used by Coons and others,[8] was not entirely suitable because its conjugation with protein was erratic and occasionally accompanied by denaturation of the antibody and reduction of its activity. Moreover, in the labeling process itself, phosgen was difficult to handle. In order to overcome these difficulties, an active search for more suitable dyes was begun and dozens of fluorescent compounds were tested. Eventually, Riggs and his co-workers[26] were able to synthesize fluorescein isothiocyanate (FITC), in which the isothiocyanate group of FIC is substituted for the isocyanate (NCO) group (NCS). This dye with its strong greenish-yellow fluorescence almost entirely fulfills all the conditions for the FA technique, and is largely responsible for its later developments and refinements. Since its successful crystallization by the Baltimore Biological Laboratory, lot to lot differences and lability of the dye have been overcome and it is now readily available commercially. One other yellow fluorescent dye, DANS[5] (1-dimethylamino-naphthalene-5-sulphonic acid), has been developed, but it has many disadvantages, such as low fluorescent efficiency as compared with FITC, and it is seldom used.

In order to analyze two antigens in tissue (double staining) or to counterstain tissue other than the antigen, red fluorescent dyes are required. Dyes of the rhodamine series are used for this purpose. Although their fluorescence efficiency and staining specificity are low, they are still indispensable at present because of the lack of any more appropriate substitute.

(b–i)   Dyes of the fluorescein series

Fluorescein isocyanate (FIC): As mentioned above, this dye was originally

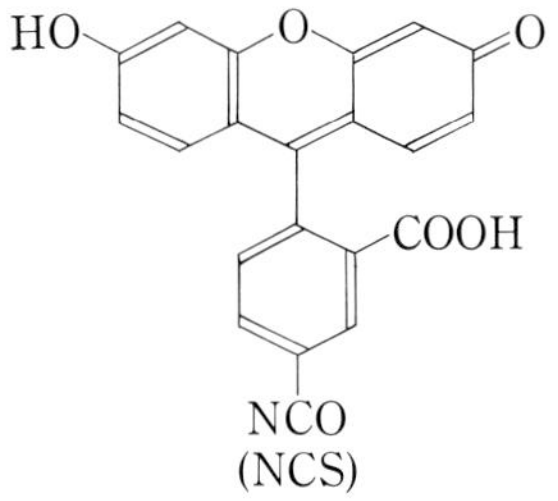

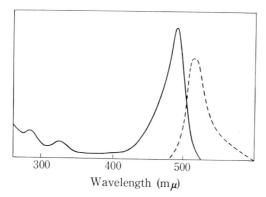

Fig. 10. Fluorescein Isocyanate (FIC), Fluorescein Isothiocyanate (FITC) $C_{21} H_{11} O_6N$ ($C_{21} H_{11} O_5NS$) (molecular weight 373 (389))
Maximum wavelength of absorption 490 mμ
Maximum wavelength of emission 520 mμ

Fig. 11. Absorption and Fluorescence
Spectra of Fluorescein at pH 7.1 (from Nairn, 1962)

introduced by Coons,[7, 8] but is seldom used at present because of its extreme lability and many disadvantages, including the use of phosgen (Figs. 10, 11).

Fluorescein isothiocyanate (FITC): This dye was first synthesized by Riggs and his co-workers[26] by treating amino-fluorescein with thiophosgen instead of phosgen, and its crystallization was accomplished by the Baltimore Biological Laboratory. The crystallized preparation is now available commercially. FITC isomer 1[21] is the best dye available for the FA technique in terms of fluorescence efficiency, stability, and combining capacity with protein. The dye has greenish yellow fluorescence and a molecular weight of 389.4; its structural formula is shown in Fig. 10 and its fluorescence characteristics in Fig. 11. When the dye is reacted with an alkaline solution of antibody protein, a thiocarbamide bond is formed with the free amino groups (mainly the ε-amino group of lysine) of the protein, forming labeled antibody. This chemical reaction can be achieved by a simple procedure. It should be remembered, however, that *all* the lysine residues of 7S γ-globulin (86 residues) are never labeled with the dye, the maximum combining number having been shown by experience to be about 15.

$$\underset{\substack{\| \\ S}}{\text{dye—N=C}} + \underset{\substack{\wedge \\ H \ H}}{\text{N—protein}} \longrightarrow \underset{\substack{| \ \| \ | \\ H \ S \ H}}{\text{dye—N—C—N—protein}}$$

A protein with many dye molecules combined with it has a strong negative charge and cannot be used in the FA technique because of its nonspecific fluorescence. For this reason, compounds with a molar combining ratio (F/P, the molar ratio of FITC to protein) of 1–2 are desirable.

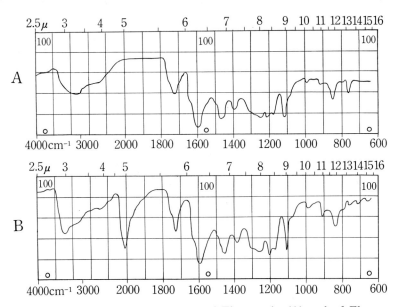

Fig. 12.   The IR Absorption Spectra of Fluorescein (A) and of Fluorescein Isothiocyanate (FITC-Crystallized Preparation of BBL) (B)

Since the melting point of FITC cannot be determined,[26] the compound must be checked by its absorption characteristics, IR spectrum, and electrophoretic pattern.[18]   Fig. 12 shows the IR absorption spectrum of fluorescein (A) and of FITC (crystallized BBL preparation) (B).   It should be noted that the only difference between A and B is the absorption at 2,100 cm^{-1}, attributable to the presence of isothiocyanate residue in the latter.   In addition, two peaks with different mobilities are found upon paper electrophoretic examination of FITC, which indicates that two components are present even in the crystallized preparation of FITC, and which also provides a probable explanation for the appearance of nonspecific fluorescence as reported by McKinney.[21]

There are still a number of unsolved problems with respect to the present crystallized FITC isomer 1 product, but no FITC preparation other than that of the Baltimore Biological Laboratory is available at present.

(b–ii)   Dyes of the rhodamine series

Tetramethyl rhodamine: The early isocyanate preparations of this dye[16] had many drawbacks and were of little practical value.   Recently an isothiocyanate

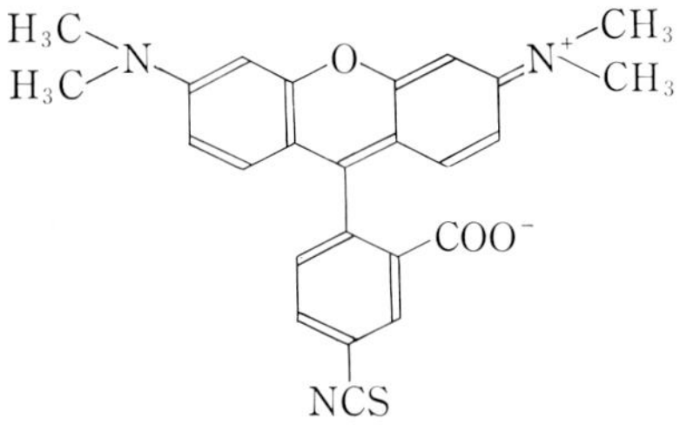

Fig. 13. Tetramethyl Rhodamine Isothiocyanate $C_{25} H_{21} O_3$ NaS (molecular weight 443)
Maximum wavelength of absorption 550 mμ
Maximum wavelength of emission 620 mμ

derivative was manufactured by the Baltimore Biological Laboratory.   It is not as stable as FITC and only weakly fluorescent, but since it is the safest of the red fluorescent dyes, it is now commonly used in double staining.   It is a dark red-brown powder and has an orange-red fluorescence (Fig. 13).
Tetraethyl rhodamine compounds: These are also dark orange-red powders, soluble in water, and with various uses.   They are available commercially under various trade names from a number of firms, e.g. lissamine rhodamine B 200 (RB 200)—Imperial Chemical Industry, England; Xylene Red B—Sandoz; Sulphorhodamine B—Bayer, etc.   Since the dye cannot combine with protein by itself, it must be used for labeling after prior treatment with phosphorus pentachloride (PCl$_5$) according to the method of Chadwick et al.[1] (see below). This reaction can be written as follows:

$$Dye—SO_3Na + PCl_5 \longrightarrow Dye—SO_2Cl + PCl_3 + NaCl$$

The protein is labeled by the formation of a sulfonamide linkage between the SO$_2$Cl residue and the NH$_2$ of the protein:

$$Dye—SO_2Cl + NH_2—Protein \longrightarrow Dye—SO_2—NH—Protein$$

Although the labeling efficiency of this dye is fairly good and its deleterious

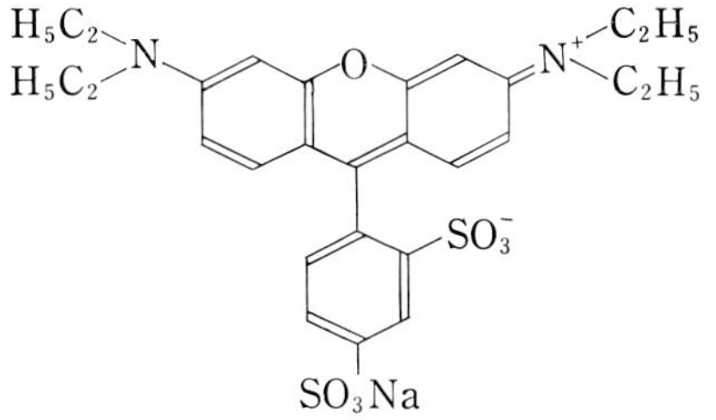

Fig. 14. Tetraethyl Rhodamine Compounds (Lissamine rhodamine B 200, etc.)
$C_{27}H_{29}O_7N_2NaS_2$ (molecular weight 580)
Maximum wavelength of absorption 570 mμ
Maximum wavelength of emission 600 mμ

effect on protein not marked, it is nevertheless inferior to FITC for general staining purposes.

Tetramethylrhodamine is more commonly used for double staining, but because the fluorescence of the tetraethyl rhodamine compounds is brighter and clearer, they are preferred for use in counterstaining (Fig. 14). Recently, the method of purification of antibody labeled with this dye has been reexamined by the authors in the hope of removing the nonspecific fluorescence. Such an attempt, if successful, would increase the importance of this dye in double staining.

B. Method of Labeling

The purified antibody protein prepared as described in the foregoing section is now ready for labeling with fluorescent dye. It is possible to treat the whole serum first with the dye and then purify the labeled antibody, but this method has certain drawbacks since the altered physicochemical properties of the labeled antibody, especially with respect to chromatographic behavior in DEAE cellulose chromatography, make it difficult to determine the optimum condition for its purification.

First, the particular dye to be used for labeling must be selected. Then, the actual procedure is begun under optimum conditions for the individual case. Special attention should be paid to the protein-dye ratio, pH, temperature, and reaction time.

(a)   Labeling with isothiocyanate (NCS) dyes.

This includes labeling with the greenish-yellow FITC and orange-red tetramethylrhodamine and covers most of the cases in which the FA technique is used at present.

(a–i) FITC

The method generally used is a modified Marshall's method[19] with some improvements, introduced by Kawamura and others.[13, 18, 21]

Materials: Antibody solution, FITC isomer 1 (crystallized preparation, BBL), saline, 0.5 M carbonate-bicarbonate buffer, pH 9.5 (see below), 0.005 M phosphate buffer, pH 7.0 (see above, p. 32), Sephadex G-25 (or G-50), DEAE cellulose, magnetic stirrer, small weighing bottle, and glass columns for chromatography.

Preparation of 0.5 M carbonate-bicarbonate buffer (pH 9.5)

$$
\left.\begin{array}{ll}
\text{0.5 M } Na_2CO_3 \text{ solution} & \text{1 vol} \\
\text{0.5 M } NaHCO_3 \text{ solution} & \text{3 vols}
\end{array}\right\}\text{mixed}
$$

Calculation: Protein solution .... A mg/ml, B ml

Total protein .... $A \times B = C$ mg

Volume of 2% protein solution .... $C/20 = D$ ml

Amount of FITC .... $C/100 - 150 = E$ mg

Volume of carbonate-bicarbonate buffer .... $D/10 = F$ ml

Volume of saline to be added to protein solution ....

$\quad D - (B + F) = G$ ml

Solution of immunogloblin
  +
1/100 to 1/50 FITC to the amount of protein by weight is dissolved in
carbonate-bicarbonate buffer (pH 9.5, 0.5 M) in 1/10 the volume of the
2% protein solution

The final concentration of protein is adjusted to 2% by the addition
of saline

Incubate for 4 hours at 7–9°C with gentle stirring

Gel filtration through Sephadex G-25 or G-50 in 0.1 M NaCl containing
0.005 M phosphate buffer (pH 7.0)

Column chromatography on DEAE cellulose in 0.1 M NaCl containing
0.005 M phosphate buffer (pH 7.0)

Collect fraction of fluorescent antibody (F/P molecular ratio 1–2)

Absorbed with aceton powder of organs to remove nonspecific staining
activity

Storage

Fig. 15.   Method of Labeling of Antibody with FITC Solution of Immunogloblin

Procedure: The steps are outlined in Fig. 15.

Step I Labeling: The concentration of antibody solution is first determined
using a refractometer (A mg/ml). A times the volume of the solution gives the
total amount of protein ($A \times B = C$ mg). E mg of FITC corresponding to
1/100—1/150 that of the protein is dissolved in F ml of 0.5 M carbonate-bicarbonate buffer. F can be calculated by dividing the volume of 2% protein solution (D ml).   When the concentration of the original antibody solution is smaller
than 2%, D is considered equal to B.

When dissolving the FITC, care should be taken to avoid foaming.   The
FITC solution is added with stirring to the protein solution, adjusted to 2%
by prior addition of G ml of saline to Bml of protein solution.   Both the FITC
and protein solutions should be kept at 2°C.   The pH of the reaction mixture
should be 9.5.   Stirring is continued (using a magnetic stirrer at 7–9°C) for 4
hours without foaming.   A temperature of 7–9°C is easily obtained by keeping
the solution in an ordinary ice-box, the amount of FITC and the duration of
the reaction being optimal at this temperature.   At 2–4°C the amount of FITC
should be 1/100 that of the protein, with a reaction time of 6 hours.

In another method, the reaction is allowed to proceed at 20–25°C immediately
after the addition of FITC to the protein solution.   In this case, the amount
of dye should be 1/200–1/250 that of the protein, with a reaction time of 1–2
hours.   Since only a very small amount of protein is used for labeling in general,
use of such a small amount of dye is apt to invite errors.   However, contaminants

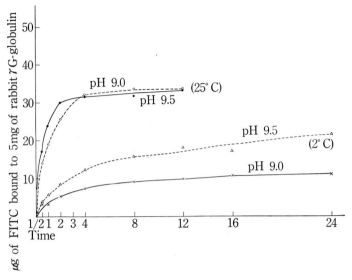

Fig. 16. Kinetics of Conjugation of FITC with Rabbit γG at 25° and 2°C
One mg of FITC in 1.0 m*l* of 0.5M carbonate-bicarbonate buffer (pH 9.0 and 9.5 respectively) was added to 100 mg protein solution of rabbit γG in saline with stirring at 2°C, then these mixtures were immediately divided into two parts. One part of each reaction mixture was incubated at 25°C and the other was left at 2°C. At the time indicated on the abscissa, a half m*l* aliquot of the reaction mixture was taken up and passed through a Sephadex G–25 column to separate unreacted free FITC. The amount of FITC bound to 5 mg of rabbit γG was calculated as shown on the ordinate. (Kawamura, 1964)

(denatured products of the dye, etc.) are prevented from combining with the protein in this method, and thus the nonspecific fluorescence is minimized.[21]

It should be apparent that there is a definite correlation between the amount of FITC, the temperature and the reaction time (Fig. 16).[18] There is one further method[27] in which the dye is adsorbed onto celite and then reacted with the protein for short time intervals. This method, however, is not recommended because of its poor combining efficiency.

Step II Removal of free dye: It is essential to remove the unreacted free dye on completion of the reaction. Otherwise, the reaction proceeds beyond the optimum. This is minimized by allowing the mixture to stand at 0–2°C. However, Steps I and II should be carried out in succession. The removal of free dye by dialysis in the original method required almost one week (even with combined use of activated carbon, 3 days were required). At present, it can be carried out within 30 minutes by using Sephadex.

The Sephadex column is prepared during the labeling procedure and, for the next procedure, the gel is equilibrated with 0.005 M phosphate buffer, pH 7.0. As illustrated schematically in Fig. 17, a zone of carbonate-bicarbonate buffer, 0.1 M NaCl used in labeling (invisible but detectable by pH testing), lies be-

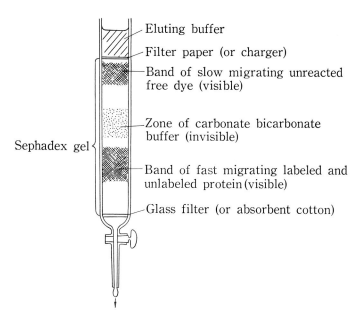

Fig. 17.   Removal of Free Dye using Gel Filtration through Sephadex

tween the advancing band of labeled (and unlabeled) protein and that of slow migrating unreacted free dye (clearly indicated by its yellow color).

Thus, it is possible to collect, by visual checking, the fast migrating fraction which is the solution of labeled protein free from unreacted dye (the protein is usually diluted more than 1.5 times).   It should be noted that the buffer of this fraction is replaced by the buffer with which the cellulose was equilibrated.   The amount of dye conjugated with the protein can be calculated by determining spectrophotometrically (490 mμ) the amount of unreacted dye eluted in the last fraction.

The procedures in Step II should be carried out in a cold room (2–4°C). If all labeling steps cannot be completed at one time, the preparation may be stored in the cold at this stage.

Step III Purification of labeled antibody: The labeled protein obtained in Step II is fractionated by DEAE cellulose column chromatography to obtain the fraction with the F/P molar ratio of 1–2.   Fractionation should be carried out in the cold (2–4°C).

The techniques of chromatography were discussed in the preceding section. After application of the labeled protein to the DEAE cellulose column previously equilibrated with 0.005 M phosphate buffer, pH 7.0 (containing 0.1 M NaCl), it can be observed visually that the fractions with strong nonspecific fluorescence (i.e., strong negative charge) are more firmly adsorbed to the cellulose and migrate slowly.   Thus, the general behavior of protein labeled to various degrees can be observed—the unlabeled protein fraction being eluted first, followed by fractions with an F/P molar ratio of 1, 2, 3, etc.   This behavior can be confirmed by examining the properties of fractions obtained by a gradient elution with increasing salt concentration starting from 0.005 M. The first fraction, with a light greenish-yellow tone, is largely unlabeled protein; this is followed by a brightly colored peak with an F/P molar ratio of 1–2 and subsequent fractions with increasingly large F/P molar ratios. Upon elution with 0.5–1.0 M NaCl, an additional fraction with a strong greenish-yellow color comes out, followed by less and less strongly colored fractions. These fractions have an F/p molar ratio over 3–5, a strong negative charge, and of course cannot be used in the FA technique.

Thus, it can be seen that with the γG antibody, the fraction with an F/P molar ratio of 1–2 can be obtained by collecting the strongly colored fractions of the first peak. Usually, it is not necessary to concentrate this fraction further. When dealing with antibodies of the γA or γM, the type of chromatographic separation suitable for each should be used, i.e. the concentration of eluent should be increased stepwise from 0.01 M to 0.1 M using a DEAE cellulose column equilibrated with 0.005 M phosphate buffer, pH 7.0.[18] The exact conditions

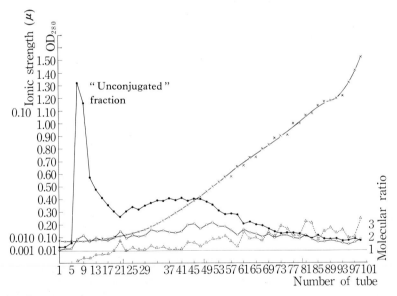

Fig. 18. Separation of FITC Conjugated Rabbit γG (anti BSA) by DEAE Cellulose Column Chromatography (III) Using a Continuous Gradient Flow With Sodium Chloride (Kawamura, 1964)
Eluting buffer: 0.005M Na-phosphate buffer (pH 7.0)
BSA: bovine serum albumin
100 mg of globulin conjugated with 400 μg FITC at pH 9.5 for 120 min at 25°C. 77.2% of the FITC was bound to the protein   column: 1.5×13 cm
○———○: OD at 495 (amount of FITC)
●———●: OD at 280, corrected (amount of protein minus amount of FITC in each fraction)
×———×: Ionic strengh (μ)
△--------△: Molecular ration of FITC to protein

for optimum labeling of IgM antibody are still to be determined, but the general method may be similar to IgG. The chromatographic patterns of labeled IgG and IgA rabbit anti-BSA antibodies are shown in Fig. 18–21 and Table 2.[18] A schematic representation of the chromatographic pattern of labeled antibody of each immunoglobulin class is shown in Fig. 22.

The method outlined above is that developed by the FA technique study group of the Institute of Medical Science.[18] In the following paragraphs we will discuss the method used by Coons[20] and Clark and Shepard.[4] In Coon's procedure, DEAE cellulose is equilibrated with 0.005 M phosphate buffer (pH 8.1, no NaCl added). The labeled protein in the same buffer, which replaces the carbonate buffer when the free dye is removed by gel filtration or is exchanged by dialysis after removing the free dye, is applied to the DEAE cellulose column and eluted with about 2 bed volumes of the same buffer. The eluate thus

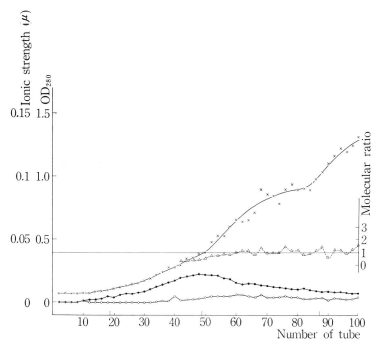

Fig. 19. Separation of FITC Conjugated Rabbit γA (anti BSA) by DEAE Cellulose Column Chromatography (IV) Using continous Gradient Flow with Sodium Chloride (Kawamura, 1964)
Eluting buffer: 0.005 M Na-phosphate buffer (ph 7.0)
BSA: bovine serum albumin
40 mg of globulin conjugated with 160 ug FITC at pH 9.5 for 120 min at 25°C.
63.1% of the FITC was bound to the protein column: 1.5×13 cm
○————○: OD at 495
●————●: OD at 280, corrected
×————×: Ionic strength (μ)
△--------△: Molecular ratio of FITC to protein

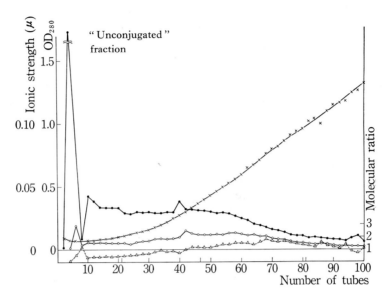

Fig. 20. Separation of FITC Conjugated Rabbit γG (anti BSA) by DEAE
Cellulose Column Chromatography (VI) Using a Continuous Gradient Flow
with Sodium Chloride (Kawamura, 1964)
Eluting buffer: 0.005M Na-phosphate buffer (pH 7.0)
BSA: bovine serum albumin
100 mg of globulin conjugated with 400 μg FITC at pH 9.5 for 6 hours at 9°C.
69% of the FITC was bound to the protein   column: 1.5×11 cm
○———○: OD at 495
●———●: OD at 280, corrected
×———×: Ionic strength (μ)
△--------△: Molecular Ratio of FITC to protein

obtained is discarded. Next, the strongly fluorescent fractions eluted with 0.05 M
phosphate buffer (pH 6.3, without NaCl) are collected and designated Fr. 1.
Fr. 2 is obtained by increasing the concentration of phosphate buffer to 0.1 M
(pH 6.3, without NaCl). Finally Fr. 3 is obtained by elution with 1 N NaCl.
Usually, Fr. 1 is the purified labeled antibody with the least nonspecific fluorescence. Fr. 3 shows intense nonspecific fluorescence (due to its strong negative charge) and cannot be used. Fr. 2 is intermediate between the two.

In Clark and Shepard's method, the purified IgG is dissolved in 0.025 M
carbonate buffer at a concentration of 1%. The solution is dialyzed in cellophane
tubing against 10 volumes of the same buffer containing 0.1 mg/ml of FITC at
4°C for 24 hours with continuous stirring. Dialysis is continued against phosphate buffered saline until no fluorescence is found in the diffusate. The labeled
antibody prepared in this manner is claimed to have negligible nonspecific
fluorescence without further treatment. Our experiments have proved otherwise,
however. Nevertheless, the procedure is simple, and may be used when dealing
with a small amount of antibody solution.

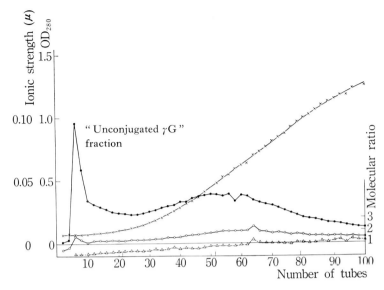

Fig. 21. Separation of FITC Conjugated Rabit γA (anti BSA) by DEAE Cellulose Column Chromatography (VII) Using Continuous Gradiet Flow with Sodium Chloride (Kawamura, 1964)

Eluting buffer: 0.005M Na-phosphate buffer (pH 7.0)

BSA: bovine serum albumin

100 mg of globulin conjugated with 400 μg FITC at pH 9.5 for 120 min at 25°C

69% of the FITC was bound to the protein   column: 1.5×11 cm

○———○:   OD at 495

●———●:   OD at 280, corrected

×   ×:   Ionic strength (μ)

△·······△:   Molecular ratio of FITC to protein

(a–ii)   Tetramethyl rhodamine isothiocyanate

In general, the same procedures used for FITC may be applied.   Since the fluorescence efficiency of this dye is poor, however, it is necessary to increase the ratio of dye to protein to about 1: 20, despite a possible increase in negative charge.   The reaction time is 18 hours at 7–9°C.   The unreacted free dye is removed by gel filtration with Sephadex.   Even with a longer column, however, efficient separation is difficult.   A certain amount of protein is usually lost.

(b)   Labeling with fluorescent dyes having an SO_2Cl residue (tetraethyl rhodamine compounds such as RB 200, etc.)

The first step is to substitute the SO_2Cl group for the SO_2Na group of the dye by treatment with PCl_5.   Labeling is carried out in the second step.   Free dye is removed in the third step, and lastly the labeled antibody is purified.   Because of its poor fluorescence and its bright color, this dye is more often used as a counter-stain than as the labeling agent for antibody.   It would be possible to use it in the FA technique, however, if a more suitable method of purifying the labeled antibody could be found.   For use as a counter-stain, it is necessary to introduce as many dye molecules as possible in order to increase nonspecific

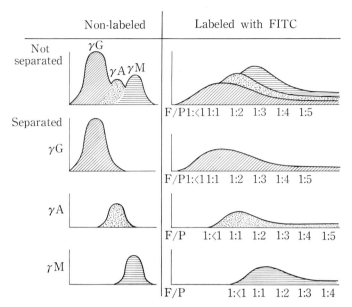

Fig. 22. Elution Characteristics of Rabbit Antibody of Each Immunoglobulin Class from a DEAE Cellulose Column
F/P: Ab labeled with FITC at the average molecular ratio of FITC/Protein indicated in the figure.

Table 2. Characteristics of Labeled Anti-BSA Rabbit Antibody

Fraction	Chromatography Fractions					Concentrated with PVP		Mg of Labeled Ab Protein Giving Specific Positive Staining of BSA Incorporated into Mouse Kidney or Liver	Molar Ratio F/P
	Chromatography No.	Tube No.		Volume (ml)	Volume (Ratio)	Total Protein (mg/ml)			
γG	III	8, 10		8.5	1/15	9.50		trace with 3.0	0.39
		38, 40		8.0	1/10	3.12		0.8	1.12
		82, 84, 86		15.0	1/32	3.98		1.3	2.77
γA	IV	47, 49		9.5	1/10	1.71		1.7	0.50
		77, 79		9.5	1/20	1.76		0.9	1.17
γG	VI	13, 15		9.0	1/10	3.01		1.5	0.48
		45, 47		9.0	1/12	3.03		0.5	1.19
		69, 71		9.0	1/20	2.71		0.9	1.69
γA	VII	25, 27		10.0	1/5	4.75		negative with 2.0	0.39
		65, 67		10.0	1/15	3.88		0.6	1.04

BSA : bovine serum albumin   (Kawamura, 1964)

ionic adsorption by the tissue containing none of the antigenic determinants in question. On the other hand, a conjugate showing as little nonspecific staining as possible must be used in labeling the antibody. Therefore, it is necessary to set up certain conditions to insure that the whole serum is sufficiently labeled in the counter-stain, and different conditions to label the purified antibody. Our general procedure follows Chadwick's method[1] with a few minor improvements.

0.5 g of dye and 1 g of PCl_5 are placed in a mortar and ground together for a few minutes. Since irritating fumes may be formed, the mixing should be done under a ventilator hood. An SO_2Cl residue is formed by this reaction. The reaction product can be extracted with acetone by adding 5 ml dry acetone (obtained by adding completely dry calcium sulfate to acetone) and mixing for several minutes. The solution, dark wine in color, is quickly separated by filtration to avoid evaporation of acetone and used immediately for labeling. The following procedures should be carried out in the cold room (2–4°C). One volume of the purified antibody solution is mixed with 2 volumes of 0.5 M carbonate buffer (pH 9.5); care should be taken not to reduce the protein concentration below 1%. To this mixture 0.1 ml per 60 mg protein of the dye solution prepared as above is added drop by drop, using a capillary pipette, with stirring. Stirring is continued for 30 minutes with an occasional pH check. Active carbon (0.5 mg per 1 mg of protein) is also added at this time. After further stirring for 60 minutes, the mixture is centrifuged at 7,500 rpm for 15 minutes to remove the carbon. Ammonium sulfate is added to the supernatant to a 40% saturation. The precipitates that are salted out are collected by centrifuging at 9,000 rpm for 15 minutes, then dissolved in as small an amount of saline as possible, and subjected to gel filtration with Sephadex for desalting and removal of the free dye. This is followed by DEAE cellulose chromatography, which should produce a fraction with an F/P molar ratio of 1–2. To prepare the labeled protein for counter-staining, the reaction time with protein should be prolonged to 24 hours. Removal of free dye by gel filtration or dialysis after treatment with active carbon may be sufficient. Although acetone extracts of the dye cannot be stored as is, they can be kept for about one month when adsorped onto filter paper and stored in a desiccator. To label the protein, the filter paper is cut into small pieces and the pieces dipped into the solution. The filter paper is then removed by centrifugation after the reaction is completed.

C. The Properties of Fluorescent Antibody

So far, we have described the preparation of fluorescent antibody to be used for labeling without further treatment. Let us now examine some of its properties, such as antibody titer (staining potency), specificity, and F/P molar ratio, in order to determine any specific uses to which it can be put. We should note, also, that absorption with powdered tissue prepared from the organs of animals of the same species from which the section was prepared is frequently used at present to increase staining specificity and to obtain a clearer picture.

(a)   The molar ratio of fluorochrome to protein.

In order to prevent the occurrence of nonspecific fluorescence, it is necessary to remove fractions with a strong negative charge.   Fractions containing un-labeled antibody, which acts as a blocking agent in staining, must also be removed from the solution of fluorescent antibody.   As stated in the first section, the dye-protein which shows the minimum nonspecific staining and has at least an ade-quate specific fluorescence is the one with an F/P molar ratio of 1–2.

Estimation of fluorochrome: When conjugated to protein, the absorption spectra of all fluorescent dyes have different patterns than those of the free dyes, showing a shift in the wavelength of their maximum absorption.   The absorbancy (optical density) at the same wavelength also varies, depending on the pH of the medium. For example, the wavelength of the maximum absorption of a pure FITC solution is 490 mμ.   When conjugated with protein, it shifts to 495 mμ.   Standard curves (Fig. 23) can be prepared by determing the optical densities of a log dilution series of the original FITC solution at 490 and 495 mμ, using a spectro-photometer.   The FITC solution is prepared by completely dissolving an exact

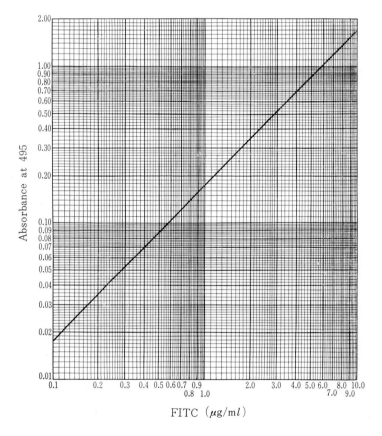

FITC $(\mu g/ml)$

Fig. 23.   Standard Absorption Curve of Fluorescein Isothiocyanate (FITC) (pH 7.0) at OD_{495} mμ (OD_{495}/FITC $\mu g = 0.175$)

amount of FITC in carbonate buffer.   The curve at 490 mμ can be used to determine the amount of free dye.   From the standard curve at 495 mμ, the average absorbance (OD) per 1 μg of conjugated dye can be calculated (OD$_{495}$ /μg FITC$=0.175$).   The amount of FITC in a preparation, the F/P molar ratio of which is to be determined, is obtained either by dividing its OD$_{495}$ value by the above value or directly applying the observed value to the standard curve......(A) *Estimation of protein*:   In general, the micro-Kjeldahl method, Folin or biuret reactions are used......(B)   All of these methods have certain disadvantages, such as troublesome procedures, too low sensitivity, or overlapping absorption at longer wavelengths.

Although the amount of unlabeled protein can be determined from the standard curve drawn from OD$_{280}$ values of known amounts of protein, the absorption of FITC itself at 280 mμ interferes with the calculations.   This can be avoided by

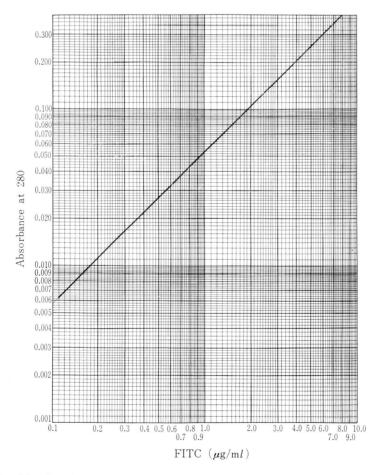

Fig. 24.   Standard Absorption Curve of Fluorescein Isothiocyanate (FITC) (pH 7.0) at OD$_{280}$ mμ (OD$_{280}$/FITC μg$=0.0530$)

assuming that the OD_{280} of a conjugated protein is the sum of the OD of the protein itself and that of the labeled dye. First, the standard absorption curve of FITC is drawn (Fig. 24), the average absorbance of FITC is expressed as OD_{280} $/\mu g$ FITC$=0.0530$, and the OD_{280} due to the conjugated FITC of the preparation is determined from the amount of FITC obtained in (A) and this standard curve......(C). Next, the OD_{280} of the preparation is determined in a separate experiment......(D). Thus, D-C represents the OD_{280} value of protein in the preparation and the amount of protein can be calculated from this value. Since the OD_{280} of a solution of mammalian γG at a concentration of 10 mg/ml is almost invariably 13, $(D$-$C)\times0.75$ will give the amount of γG in mg......(E). In actuality, however, the OD_{280} of a labeled protein is greater than the sum of the respective values of the protein and the dye. Our object is to discover the strength of the negative charge of the preparation from the relative amount of protein and dye, and therefore it is not essential to know the absolute value of the amount of protein. Taking possible errors in other methods of measurement into account, the F/P molar ratio can be calculated directly from the OD values according to the following equation:

$$\text{F/P molar ratio} = \frac{A\mu g}{\text{Mol. Wt. of}} \bigg/ \frac{B(\text{or } E)\,\mu g}{\text{Mol. Wt. of}}$$
$$\text{FITC} \qquad\qquad \text{Protein}$$

(b)   Determination of antibody titer (staining titer)

The antibody titer of fluorescent antibody is expressed in terms of the amount of antibody protein in the original antiserum. The complement fixation test, precipitin test (antibody dilution method), and passive hemaglutination can be used to measure the titer. A two-fold dilution series of the preparation of fluorescent antibody can also be reacted with the corresponding antigen and the maximum dilution determined, which gives the visible specific fluorescence or determination of staining titer (a dilution containing 2–4 units is used in the actual staining).

(c)   Criteria for the specificity of the fluorescent antibody preparation

The specificity can be determined by using immunoelectrophoresis and/or agar gel diffusion tests against various control antigens and also by inhibition tests.

D. Absorption with Tissue Powder.

Fluorescent antibody prepared and examined by our method shows markedly reduced nonspecific fluorescence, at least with regard to that due to the labeling of antibody, as compared with that of a preparation prepared by the classic methods. Direct use of such a preparation without further scrutiny, however, may not be sufficient for tracing a very small amount of antigen or for a preparation at a concentration of 2–4 units used for diagnostic purposes, and further treatment to remove the nonspecific fluorescence as completely as possible may be required. With tissue sections especially, nonspecific staining may cause difficulties in interpretation. When an antiserum showing cross-reaction with the tissue antigens of the section to be examined is the starting material for fluorescent antibody, absorption with the same tissue or with another tissue of an animal of the same species may be necessary for complete removal of such non-specific fluorescence and for use in the FA technique.

Although the tissue powder used for absorption is usuallly from the tissue to be examined or from another organ of an animal of the same species, mouse liver tissue is frequently used for efficient and universal absorption of nonspecific fluorescence. Treatment with acetone is the usual procedure for preparation of the tissue powder, but other means may also be used, since there are cases in which complete absorption cannot be achieved with such a preparation. For example, there are cases in which the specific fluorescence could be detected only after absorption with powder prepared by treatment with fluorocarbon, as will be described in the next section on the pretreatment of antigen.

(a) Preparation of acetone-dried powder

The preparation of powdered tissue from mouse liver can be taken as an example of the method. Livers are collected from large mice after exsanguination. If not used immediately, they are stored in a deep-freezer. A quantity of liver $(x$ g$)$ is cut into small pieces, washed with distilled (deionized) water several times, and homogenized in a Waring blender with an equal volume of saline $(x$ ml$)$, with care taken to avoid generation of heat. After the homogenate is poured into a beaker, 8 volumes $(8x$ ml$)$ of acetone are added with stirring. The precipitate is collected by centrifugation (3,000 rpm, 10 minutes) and resuspended in $4x$ ml of saline and kept in the cold room overnight. Sediments are collected either by centrifugation or suction through a Buchner funnel, and suspended again in x ml of saline followed by a second addition of $8x$ ml of acetone. The resultant precipitates are collected similarly. Resuspension in saline $(x$ ml$)$ and treatment with acetone $(8x$ ml$)$ are repeated until hemoglobin pigment is no longer discernible in the supernatant (no soluble protein should be present). After the washing, $4x$ ml of acetone are added directly to the final sediment, the solution is allowed to stand for a while, stirred, and then the supernatant is removed. This procedure is repeated, then the sediment is further washed in the funnel and suction is applied to remove the acetone as completely as possible. A dry powder is obtained by spreading the material on filter paper and drying in an incubator or desiccator. The yield of powder should be about 1/20 of the starting material. This is a modification of Coons' method, and is used routinely in our laboratory.

(b) Absorption procedure for labeled antibody

There are two methods of absorption, using either dry or wet powder.

Dry powder method: 100 mg/ml of dry powder is added to the solution of conjugated protein adjusted to a staining titer of 4 units, mixed thoroughly and centrifuged at 12,000–16,000 rpm for 20–30 minutes after standing for about 1 hour at room temperature. A second portion of 50 mg/ml of powder is added to the supernatant, and the procedure repeated. The supernatant is carefully collected with a pipette, taking care to avoid contamination with sediment, and distributed in small amounts into ampules or small test tubes which are frozen and stored after sealing. About 60% by volume is recoverable by this method, but the staining titer of the solution becomes concentrated. The absorbed fluorescent antibody becomes denatured if stored at room temperature. This may happen even in the cold room due to contaminating enzymes from the powdered tissue. This is why the absorbed preparation must be divided into small amounts, and frozen without delay after each use (freeze-thawing should not be repeated more than 10 times). The addition of 0.1% sodium azide (NaN_3) prevents bacterial contamination.

Wet powder method: In the dry powder method, there is some loss of solution. In order to avoid this, aliquots of weighed amounts of dry powder are added to the solution to be absorbed (first and second absorption, respectively) and are treated with about the same volume of phosphate buffer or saline as in the wet powder method, giving 2 preparations of wet powder after centrifugation under the same conditions. The solution of labeled antibody is treated twice, as in the first method, with this wet powder. When done properly, neither loss nor dilution of the solution results. For preservation of the absorbed solution, the same precautions should be taken as in the first method.

If nonspecific fluorescence still remains even after absorption with tissue powder as described above, repeated absorption or absorption with powders of different kinds of tissue or treated with different solvents may be tried.

(c) Other methods

(c-i) Absorption with sediments of tissue powder at high speed centrifugation.

Tissue powder prepared by treatment with acetone is washed repeatedly with saline, and the suspension is centrifuged at 15,000–16,000 rpm for 30 minutes. The sediment can be used directly for absorption. The solution of labeled antibody treated in this way is not suitable for storage owing to heavy contamination with tissue enzymes. Enzyme inhibitors such as ethylene diamine tetraacetic acid ($0.2\ \mu g/ml$) or soy bean trypsin inhibitor ($3\ \mu g/ml$) may be used.

(c-ii) Absorption with cultured cells

In virus studies, investigations of the antigens of cultured cells may be required, and in some cases absorption with tissue powder prepared as described above will fail to eliminate the nonspecific fluorescence. In such a case, a normal culture of the same cells or of the same animal species is used for absorption, although difficulty may be encountered in getting enough cells. The cells are used directly without any further treatment, or cell powder prepared by treatment with acetone may be used for absorption. Large amounts of cells are required for satisfactory results.

E. Storage of the Labeled Antibody

Care should be taken not to reduce the antibody activity or invite denaturation. Since no special precautions are taken to prevent bacterial contamination in the FA technique, the main problem is storage. Preservation of the solution at 4°C with the addition of 0.1% sodium azide is preferred. It should be noted, however, that the addition of sodium azide before labeling has an unfavorable effect on the labeling reaction. Storage of frozen material at $-20°C$ gives poor results. Storage at $-70°C$ is problematical because of the need to thaw and refreeze the material for each use. It is also possible to store the labeled antibody in the lyophilized state with appropriate stabilizers, but there is some reduction in antibody activity within 1–2 years. The preservation without reduction of activity of labeled, absorbed antibody is far more difficult than the preservation of untreated antibody because of partial insolubilization, appearance of nonspecific fluorescence, reduction in staining titer, etc. Preservation by lyophilization is possible with the addition of such substances as glycin, sodium glutamate, lactose or saccharose, when the concentrations of protein and selected additive are appropriately balanced.

Another possible method is storage of the material in sealed ampules in vacuo; these too, however, show a reduction in staining titer after storage at $4°C$ for 1 year. Sealed ampules with small amounts of material stored at $-70°C$ are preferable if facilities are available.

4. Preparation of Substrates and Fixation

The tissue sections or smears to be examined must be prepared and fixed (pretreated) in such a way that the antigen keeps its antigenicity and remains in its original site without diffusing out or being stripped off from the tissue or cells. The formation of the antigen-antibody complex must also be facilitated by preparing very thin sections and removing agents that inhibit the reaction and formation of the complex, by expelling the antibody solution, masking the antigen, or inhibiting the combination per se. The kind of antigen (bacteria, virus, enzyme, etc.), and the properties of the tissue or cells in which the antigen is present should also be taken into consideration.

Infectious microbes sometimes withstand the rather mild preparative procedures adopted to avoid antigenic deterioration, and retain their infectivity. Care should be taken in these cases to avoid infection (by vaccination, determination of antibody titer, etc.).

A. Slides and Cover Slips

These must be thin and of good quality, showing no fluorescence. The tissue section is generally placed on the cover slip and mounted upside down on the slide after staining (a tissue culture can be treated in the same way). Smears and impression preparations are made on the slide and the cover slip is applied afterwards. It should be remembered that the working distance of a dark-field condenser (which fluorescent antibody preparations are usually observed with) is less than 1.2 mm and occasionally as short as 1.0 mm, except that of the Tiyoda Optical Co. which is 1.4 mm. Therefore, a slide thinner than this must be used. A normal slide is about 1.5 mm thick. Slides 1.0 ± 0.2 mm thick can generally be used, although some condensers, e.g. the Reichert and Weiss models, require even thinner ones. Adequate slides can be obtained from the Matsunami Co. in Japan. Smear preparations can be made by applying the material to circles previously marked on a slide, 4 circles (about 1 cm in diameter) to a slide.

Clearing of slides: Glass slides are first washed thoroughly in neutral cleanser, soaked in ethanol containing 3% hydrochloric acid for 12–24 hours, and stored in pure ethanol. Before use, they are dried by holding them for a few seconds in the burner flame. After use, they can be cleaned by soaking in water to remove the mounting agents, followed by treatment with cleanser and a potassium dichromate-sulfuric acid mixture.

B. Tissue Sections

Sections must be cut as thin as possible from materials taken in autopsy or biopsy or from experimental animals. If the sections are too thick the specific fluorescence may be masked by the increase in auto- and nonspecific fluorescence. Normal paraffin embedding may result in a marked or complete loss of antigenicity. Ordinary sectioning of CO_2-frozen tissue does not provide sufficiently thin sections for the purpose. The most desirable method of tissue sectioning at present is with a cryostat. However, with certain antigens, a modified paraffin-sectioning, carbowax or lyophilization may be used.

(a) Snap-freezing method

(a–i) Freezing

Fresh tissue material is frozen directly, for if the material is allowed to stand, it frequently loses its antigenicity. Influenza virus material aged more than 18 hours has been used successfully in cold weather, but material from mice infected with Japanese encephalitis virus and allowed to stand at 37°C for 24 hours completely lost its viral antigenicity. Freezing below −70°C is desirable, but too rapid freezing with liquid nitrogen must be avoided. In general, use of a dry ice-acetone mixture (−70~−72°C) may be recommended. Tissues are cut into pieces of appropriate size (1.5 cm² × 3 mm), wiped clean and fixed to a piece of filter paper. The description and identification of the specimen should be written in pencil (not ink) on the paper. As shown in Fig. 25, dry ice and acetone are placed in a wide-mouthed vessel in which a large test tube containing *n*-hexane or iso-pentane is immersed. Prior cooling of these solvents to −70°C minimizes the formation of ice crystals. The solvents do not damage the tissue. The tissue fixed on filter paper is gently immersed in the solvent in the test tube. 5 to 10 minutes are sufficient for freezing. If the tissue is left in the solvent for a longer period of time, it dries out and turns to powder on sectioning. As soon as the tissue is completely frozen it is removed from the test tube with forceps, placed in another test tube and stored after sealing in a dry ice-acetone mixture, in dry ice, or below −20°C. Use of cooled iso-pentane (−160°C) may be preferable for freezing with liquid nitrogen. Frozen tissue should be cut as soon as possible, but with careful storage it may be used more than a year later. If the frozen pieces are allowed to melt they cannot be refrozen. Tissues which are difficult to section (e.g. lung tissue) or very minute materials (e.g. mosquito

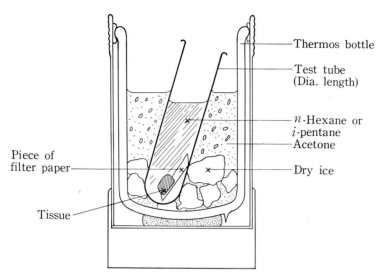

Thermos bottle

Test tube
(Dia. length)

n-Hexane or
i-pentane
Acetone

Dry ice

Piece of
filter paper

Tissue

Fig. 25.   Tissue-freezing Method

tissue) are immersed into albumin solution prior to freezing or inserted into a small cut made in mouse liver, frozen and sectioned together with the liver.   In the first method, the material is placed on the surface of frozen albumin solution in a small cup made of zinc foil, about 1 cm in diameter, and frozen after further addition of albumin solution.

(a–ii)   Preparation of tissue sections

A cryostat is used for sectioning.   The instrument consists of a refrigerated cabinet, the temperature of which can be lowered to between 0° and −30°C and in which a microtome is housed.

While tissues are usually sectioned at −18° to −20°C, other temperatures may be optimal for some tissues (e.g. −15°C for plant tissues).   Thin sections of not more than 4 μ should be cut and fixed to the slide without creasing or overlapping, which would intensify the auto- and nonspecific fluorescence.   Control of the humidity is important in humid areas such as Japan (a 55% humidity is most favorable; over 60% should be avoided).   Working in a small air-conditioned room is best.   A hydrophilic absorbant like silica gel should be placed in the cabinet.   Various types cryostats are available: of a remote control model, a manually operated one (the hands are inserted through holes on both sides of the instrument), and one with an air-curtain device; the first type is the most convenient.   There are two major types of microtome: in one, a fixed tissue block is sectioned by moving the knife, and in the other, sections are made by moving the block against a fixed knife.   Jung's sliding model belongs to the former, Minot's revolving model and Kembridge's rocking and rotary models belong to the latter.   While exchange of the specimen is easier with the former, a certain amount of friction cannot be avoided even with oil of a low freezing point.   The latter, especially the rocking and rotary types, have only negligible friction, but exchange of the specimen is troublesome and the rocking type will not take large tissue fragments. The cryostats manufactured by Pearse-SLEE (England) (Fig. 26), Harris, Lipshow (U.S.A.), Linde (West Germany) and Sakura (Japan) are popular at present.

The frozen tissue fragments are quickly frozen on to an object holder, precooled to −20°C, by applying a very small amount of water or saline round its base. With too much water or prolonged manipulation, the frozen tissue becomes water-logged. If this happens, the base of the object holder can be immersed in a dry ice-acetone mixture. This can be done by hanging the holder as shown in Fig 27A (the Pearse holder has holes for hanging). It should be kept in mind that too strong cooling may result in detachment of the tissue from the holder. The holder with the tissue fragments is then positioned on the microtome for cutting. The section curls upwards from the temperature difference between it and the knife and from the heat of fusion. The instrument is constructed so that the sectioned, frozen sheet of tissue is inserted into the gap between the knife and the antiroller which is fixed either directly to the knife (Jung type) or adjacent to it (Minot and Kembridge types), as illustrated in Fig. 27 B. When the antiroller is removed, the section lies flat on the knife surface. It is then transferred, by touching the surface lightly, to a cover slip fixed by suction to a rubber sucker attached to the tip of a specially designed pipette, as shown in Fig. 27C. The section smoothes out on the cover slip, whose temperature is considerably higher (room temperature) than the section. After removing it from the cryostat cabinet,

Fig. 26. Cryostat (Pearse-SLEE)

the section is allowed to stand at room temperature until dry.   In humid weather, however, the section should be dried rapidly with a dryer.

By this method, it is possible to make serial sections and to process some 20 samples per hour.   When working with an instrument lacking the antiroll device, the sheet of sectioned tissue is carefully picked up with a soft brush and placed on a pre-cooled cover slip.   The section will extend slowly on the glass when the back side of the cover slip is warmed with a finger tip, although this procedure requires some skill.   Some workers recommend using an egg albumin-glycerin mixture or adhesive cement to fix the section to the glass.   If the glass is sufficiently clean and the section sufficiently thin no adhesive is normally needed.   In general, it is more convenient for later handling to attach the section to the cover slip than to the slide.

The prepared section should be fixed and stained immediately if possible. If the section must be stored for a short period (about 1 week), it should be stored before fixation in a cold room ($-5°C$) or at $-20°C$ after having been completely dried and sealed.   When ready to use, the seal should not be opened until the section has come to room temperature.   If longer storage (several weeks) is necessary, the specimen should be treated as above after fixation.

(b)   Sectioning of tissue embedded in paraffin

Using paraffin sections in the FA technique would probably increase its availability and would also permit thinner sections with finer structure than the frozen ones.   Although fairly good results have hitherto been obtained with this method with certain stable antigens (bacteria, etc.), they were not comparable to those obtained by frozen section.   This was due to the deleterious effects of the fixation, embedding in paraffin, and treatments with xylene to remove the paraffin.   Consequently, the method could not be applied to a labile antigen like that of viruses.   Recently, however, an improved method for carrying out the processes at low temperatures was developed by Saint-Marie[28] and applied successfully to certain viral antigens.   Since then, the paraffin method attracted renewed interest.

The improved method[28]—Small fresh fragments of tissue are fixed with an appropriate solution for 1 to 2 hours at about 4°C.   In order to get adequate fixation, the fragments are then cut into smaller pieces, 3 to 4 mm thick, and treated with the solution overnight at 4°C, followed by the usual treatments with ethanol and xylene and by embedding in paraffin (at 53° to 56°C).   Except for the embedding, all procedures are carried out at 4°C.   Then the tissue is sectioned and finally treated with ethanol after removing the paraffin.

The section should be allowed to float out on water for only a short time. Adequate washing of the section in phosphate buffer at pH 7.0 will reduce its auto- and nonspecific fluorescence.   Sections embedded in paraffin are fairly stable.

(c)   Other methods

(c–i)   Freeze-substitution

Frozen tissue fragments are dehydrated by treating with absolute ethanol,

(A) Hanger for object

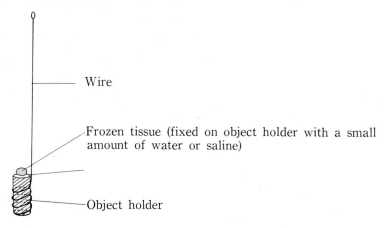

(B) Antiroller When correctly positioned, controls the initial tendency of the section to roll up and guides the section, as it is cut, down the face of the knife.

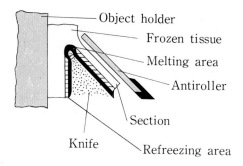

(C) Suction holder

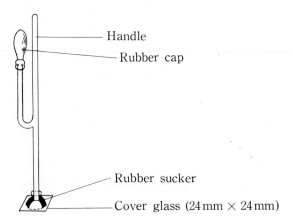

Fig. 27. Accessories for Cryostat

butanol, or propanol at $-35°$ to $-40°C$ for 48 to 96 hours and treated like lyophilized material (embedding in polyester wax⟶sectioning). The use of this method has not yet been fully studied, however, with the FA technique.

(c–ii) Carbowax method

Because the melting point of carbowax is below $50°C$ and it is soluble in water and ethanol, the fixed tissue fragments can be embedded in carbowax after the solution used in fixation has been washed off.   Treatment of the sectioned tissue with only ethanol and phosphate buffer is also possible.   The advantages of this method compensate for the drawbacks of paraffin embedding.   Furthermore, by combining different kinds of carbowax of different molecular weights, a block of good consistency can be obtained.   The carbowax sections are fairly stable.

C. Smear and Impression Preparations

These preparations are used frequently for diagnostic purposes.   First, a thin clean slide is passed slowly through a burner flame and allowed to cool. Blood or exudate samples are spread thinly on these slides as usual.   Samples of pus, fetus, or urine sediments are spread over an appropriate area on the slide. For ciliated epithelial cells, which are frequently studied for diagnosis of viral diseases, a direct sampling with a cotton swab from the *concha inferior* is made, using a rhinoscope, after removing any viscous secretions, and the swab is spread carefully over a circle about 1.5 cm in diameter marked on a slide with blue glass pencil (red pencil does not work well).

The same method can be used for pharyngeal mucous membrane.   However, since this type of membrane is covered with nonciliated, keratinized, flat epithelial cells, peeling off the basal cells for a smear is more complicated.   With a specimen from a test incision or autopsy material, a small cut is made on the tissue with a sharp knife and the fresh surface is pressed against the glass so as to leave at least one layer of cells (Fig. 28A).   Next, the tissue is rubbed strongly against the glass as shown in Fig. 28B.   The preparations are dried at room temperature with a hair-dryer (cold air) or an electric fan, placed in polyethylene bags, sealed tightly, and stored at $-20°C$ until use.   (Storage for 1 or 2 weeks in a cold room does not cause serious deterioration.)   These preparations are preserved without fixation and the bag is opened only after the slide has come to room temperature.

This method is used for testing unknown material with a known test serum. When an unknown antiserum is tested against a known antigen, a fresh culture of bacteria is used for the smear.   In the case of leptospira or treponema, which are fragile and apt to be stripped away, an appropriate adhesive such as 2–5% egg albumin is added to the suspension before making the smear.

Fig. 28.   Impression Preparation (A) and Smear Preparation (B)

D. Preparation of Tissue Culture Cells

Tissue culture cells are frequently used in virus studies with the FA technique. Usually, a small piece of glass is inserted in a tissue culture tube (a Leighton or angular tube) to obtain a monolayer of cells. If a CO_2-incubator is available, the cells may be cultured in a Petri dish, the bottom of which is covered with cover slips. The cells grown on the cover slips are infected with virus and, after a given interval, the cover slips are taken out and rinsed in phosphate buffer to remove the culture medium. This may be done by placing the cover slip in a test tube with a hole at the bottom and repeatedly dipping the tube in buffer. Alternatively, the tube may be stood in a tray containing phosphate buffer and gently vibrated mechanically as shown in Fig. 32B. The preparation is dried after washing and preserved as in the previous procedure or it may be stained immediately. A thin sheet of cells can readily be examined by the FA technique but compact layers of piled-up cells present numerous difficulties. Usually, tissue culture cells are well spread, and are therefore highly suitable for investigating the intracellular distribution of antigen, often showing a clear and detailed pattern of antigen distribution in the cytoplasm and/or nuclei.

E.   Fixation (pretreatment)

Fixation of tissue sections or cells containing antigen is indispensable to subsequent staining for two reasons. First, it prevents the tissue from being pulled off the glass, and second, it facilitates the formation of the antigen-antibody complex by eliminating agents (for example, lipid) which prevent the antibody from gaining access to the antigen and/or inhibit the antigen-antibody reaction. The treatment should not, however, enhance nonspecific fluorescence due to the antigen or tissue.

Without appropriate fixation, staining of tissue containing antigen with corresponding labeled antibody frequently fails. Changes in the distribution and shape of the antigen may occur depending on the treatment used. The method must be suited to the nature of the antigen and to the tissue. Care should be taken not to lose an antigen or reduce its antigenicity by improper fixation. Occasionally, however, when dealing with a superficial and labile antigen, it may be best to omit fixation and to stain the section directly with labeled antibody.

(a)   Selection of solvent for fixation

Protein antigen: Treatment with 95% ethanol should be tried first. 100% methanol has been reported to give good results for serum proteins, and ethanol for antibody. Acetone or carbon tetrachloride is more frequently used for microbial antigens, including viruses. In order to eliminate the protein coat masking the antigen, the material is treated with proteases such as nagarse or trypsin.

Polysaccharide antigen: This antigen is normally relatively stable. Occasionally, however, it may be difficult to fix the antigen if pretreatment of the frozen section has been omitted. In such a case, the tissue is first treated with acetone, followed by sectioning of the frozen tissue or of tissue embedded in paraffin.

Treatment of bacterial polysaccharide antigens with 8 to 10% formalin (in neutral phosphate buffer) and subsequent embedding in paraffin will give fairly good preparations with good contrast. Unfortunately, however, such a treatment often enhances auto- and nonspecific fluorescence.

Fixation by heating over a flame may be used for bacterial smears. In order to remove the mucinous substances covering the antigen the material is treated with enzymes such as RDE, hyaluronidase, or mucinase.

Lipid antigen: Forssman and similar antigens are soluble in ethanol. Frozen sections of tissues containing these antigens are treated with 8–10% formalin or sodium hyposulfite. Pretreatment with organic solvents (ether, acetone, fluorocarbon), surface active agents, including cleanser, or enzymes (phospholipase, etc.) should be used for antigens in tissues rich in lipid.

(b) Conditions of fixation

pH: When there is a possibility of in vivo formation of an antigen-antibody complex, dissociation should first be attempted with hypertonic salt solution or enzymes or by changing the pH. It should be noted, however, that the use of strong acids or alkali will result in an increase in auto- and nonspecific fluorescence. Adequate washing with phosphate buffer is needed after such treatment. For treatment with enzyme, the optimum pH should be taken into consideration.

Temperature: Normally fixation is carried out at room temperature. Some enzymes are used at 37°C. For certain viruses, fixation with organic solvent at low temperatures is often required. For example, treatment with acetone at −20° to −40°C for 30 minutes is the best method for measles virus.

Time required for fixation: 5 to 10 minutes at room temperature are generally sufficient. Fixation at low temperatures requires a longer time.

Drying: The N antigen of polio virus grown in HeLa cells converts into H antigen when dried at room temperature and treated with acetone. It remains unchanged when treated with acetone at −20°C without desiccation.

Washing: When sections are dried immediately after fixation or washing, substances that have diffused out in the fixation process sometimes cover the surface, thereby inhibiting the reaction or increasing nonspecific fluorescence. The diffusing substances should therefore be removed by pouring phosphate buffer over the section while it is still immersed in solvent, followed by repeated rinsing and drying. Alternatively the specimen may be thoroughly washed immediately after removing it from the solvent. In order to make sure that the fluorescence developed by the staining is specific, various controls for fixation should be set up, and absorption of labeled antibody with powdered tissue treated with the same solvent as used for fixation should be carried out. A summary of the general procedures for fixation is given in Table 3. Some of the problems which we encountered in special situations will be discussed next.

In a study on globulins, protein was found in all areas, as expected, when the tissue was treated with acetone as usual. However, when it was treated with fluorocarbon only globulin bound to the tissue was stained, all free globulin, including plasma globulin, having been eliminated. Similarly, pretreatment of

Table 3. Fixation (Pretratment) of Various Antigens

Antigens	Fixed with	Conditions of Fixation
Protein		
Enzyme	⎫ 95% ethanol (100% ethanol)	
Hormone	⎪ (methanol), acetone	
Immunoglobulin	⎬ carbon tetrachloride (10% formol)	3–10 minutes at room temperature or 30 minutes at 4°C
Albumin	⎪ 95% ethanol with 1–5%	
Fibrinogen	⎭ glacial acetic acid	
Virus	acetone carbon tetrachloride 100% ethanol (methanol) (ether)	5–10 minutes at room temperature or 30–60 minutes at 4°C or a long time at −20°C
Polysaccharide		
Bacteria, etc.	acetone, methanol 10% formol carbon tetrachloride heat (chloroform-methanol)	3–10 minutes at room temperature or 30 minutes at 4°C
Lipid		
Forssman antigen	10% formol sodium thiosulphate untreated	3–10 minutes at room temperature

Solvents in parentheses are useful for some antigens.

autopsy specimens or specimens from experimental animals infected with Japanese encephalitis Virus with carbon tetrachloride at 5°C for 30 to 60 minutes made it possible to detect traces of antigen which remained masked after fixation with acetone. These results are easily explained by the following experiments:

(b-i) What substances diffuse out during fixation? Serial sections ($4\,\mu$ thick) of a normal mouse brain were prepared and placed in weighing bottles to which 0.3 ml of acetone, fluorocarbon, methanol, or chloroform-methanol mixture (2:1) were added. After shaking for 10 minutes at room temperature (20°C), the sections were taken out and the remaining solvent analyzed by thin layer chromatography. Staining with anthrone reagent gave spots as illustrated in Fig. 29. Left white matter shows the pattern produced by a lipid fraction obtained by exhaustive extraction with the choloroform-methanol mixture (2:1) from the white matter of human brain. The spots, from top to bottom, represent cholesterol, cerebroside, cephalin, lecithin, cerebroside ester, and sphingomyelin. The results clearly demonstrate that these lipids were extracted by carbon tetrachloride and other solvents, while only cholesterol was extracted by acetone under the same conditions (20 minutes at 20°C).

(b-ii). Reduction in antigenicity

Table 4 shows the relationship between the time of treatment with various solvents and the reduction in antigenicity. Treatment with carbon tetrachloride at 20°C for 30 to 60 minutes gave the best results for lipid extraction, although

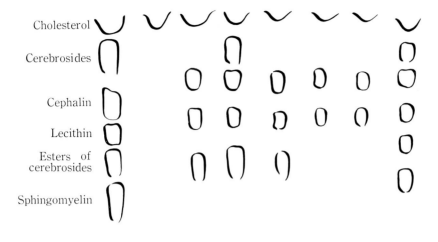

W.M.* Acetone Fluoro- CCl₄ Ether Ethanol Methanol Chloroform-
carbon   methanol (2:1)

Fig. 29. Thin Layer Chromatography of Various Solvent Extracts of Normal
Mous Brains
* Chloroform-methanol extract of the white matter of human brain

a temperature of 5°C minimizes denaturation of protein. The chloroform-
methanol mixture was quite effective in removing lipid but destroyed the antigenicity within a very short time.

Using fixation with carbon tetrachloride at 5°C for 30 to 60 minutes, viral
antigens in the cytoplasmic projections of nerve cells have been clearly demonstrated. Excellent preparations of brain cells from encephalitis patients have
also been obtained by a smilar treatment while acetone fixation gave preparations

Table 4. Relationship between Time of Treatment with Various Solvents
and Reduction in Antigenicity

Solvents \ Time of Treatment	5 min.	15 min.	30 min.	60 min.	3 hours	6 hours	12 hours	24 hours
Acetone	+	+	±	±	−	−	−	−
Fluorocarbon	+	+⊦	++	++	+	±	−	−
Carbon tetrachloride	+	++	+++	+++	++	+	±	−
Chloroform-methanol	±	−	−	−	−	−	−	−
Pyridine	±	−	−	−	−	−	−	−
Methyl cellosolve	±	−	−	−	−	−	−	−
Tetrahydrofuran	±	−	−	−	−	−	−	−

Frozen brain sections (4μ in thickness) were prepared from a mouse four days after
intracerebral infection with Japanese encephalitis (JB) virus. These were stained with
labeled anti-JB rabbit γG (4 units) after fixation with various solvents. ⫲ indicates
the intensity of specific fluorescence.

with poor contrast and less intense specific fluorescence.

(3)   Method of fixation

Solvent may be poured gently over tissue sections or cells attached to cover

1.   Direct method

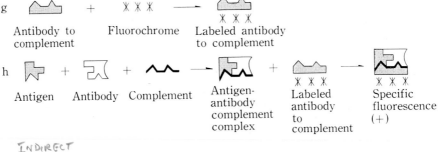

a   Antibody   Fluorochrome   Labeled antibody

b   Antigen   Labeled antibody   Specific fluorescence(+)

c   Antigen   Heterologous antibody   Specific fluorescence(−)

d   Antigen   Antibody   Antigen-antibody complex   Labeled antibody   Specific fluorescence(−)

COMPLEMENT

2.   Indirect method

g   Antibody to complement   Fluorochrome   Labeled antibody to complement

h   Antigen   Antibody   Complement   Antigen-antibody complement complex   Labeled antibody to complement   Specific fluorescence (+)

INDIRECT

3.   Complement method

e   Antibody to normal γG-globulin   Fluorochrome   Labeled antibody to normal γG-globulin

f   Antigen   Antibody   Antigen-antibody complex   Labeled antibody to normal γG-globulin   Specific fluorescence (+)

Fig. 30.   Fluorescent Antibody Techniques

33

slips, or these may be placed in a rack, as shown in Fig. 30, and immersed in the solvent in a shallow tray. After treatment, the sections or cells are washed repeatedly in phosphate buffer with a Pasteur pipette or in the tray by repeated addition of fresh buffer or shifting to another tray with fresh buffer. Cover slips are washed in a test tube with a hole at the bottom as described earlier. Slides are washed with buffer in a shallow tray as above. After washing, every specimen is completely dried in an air current. In order to avoid confusion, the treated (specimen) sides of cover slips should be marked with a small piece of adhesive, or by breaking one corner or the cover slip of some other such means.

CHAPTER IV

STAINING METHODS

1. CONDITIONS

Conditions relating to the antigen, which is fixed on a slide or cover glass, may be considered as constant. The first condition of staining lies, therefore, with the antibody. A sufficient amount of antibody (two to four staining units) must be used, as calculated from the preliminary examination of the staining titer of the antibody. The pH of the antibody solution, time of incubation and temperature of reaction are all important in obtaining optimal results. When Japanese encephalitis virus in tissue is examined, for instance, a pH of 7.75 rather than the conventional 7.0 for the antibody solution and PBS gives better results. When the reaction temperature is low, a longer incubation is necessary than at higher temperatures and the most widely employed procedure is to incubate for 30 to 60 minutes at 37°C. However, overnight incubation at 5°C often gives a more sensitive or clearer result for Japanese encephalities virus and other antigens in tissues. When a very delicate examination is to be made, or when observation of the stained preparation cannot be made on the same day, it is better to incubate at 5°C overnight than at 37°C for 30 minutes. The stained preparation should be examined as soon as possible, usually on the same day. Gentle shaking during incubation, although not essential, sometimes gives better results.

2. DIRECT METHOD

The fluorochrome is conjugated directly with the corresponding antibody globulin in this procedure. It is the simplest and the most reliable of all the staining procedures, but is a little less sensitive than the indirect or complement method. An outline of the procedure is shown in Fig. 1 and Fig. 31—1. The one drawback of this technique is that each antiserum must be labeled with the fluorochrome. Nevertheless, the technique is preferred for delicate examinations due to its high specificity.

A. Procedure (Fig. 1, 31—1 and 32)
  1.   One or more serially diluted antibody solutions are placed on the specimen with a capillary tube. For staining a single specimen with different antibody solutions, transverse lines are drawn on the slide with a blue glass pencil or nail polish as shown in Fig. 32—1 and each section is stained with different solutions.

(1)

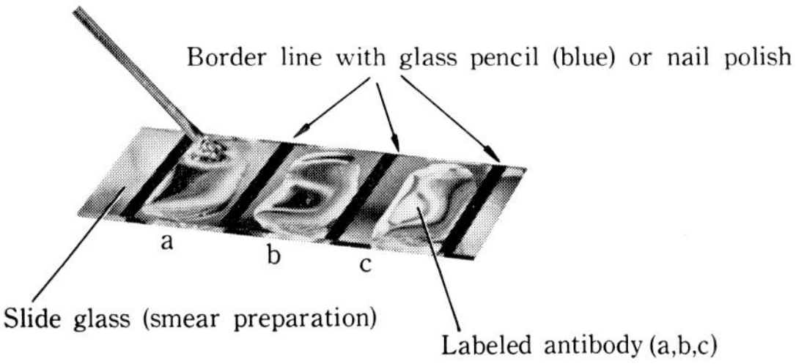

Border line with glass pencil (blue) or nail polish

a b c

Slide glass (smear preparation)

Labeled antibody (a,b,c)

(2)

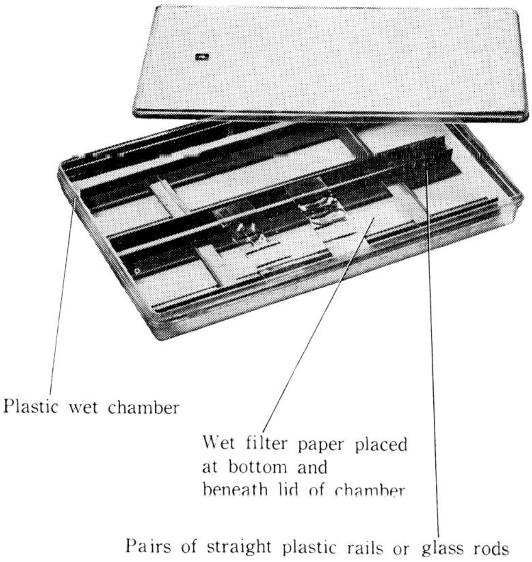

Plastic wet chamber

Wet filter paper placed
at bottom and
beneath lid of chamber

Pairs of straight plastic rails or glass rods

(3) The plastic chamber is incubated at 37°C for 30–60 minutes of in a refrigerator at 5°C overnight.

(4) Surplus labeled antibody is washed off with PBS (Fig. 32)

(5) (drying)——mounting——observation

Fig. 31. Direct Method

Care must be taken that the wax or demarcating lines do not float during incubation, or else different antibody solutions will mix with each other.   In the
experiment shown in Fig. 32–1, a corresponding antibody is placed in (a), a heterologous antibody in (b) and a mixture of labeled and unlabeled corresponding
antibodies in (c) (one step inhibition test).

2.   A plastic moist chamber is prepared by placing wet filter paper at the bottom
of the container and under the lid.   Pairs of straight plastic rails or glass rods are

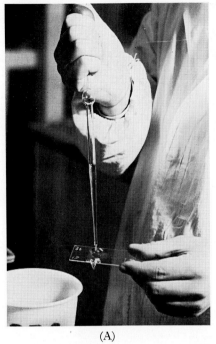 

(A)   (B)

Fig. 32.

(A)   The slide is held obliquely and the labeled antibody is washed off gently
with a Pasteur pipette

(B)   Vibrator for washing with PSB

placed in the chamber and the slides are placed on these rails. The chamber has a high level of humidity and prevents desiccation of the labeled antibody.

3. The plastic chamber is incubated at 37°C for 30 to 60 minutes or in a refrigerator at 5°C overnight.

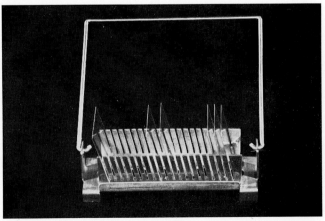

Fig. 33.   Cover Glass Rack

32—A

4.   The slide is held obliquely as shown in Fig. 33—A and the labeled antibody is washed off gently with a Pasteur pipette.   Care must be taken to avoid
mixing the different antibodies.   The slides are then placed in a glass staining
dish filled with PBS and are shaken on a vibrator (Fig. 33—B) for about 15 minutes
with three changes of PBS.   The staining dish may be shaken manually if no
vibrator is available.   The fluid is changed three times at 5 minute intervals
during the washing procedure.   The floating wax must be removed carefully.
Unreacted antibody is removed completely by this procedure.   The transverse
lines of nail polish which were drawn on the slide glass should then be removed
with a pincette, as they are an obstacle to mounting.

5.   The slides are then dried with a fan or a hair dryer.   They should not be
allowed to dry before the washing procedure is completed.

6.   A drop of mounting medium is placed on the specimen and a coverglass is
fitted over it with maximal care to avoid minute air bubbles or lint.   The specimen is now ready for observation.

Specific fluorescence should be present in the section stained with (a) but not
in those stained with (b) and (c).   A portion of the specimen not covered with
solutions a, b or c serves as an autofluorescence control for the tissue material.

Tissue culture cover slips may also be examined in a similar manner.   Test
tubes with a hole at the bottom are convenient for washing the stained cover slips.
Frozen sections fixed on cover glasses can be stained with only one antibody solution.

B. The Mounting Medium

Buffered glycerol or elvanol is commonly employed.   Fluorescence fades in a
short time (about 30% overnight and then more gradually) in glycerol but remains
for a longer time in elvanol.   The fluorochrome of the rhodamine series dissolves
in elvanol, however, and therefore it cannot be used except with FITC-labeled
antiserum.   The pH of the buffered glycerol is normally 7.0 to 7.5.   However,
we have used it at a pH of 8.5 with good results.[18]

Buffered glycerol solution

   0.5 M carbonate buffer (pH 9.5)...1 vol.

   Glycerine (reagent grade, free of autofluorescence)   ....9 vol.

The two reagents are mixed thoroughly (with a magnetic stirrer).   The final
pH should be 8.5.

Elvanol (Elvanol-buffered glycerine mixture)

   Elvanol (polyvinyl alcohol, 51–05 grade) ....1 vol.

   0.5 M carbonate buffer (pH 9.0)...4 vol.

The two reagents are mixed with a magnetic stirrer for 16 hours.   One volume
of reagent grade glycerine is mixed with two volumes of the above mixture.   The
final mixture is stirred again with a magnetic stirrer for 16 hours, centrifuged for
60 minutes at 12,000 rpm and the pH of the supernatant corrected to 8.5.

The final product should be kept in an air-tight container.   It is best stored in
tubes and kept in the dark.   It will harden under the cover glass and fix it firmly.

This is very convenient because cover glasses mounted with glycerine move over the slide.

3. INDIRECT METHOD

In this procedure unlabeled (primary) antibody is placed on the antigen and then labeled secondary antibody is brought into contact with the antigen-primary antibody complex. If there is specific fluorescence, we can identify the antigen when the nature of the primary antibody is known, or vice versa. This is an application of Coomb's technique and is called the sandwich method (Fig. 1 and Fig. 31–2). The primary antibody in this case acts as antigen. The method has wide application when labeled antibody against normal γ-globulin of humans or animals in which primary antibody is formed is available.

The merit of this method is that it is more sensitive than the direct method. Maximal amounts of primary antibody react with the antigen and again excess amounts of labeled antibody react with this excess (of primary antibody) yielding stronger fluorescence than in the direct method. Another merit of this procedure lies in the small amount of primary antibody required in the test. However, as the reacting agent is doubled, it is less reliable as regards specificity. Duplicate staining is complex and requires a longer time for preparation of stained films, thus making the procedure less desirable when many specimens are to be examined.

The same principles are applied in the demonstration of antibody in tissues and organs; this procedure is called the antibody staining method. An antigen solution is overlaid on sections of tissue in which the antibody is expected to be bound; the antigen solution in this case corresponds to the primary antibody in the indirect method. This is followed by application of labeled antibody to the antigen. It can be demonstrated indirectly that there is antibody if specific fluorescence can be observed under the microscope.

If the antigen is protein, the antibody may be traced with protein material labeled directly with fluorochrome; this is the direct fluorescent antigen method.
Procedure (Figs. 1, 31–2 and 34)
1. The specimen fixed on the slide is divided into three sections with a glass pencil or nail polish and primary antibody is placed on each section. The corresponding antibody is placed on section (a), heterologous antibody on section (b) and normal serum from the same animal source as (a) on section (c).
2 & 3. The same techniques as in the direct method are employed (p. 66).
4 & 5. Labeled secondary antibody solution is placed on sections (a_2) (b_2) and (c_2) transversely across the demarcating lines, as shown in Fig. 34–4.
6 & 7. Incubation, washing, and drying and embedding are carried out as described previously.

Specific fluorescence should be observed in section (a_2). Sections (a_1), (b_1), (b_2), (c_1) and (c_2) serve as negative controls and (a_3) (b_3) and (c_3) as auto-fluorescnece controls. Tissue culture cells on coverslips or frozen sections may be examined in the same manner.

(1)

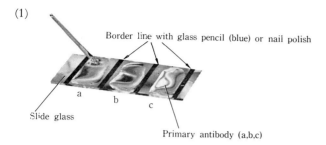

Border line with glass pencil (blue) or nail polish

a b c

Slide glass

Primary antibody (a,b,c)

(2) The staining is carried out and the slides are placed in the wet chamber (37°C, 30–60 minutes)

(3) Surplus antibody is washed off with PBS

(4)

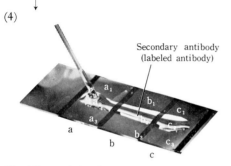

Secondary antibody (labeled antibody)

a_1 b_1 c_1
a_2 b_2 c_2
a b c

(5) The staining is carried out and the slides are placed in the wet chamber (37°C, 30–60 minutes)

(6) Surplus antibody is washed off with PBS

(7) (drying)——mounting——observation

Fig. 34. Indirect Method

The one-step inhibition test is made by mixing labeled and unlabeled secondary antibody and substituting this mixture for the antibody solution in step (4). Tissue culture cover slips or frozen sections fixed on cover glasses may be examined in a similar manner.

The procedures given for the direct and indirect method are used when the amount of antigen material available is limited. If many sections containing a sufficient amount of antigen are available, it may be simpler to use different cover slips, frozen sections or smears for the controls.

4. COMPLEMENT METHOD

This is a modification of the indirect method and was first described by

Goldwasser et al.[14] The principle is the tracing of antigen-antibody-complement complex by immunological methods (see Fig. 31–3).[30–3] The technique is theoretically feasible as long as there is labeled antibody to complement, since many antigen-antibody complexes combine with complement. It should be highly sensitive and should find wide application when perfected. At present, however, the method has a high incidence of nonspecific reaction and is rather risky except for very simple systems. Inactivated antibody, fresh guinea pig complement and labeled antibody are generally used. Use of mixtures of labeled complement component and antibody (direct complement method) and of labeled antibody to complement components in the antigen-antibody complement complex is under study at the present time.

5. SPECIFIC STAINING PROCEDURES

A. Double Staining

This procedure is used to study two different antigens in the same specimen by labeling the respective antibodies with different fluorochromes. Yellow-green fluorescein isothiocyanate and orange-red tetramethyl rhodamine isothiocyanate or tetraethylrhodamine are commonly used. Two labeled antibodies are mixed at optimal dilutions and applied in a one-step method. It is important to make sure that the antibodies do not cross-react, and to use a higher concentration of orange-red labeled antibody, because its negative charge is stronger than that of the FITC-labeled antibody and it therefore takes a longer time to react.

A two-step method of staining with one and then the other labeled antibody may also be used. Rhodamine-antibody is applied first, and during the incubation FITC-labeled antibody is added without washing off the first antibody. The concentration, temperature and duration of incubation should be optimal for each antibody. Elvanol should not be used for embedding in this procedure.

B. Counterstaining

The electric charge of a protein changes when it is conjugated chemically with a fluorochrome. Its negative charge increases in parallel with the number of fluorochrome molecules conjugated. This negatively charged protein combines readily and nonspecifically with positively charged protein, and produces nonspecific fluorescence.[13,18] Smith et al.[31] made use of this drawback to the fluorescent antibody method and developed what is now called the counterstaining method. A highly negatively charged fluorescent protein is prepared by conjugating bovine serum or bovine serum albumin with tetraethylrhodamine (lissamine rhodamine B 200, or Rb 200), an orange-red fluorochrome. This is mixed with adequately diluted FITC-conjugate and applied to appropriate tissues containing the antigen. The FITC-labeled antibody combines specifically with antigen in the tissue while the RB-200 labeled protein combines nonspecifically with other tissues. The specific antigen-antibody complex is a brilliant yellow-green on a background of orange-red tissues and can be observed very easily.

Recent improvements in the production of purified fluorescent antibody and fluorescent microscopic apparatus have brought about a marked decrease in nonspecific reactions, and observation of autofluorescence has become much easier, so that counterstaining is no longer as significant a procedure as it used to be. It is still used in many cases, however, because the strongly negatively charged RB-200 labeled antibody prevents the less negatively charged FITC-labeled antibody from combining nonspecifically with tissues.

Procedure: Properly diluted FITC-labeled antibody and RB-200 labeled protein are mixed in equal amounts and the mixture is reacted with the antigen by the direct method. RB-200 labeled protein is usually used in a 1 to 20–50 dilution(1 to 20 at 37°C is the general rule). Elvanol is not used for mounting.

C. Combination with Routine Staining

After observations and microphotography of the fluorescent stained preparations are finished, routine staining of the same preparation is often useful for comparison of pathological changes or the relationship to viral inclusion bodies. Dissociation of the antibody from the specimen is necessary for this procedure since the antibody protein impairs staining.

Method: Preparations are washed by shaking with PBS or saline in a beaker. Cover glasses are detached from the slides and the mounting medium is eluted out. The washing is continued overnight. The fluorescent antibody fixed to the specimens is dissociated by treatment with a weak acid such as acetic acid or with a hypertonic salt solution. After washing and refixing the specimens are routinely stained. With frozen serial sections, the next section can be stained instead of using this restaining method. This is preferable since restaining never produces as good results as staining of a fresh preparation.

6. Controls

Since the fluorescent antibody technique provides a means of analyzing antigen-antibody reactions, good controls are essential. For the antigen controls, normal and infected tissue fixed by various methods, untreated tissue, and identical tissue containing a different antigen should be stained. For antibody controls in the direct method, (1) the inhibition test should be successful, (2) there should be negative fluorescence with non-homologous antibody and with uninfected or unimmunized homologous labeled animal globulin, and (3) there should be negative fluorescence when the homologous labeled antibody is absorbed with specific antigen. In the indirect and complement methods, similar antigen and antibody controls should be prepared; in addition no specific fluorescence should be observed when the first antibody is replaced with PBS or physiological saline, non-homologous antibody or normal serum in the indirect method. In complement staining, more controls are needed to establish the specificity of the reaction.

In the two-step inhibition test,[3] the specimen is first exposed to specific unlabeled primary antibody, followed by the conventional direct fluorescent antibody. The same procedure is used in the indirect and complement methods. The antigen-antibody complex is in equilibrium with excess antibody, hence replacement by unlabeled molecules may occur if the reaction time or the serum titer is not properly adjusted.

The one-step inhibition test relies on the stronger reactivity of unlabeled antibody. A mixture of labeled and unlabeled antibody is applied to the tissues in the direct, indirect or complement methods, and failure of the labeled antibody to bind with the antigen, i.e. absence of specific fluorescence, is noted. If the labeled serum has a much higher concentration of antibody than the unlabeled one, however, the reaction will take place largely with labeled molecules, resulting in bright staining of the antigens. Hence a larger amount of unlabeled antibody is necessary in this test than in the two-step method.

7. Preservation of Stained Specimens

Stained preparations should be observed under the microscope immediately, as the fluorescence is at its brightest and sharpest on the day of staining. They may be stored in a box covered with a polyethylene bag, at 0–5°C, but the specific fluorescence fades 30% overnight and about 50% after a week's storage when the specimen is mounted with buffered glycerol. Specimens mounted with elvanol will keep for a few weeks with some loss in intensity and clarity of specific fluorescence.

Specimens which have been examined under the fluorescence microscope suffer a marked loss of specificity, not only in the area under observation but also in other areas. For this reason, fresh specimens should be used for photography.

8. Evaluation of Results

Evaluation of results in the fluorescent antibody technique is quite easy if properly controlled antigens and antibodies and optimal staining procedures are used, and if the microscopic examinations are carried out correctly. The importance of proper controls cannot be overstressed, as specificity is the most important aspect of this procedure. The characteristics and limitations of the procedure should be kept inmind, however, in evaluating the results. The intensity of fluorescence of the antibody depends on the amount and density of antigen present in the tissue or smear, and the specific fluorescence cannot be identified or localized unless there is a sufficient amount of fluorescence emission. Absence of specific fluorescence does not, therefore, necessarily indicate absence of antigen.

CHAPTER V

FLUORESCENCE MICROSCOPY

1. OPTICAL PRINCIPLES : DARK-FIELD FLUORESCENCE MICROSCOPY

Dark-field fluorescence microscopy is used in the fluorescence antibody techniques because the quantum efficiency of FITC is very low in the ultraviolet region. The spectra of specific and autofluorescence are spread throughout the whole visible region; hence a barrier filter that allows uniform transmission of the entire visible range is the most desirable for our purpose.

Observation of the fluorescence of the FITC conjugate (520 mμ max.) is theoretically feasible with an exciter filter (an interference filter with a narrow spectral bandwidth that transmits only the maximum 495 mμ wavelength of the exciting spectrum of FITC) and a barrier filter (an interference filter that transmits only the 520 mμ wavelength). A light source with an extremely high intensity must be used, however (see Fig. 11). For observation, with satisfactory contrast, of the specific fluorescence and autofluorescence within a specimen, it is essential to keep those parts other than the specimen itself, particularly the objective, from emitting autofluorescence through the action of the UV rays. Hence the use of dark-field illumination.

The basic principle of ordinary dark-field illumination is irradiation of a specimen with visible light in hollow cone form; the distribution of invisible phase-retarded rays then becomes visible because only the diffracted rays of higher order emitted by the specimen are observed, both the direct rays and the diffracted rays of lower order being kept out of the optical observation system. In dark-field fluorescence microscopy, irradiating the specimen with invisible UV rays by the dark-field illumination method produces the following physical phenomena: (1) The specimen that has absorbed UV rays emits fluorescence in all directions. (2) Of the UV diffracted rays caused by phase retardation of a specimen, those of higher order enter the objective while those of lower order as well as the direct beam do not go into the optical observation system. An image is formed by the collected fluorescence, but there is practically no autofluorescence caused by UV diffracted rays of higher order. (The UV diffracted rays of higher order, after passing through the objective, are absorbed by the UV barrier filter.)

Bright-field microscopy is not suitable for observing fluorescent antibody for reasons which should be evident from the preceding details. In bright-field illumination, the direct beam and the diffracted rays of lower order enter the objective while the diffracted rays of higher order do not; hence the autofluorescence of the objective becomes very noticeable and the contrast is lowered. In the case of other fluorochromes using ordinary staining (acridine orange, auramine etc.), the quantum efficiency is not as low as that of FITC. But in all possible applications of fluorescence microscopy requiring both auto- and fluorochrome-fluorescence within a visual field, dark-field is superior to bright-fluorescence microscopy.

2. IMMERSION AND DRY DARK-FIELD SYSTEMS

There are two systems of illumination used in dark-field fluorescence micros-copy, the immersion and the dry system. The immersion is the better of the two, but the dry system is sometimes used for convenience. With a dark-field con-denser designed for the dry system a specimen can be illuminated as is, without the use of immersion oil to close the space between the slide surface and the condenser. One advantage is that the focal length can be made longer and hence the field of view can be larger than with oil immersion. This is especially useful for low power objectives. Often a dry dark-field condenser is used for low magnification and an immersion dark-field condenser for high power.

The advantages of the immersion system are many. The numerical aperture (N. A.) of an immersion type dark-field condenser can be enlarged about 1.5 times more than the dry type, producing a fluorescent image 1.5^2 or 2.25 times brighter. In combination with a toric lens, the field of view can be enlarged without reducing the large numerical aperture. Since the inner N. A. can be enlarged, entrance of UV rays of lower order into the high power objective, which would reduce the contrast due to autofluorescence, is prevented. Since the aperture angles on the outer and inner sides of an immersion type dark-field condenser are larger than the total reflection angle of a cover glass, the UV direct beam and portions of diffracted rays of lower order whose angles are larger than the total reflection angle are almost all reflected back into the condenser along the illumination path. Therefore autofluorescence caused by dust or fibers on the cover glass can be minimized.

3. BACKGROUND CONTRAST

Good contrast is essential for observation of fluorescence, and therefore the darker the background of the field of view, the better. This is particularly im-portant when viewing thin smears, as the fluorescence tends to be weak in such cases. In recent years, as a result of improvements in the illuminating system as well as in dark-field condensers, the field of view in fluorescence microscopy has tended to become brighter. This has contributed to lowering the required concentrations of reaction liquids and raising sensitivity; on the other hand, it has also resulted in lowering of contrast, primarily because of the autofluores-cence of buffered glycerol.

Three possible means of increasing contrast can be suggested: (1) The BV exciting method can be used. Buffered glycerol emits practically no auto-fluorescence with a BV beam. (2) A combination of a UV exciter filter and a subsidiary UV or BV barrier filter can be used to absorb pale blue autofluorescence. (3) The buffered glycerol may be purified. In addition, the brownish autofluorescence emitted by slides and cover glasses can be reduced by using fluorescence-free glass.

4. The Fluorescence Microscope

As was mentioned earlier, the maximum wavelength of the absorption spectrum of FITC is very close, within the visible range, to the maximum wavelength of the emission spectrum. Therefore it is essential to use excitation beam wavelengths of the lowest possible quantum efficiency. The fluorescence microscope makes this possible, but certain additional requirements must be met. The object or preparation should be illuminated with as strong excitation as possible, and there should be good contrast for observation of the fluorescent image. A dark-field condenser will provide for these requirements, but the illuminating field must still be kept as large as possible. Additional accessories or components are therefore used: a super high-pressure mercury arc lamp, a concave mirror, exciter and barrier filters, etc. These, of course, must be adjusted for optimal use, and any problems that may arise—heat generated by the lamp, stray light from the lamp housing, alignment of the microscope and light source, dust on the barrier filters, immersion oil on the microscope stage, etc.—must be dealt with for maximum efficiency.

A. Excitation Systems

(a) UV System

Combinations of exciter and barrier filters are roughly divided into two types, the UV and BV systems. In the UV system, a UV exciter filter with a transmission range of 300–400 mμ and a maximum transmission at 360 mμ intercepts an illuminating beam, and the incident rays of the UV beam illuminate the specimen. A UV barrier filter that absorbs UV diffracted rays below 410 mμ is also inserted into the observation system. In this way, the UV rays diffracted from the specimen are eliminated and only the fluorescence is visible. The Wood's filter generally used as the UV exciter filter transmits a residual red range above 700 mμ in addition to the 300–400 mμ range. Because of this, when the refractive index of a specimen is high or when dust is sealed in, a residual red color will appear in the field of view. The barrier filter cannot absorb this residual red, and a blue filter is therefore used as a UV auxiliary filter, superimposed on the UV exciter filter. Simply by inserting and removing the UV auxiliary filter, it is possible to differentiate reddish autofluorescence from the residual red caused by diffracted rays.

One advantage of the UV system is that it discriminates clearly between specific and autofluorescence. Of course, one must be able to adjust the various filters according to the state of the specimen and the purpose of observation.

(b)   The BV System

In the BV system a combination of a BV exciter filter with a transmission range of 330–500 mμ and a maximum transmission at 410 mμ, and BV barrier filters that absorb at 500 mμ and above is used.   The intensity of specific fluorescence can be adjusted by using BV exciter filters of different thicknesses or by combining several filters.   Since a higher range of the absorption spectrum of the FITC conjugate is used with the BV system than with the UV system, the intensity of the specific fluorescence is high; the autofluorescence of the background, on the other hand, is weak, and therefore the contrast is quite good.   A yellow barrier filter must be used, however, making the field of view appear yellowish, and thus it is more difficult to differentiate between the pale blue autofluorescence and the specific fluorescence than with the UV system.

(c)   The UG5 System

In addition to the UV and BV systems, there is another system, which uses a Schottglasfilter UG5 as an exciter filter.   The UG5 filter has a maximum tranmission range extending over both the UV and BV spectra.   A BV filter is used as the barrier filter, and a UV auxiliary filter is often used in combination with it to eliminate residual red transmission.   The UG5 system is effective for identifying enzymes in a tissue emitting autofluorescence, and will produce a comparatively bright image even with a mercury lamp whose intensity has diminished because of long use.

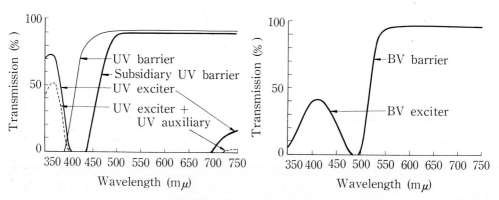

Fig. 35.   Filter Combinations

The above graphs (Fig. 35, 36) compare several relevant factors of the various systems.   The curves are all drawn in spectral form (with the wavelength as abscissa); in order, from top to bottom, they indicate the image, barrier filters, absorption and emission of specimens, excitation beam, exciter filters, and light source.

B. Light Source

A super high-pressure mercury arc lamp is generally used as light source for

Principle of Fluorescence Microscopy

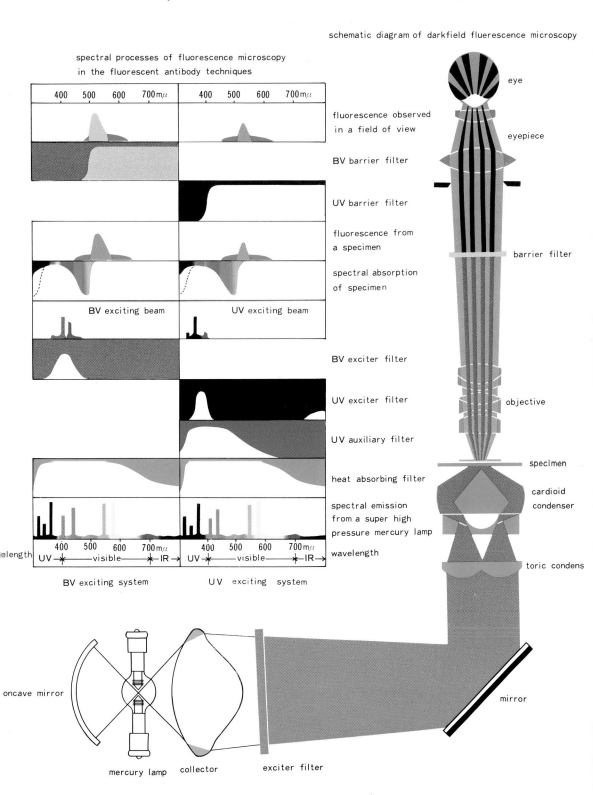

schematic diagram of darkfield fluerescence microscopy

spectral processes of fluorescence microscopy
in the fluorescent antibody techniques

eye

eyepiece

fluorescence observed
in a field of view

BV barrier filter

barrier filter

UV barrier filter

fluorescence from
a specimen

spectral absorption
of specimen

BV exciting beam   UV exciting beam

objective

BV exciter filter

UV exciter filter

specimen

UV auxiliary filter

cardioid
condenser

heat absorbing filter

spectral emission
from a super high
pressure mercury lamp

toric condens

wavelength

elength UV → visible → IR →   UV → visible → IR →

BV exciting system   UV exciting system

oncave mirror

mirror

mercury lamp   collector   exciter filter

Fig. 36

fluorescence microscopy because it produces a compact arc rich in UV-BV
beams of 360–410 mμ.   The mercury vapor within the lamp reaches a pressure of
more than 60 atmospheres.   The globe of a mercury lamp is made of anhydrous
quartz, which is more durable than ordinary quartz.   The lifetime of the lamp

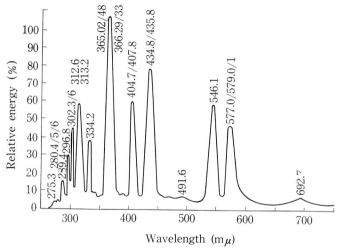

Fig. 37.   Spectrum of Super High-Pressure Mercury Arc Lamp (Osram HBO
200w)

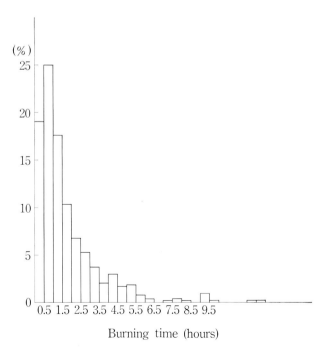

Burning time (hours)

Fig. 38.   Burning Frequencies of Mercury Lamp

depends on the frequency of firing or ignition.   Discrepancies in lifetime among individual lamps are probably caused chiefly by extremely slight differences in the treatment of electrodes.   The firing frequencies of typical Osram HBO 200W lamps, based on data supplied by the Institute of Medical Science, University of Tokyo, are given in Fig. 38.

The starter generates a high tension of approximately 3 KV.   Photomicrography and determination of the activity of an antibody by indirect methods such as the fluorescent treponemal antibody test are most affected by a decrease in light intensity.   For this reason, the UV intensity can be measured on the stage of a microscope by means of a UV meter (Fig. 39).   The UV meter, which is

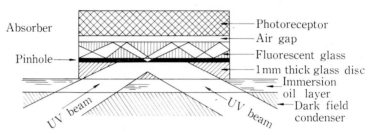

Fig. 39.   Photometric Element of UV Meter

shaped like a slide, comprises an ammeter and a photometric element made up of a 1 mm thick glass disc, a pinhole, a fluorescent glass and a photoreceptor superimposed at the center of a 25×75 mm plastic plate.   Most of the UV hollow cone beam entering the pinhole through the glass disc from an immersed dark-field condenser is converted into fluorescent light.   Since there is an air gap between the photoreceptor and the fluorescent glass, the rest of the UV beam is wholly reflected by the air gap.   The photoreceptor, which is sensitive only to visible light, transmits the intensity of the fluorescent light to the ammeter.

C. Lamp Housing

The requirements for a good lamp housing are as follows:

a.   The housing should provide adequate ventilation for the lamp.   This is important for its efficiency and lifetime.

b.   There should be no leakage of direct light.

c.   A concave mirror should be built into the housing to reflect the back beam of the lamp at the position of the arc.

d.   The centering device of the lamp should permit its adjustment in all directions.

e.   The housing should have a quartz or UV-free glass collecting lens of satisfactory correction—in most cases, aspheric—with a focusable mount.

f.   The knobs attached to the lamp housing should never be made of metal, but preferably of heat resistant plastic.

g. The exciter filter holder should be capable of accommodating a number of superposed exciter filters.   This is especially important in measuring the activity of an antibody by the indirect method.   The knobs of the holders should not get too hot to handle, and no stray UV light should leak from them.   It is convenient if standard size filters can be freely interchanged.

h. The housing should be equipped with a shutter to allow the beam to be interrupted at will.

D. Dark-field Condenser

Cardioid condensers are chiefly used as dark-field condensers, as the cardioid curve satisfies the sine condition in the theory of aberrations—i.e., it allows a composition of aplanatic condenser, and is very effective.   The numerical aperture (N.A.) of a dark-field condenser is 1.4 on the outer side and 1.2 on the inner side, hence the aplanatic type is excellent for the concentration of light.   The N.A. of a dark-field condenser as used here means the value obtained by multiplying the sine of the outer and inner half angles of a hollow cone beam concentrated at an object by the refractive index of the medium.   For example, with a mean refractive index of 1.51525, an outer N. A. of 1.4 and an inner N. A. of 1.2, the hollow cone has an outer angle of 135° and an inner angle of 104.8°.

The intensity I of a UV beam on a specimen is expressed by the following equation:

$$I = k(\text{N. A.}^2 \text{ out} - \text{N. A.}^2 \text{ in})TR \tag{1}$$

where k=the proportional constant
   N. A. out=the outer N. A. of a dark-field condenser
   N. A. in=the inner N. A. of a dark-field condenser
   T=the product of the transmissions of the collecting lens, exciter filter, dark-field condenser and other glasses interposed
   R=the reflectivity of a 45° reflex mirror.

and the diameter d of an illuminating field of view is expressed by

$$d = D \frac{fd}{L} \tag{2}$$

where D=the effective diameter of a collecting lens
   fd=the focal length of a dark-field condenser
   L=the distance between the back focal point of the collecting lens to the front focal point of the condenser.

Equation (1) shows that the intensity is greater when the outer N. A. is large and the inner N. A. small.   Although the transmission of a quartz condenser is high, its N. A. is small because of its low refractive index.

From Equation (2) it would appear that increasing D and fd while decreasing L would give a larger diameter d.   However, the distance L is governed by another equation (3) as follows:

$$L = fc\frac{Pec}{a} \tag{3}$$

where fc = the focal length of the collecting lens
        Pec = the outer diameter of the entrance pupil of the condenser
        a = the arc length.

Equation (3) indicates that the arc image must cover the entrance pupil of a dark-field condenser. Pec is expressed by

$$Pec = fd \cdot \text{N. A. out} \tag{4}$$

Since large values of fd and N. A. out are used, Pec naturally becomes large. Consequently, in order to make L in Equation (3) smaller, the focal length fc of the collecting lens must be smaller. On the other hand, its effective diameter D must be kept large. Therefore, the effective aperture ratio of the collecting lens must be as small as possible. This limit is subject to the diameter of the lamp globe. In other words, it must reduce fc to such an extent that the collecting lens does not come in contact with the lamp. In a normal multiple lens system, a small aperture ratio fc/D makes it difficult to correct spherical aberrations. A cemented lens system which collects UV beams is not satisfactory either. Instead, an aspheric single lens made of UV-free glass or quartz is used.

As previously mentioned, it is desirable to use a single immersion system with dark-field condensers. Most cardioid condensers have an fd of approximately 3 mm. This corresponds to the field of view of immersion objectives. To enlarge the fc while keeping the N. A. out at 1.4 it is only necessary to increase the diameter of the lens up to the very limit of the substage mount, to an fc of 8 mm. This corresponds approximately to the field of view of a 20X objective. For observing a specimen, it is preferable to have a field of view equivalent to a 10X objective illuminated.

In bright-field illumination, the low power system can be realized by inserting an auxiliary low power condenser between the collecting lens and the substage condenser, expanding the field of view and reducing the entrance pupil of the substage condenser. In the immersion dark-field system, however, although the field of view must be expanded, the entrance pupil of the dark-field condenser cannot be decreased. Since the entrance pupil of the dark-field condenser is annular in shape, when the arc image is reduced, it gets inside the inner diameter of the aperture and interferes with the beam directed towards the plane of the object.

We designed a new type of dark-field condenser consisting of an auxiliary toric (or annular) condenser set up beneath a cardioid condenser with $fd = 8$ mm. This is called a UV superwide dark-field condenser (or SW for short). With an SW condenser, a cylindrical UV beam sent out from the collecting lens is first concentrated into annular form by the toric condenser. The size of this annular image is kept exactly the same as the annular entrance pupil of the cardioid condenser. Consequently, most of the UV beam passing through the cardioid con-

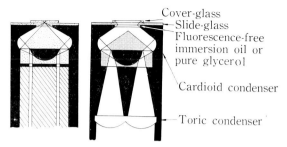

Cover-glass
Slide-glass
Fluorescence-free immersion oil or pure glycerol

Cardioid condenser

Toric condenser

Fig. 40. Comparison of Two Types of Dark Field Condenser

denser can irradiate the plane of the object. With only a cardioid condenser, the UV beam passing through the annular entrance pupil is extremely small, all the rest being reflected. The following figure compares the two types of condensers. (see Fig. 40)

E. Microscope Stage

In the fluorescence antibody method, it is often necessary to compare a number of specimens placed on a single slide. Because of this, the area in which slides are moved about on the stage of a fluorescence microscope is considerably larger than with an ordinary microscope. When the immersion system is used, the immersion oil tends to spread out on the surface of the stage, impeding the movement of the slide. In other words, if the adhesion produced by the viscosity of the oil is greater than the pressure exerted by the spring of the object holder keeping the slide in place, the spring-loaded object holder will not function properly and the specimen will only move in the opposite direction.

Two methods can be used to solve this problem: (1) A grooved stage (a stage with numerous grooves engraved crosswise on its surface, as shown in Fig. 41) can be used. With such a stage, the excess immersion oil flows into the

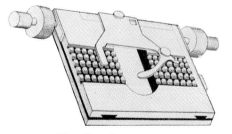

Fig. 41. Grooved Stage

grooves; the contact area between the slide and the stage surface is small; the direction of the grooves is parallel to the direction of movement of the slide; and the oil can easily be wiped off. (2) The movable part of the object holder can be fixed by means of a small bolt to the main part while the slide is held down by the elastic force of the spring. This reduces the effect of the oil on the stage.

F. Objectives

Most specimens used in the fluorescent antibody technique are not fixed but merely sealed in buffered glycerol by a cover glass.   Dry high power objectives such as 40X, 60X, etc. are best for viewing such specimens, but residual spherical and chromatic aberration in these objectives is more pronounced with the fluorescence microscope than with the ordinary microscope, because the specimen itself is an illuminant.   The ordinary microscope has " partially coherent illumination," and its image can be improved by stopping down the condenser aperture a little more than the objective aperture.

Figures 42 and 43 give the aberration curves of various objectives, indicating their suitability for fluorescence microscopy.

The suitability of an objective for fluorescence microscopy can readily by determined by using a good quality achromatic aplanatic condenser (N. A. 1.4) and an Abbe's test plate.   A detailed description of the principles of Abbe's test plate may be found in any general microscopy book, and will not be gone into here.

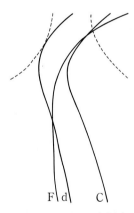

Fig. 42.   Spherical Aberration of Objective (unsuitable)

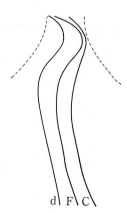

Fig. 43.   Spherical Aberration of Objective (suitable)

But for a suitable objective, briefly, the blur or spread of wine-red color around the silvery striped edges should be as slight as possible. The portion exceeding Rayleigh's limit of spherical aberration appears as a violet mist from the silver-striped edges to the silvery inside. This testing can be carried out with ease with a high power eyepiece of about 32X if the procedures for using Abbe's test plate are strictly observed. It should be noted, however, that the cover glass of the Abbe's plate is made by polishing a piece of optical glass into a wedge shape, hence its refractive index sometimes differs from that of commercial cover glasses. It may be more practical, therefore, to take a plain, 0.17 mm thick cover glass, silver it, rule it and fix it to a slide with balsam.

Generally, there is practically no aberration with a semi-apochromat or an apochromat, but there may be some with an achromat. And since the brightness of an objective is directly proportional to N. A.^{2}, as long as the magnification remains the same, a semi-apochromat or an apochromat is far brighter than an achromat. It is therefore preferable to use the former for magnifications of 40X or above, and with the fluorescence microscope. In dark-field fluorescence microscopy, the autofluorescence of a lens within the objective almost never detracts from the quality of the image.

Immersion objectives should, of course, be provided with an iris diaphragm, as in ordinary dark-field microscopy.

G. Eyepieces

A wide-field, compensating eyepiece, with an anti-reflection coating on the upper surface of the eyelens, is satisfactory. Those provided with eye shades are preferable since they protect the viewer from the table light. The high eyepoint type which permits observation while wearing eyeglasses is also desirable. Ordinary eyepieces are designed so as to permit the insertion of an eyepiece micrometer disc over the field diaphragm. In certain cases fluorescent antigens of similar intensity are counted with a rectangular aperture mask with the same outer dimension as the disc attached over the field diaphragm. An eyepiece with a mechanism that permits complete fixing of the mask over the field diaphragm is therefore desirable.

Eyepieces used in combination with a semi-apochromat or an apochromat, naturally, need only be of the compensating type.

H. Barrier Filter Holder

The holder should be completely dustproof, and permit the easy interchange of standard size filters.

5. FLUORESCENCE PHOTOMICROGRAPHY

The most important considerations in fluorescence photomicrography of fluorescent antibody staining are the use of high-speed films and of a swing-out prism type photomicrographic apparatus.

A. Selection of Films

Anscochrome ASA 200 is the best film for 35 mm color transparencies for projection. While a mercury lamp is still new, a shutter speed of less than two minutes can be used with the UV system, provided a 40X achromat, a 10X eyepiece and a photo factor of 0.5X are used. For a lamp used up to 200 hours, a shutter speed of six minutes or less is acceptable under the same conditions.

Color films made in Japan cannot be recommended, as the color development and sensitivities are not satisfactory.

B. Photomicrographic Apparatus

An apparatus of swing-out prism type is used so that all the light can be transmitted to the viewfinder and the film. A half-prism system is satisfactory for bright-field photomicroscopy but is not suitable for fluorescence photomicrography.

To govern the shutter speed, the " B " setting can be used in all cases. The " T " setting is not necessary; a long exposure can be made simply with a cable release and stopper.

The higher the magnification of the viewfinder, the better; a total magnification of 4X is sufficient, however. With a viewfinder of low magnification the focusing may become unstable when photographing with a low power objective. An apparatus with a viewfinder of this type is ordinarily provided with a frosted glass screen for bright-field photomicrography, but not for fluorescence photomicrography.

C. Magnification

The diagonal length of a 35 mm film is about 43 mm. What magnification should be selected for the eyepiece in order to make this diagonal coincide with the field of view within the eyepiece of the observation tube? Assuming that the field number of the observation eyepiece, i.e. the diameter of the image within the eyepiece, is 18 mm, and the photofactor of the apparatus is 0.5X, the required magnification for the photo eyepiece will be

$$m = \frac{43}{0.5 \times 18} = 4.8 \fallingdotseq 5$$

In other words, a 5X eyepiece is satisfactory.

D. Exposure Time

From the point of view of sensitivity, an exposure meter with a photomultiplier as receptor meets the needs of fluorescence photomicrography. This does not give an accurate exposure, however, but partial brightness measuring devices are difficult to obtain and expensive. On the other hand, because of the limitation of the subjects taken into consideration in fluorescence microscopy, determination of the exposure time is far easier than for bright-field microscopy.

The factors contributing to changes in the intensity of an image are limited to the following two: (1) decrease in the intensity of a mercury lamp; and (2) change in magnification, chiefly of the objective. The first can be measured by such devices as the UV meter mentioned earlier. As for the second factor, when the proper exposure time has been determined by making test exposures with a specific objective, whenever the magnification is altered because of a change of objective or eyepiece, a conversion can be made, keeping in mind the fact that the following factor determines the intensity of the image:

$$\text{Image intensity} \propto \frac{\text{N.A.}^2}{(M+1)^2}$$

where $M=$the total magnification.

E. Stability

The focusing must of course remain stable for long exposures, hence a microscope stand of the type in which the stage may be moved up or down is most desirable.

GENERAL REFERENCES

1) Ackroyd, J. F.: Immunological methods. A symposium organized by the Council for International Organizations of Medical Sciences, Blackwell Scientific Publications, Oxford, 1964.

2) Beutner, E. H.: Immunofluorescent staining: The fluorescent antibody method, *Bact. Rev.*, **25**, 49–76, 1961.

3) Cherry, W. B.. Goldman, M. and Carski, T. R.: Fluorescent antibody techniques in the diagnosis of communicable diseases, U. S. Govt. Printing Office, Washington, D. C., 1960.

4) Coons, A. H.: Fluorescent antibody methods (General Cytochemical Methods, Vol. 1, ed. by J. F. Danielli) 399–422, Academic Press Inc., New York, 1958.

5) Goldman, M.: Fluorescent antibody methods, Academic Press, New York and London, 1968.

6) Kabat, E. A. and Meyer, M. M.: Experimental immunochemistry, 2nd ed., Charles C. Thomas Publisher, Springfield, Illinois, 1961.

7) Kawamura, A. Jr.: Fluorescent antibody methods, Protein, Nucleic Acid & Enzyme, **11**, 1621–1634, 1966 (in Japanese).

8) Nairn, R. C.: Fluorescent protein tracing, 2nd ed., E. & S. Livingstone Ltd., Edinburgh and London, 1964.

9) Neurath, H.: The proteins: Composition, Structure and Function, 2nd ed., Vol. III, Academic Press, New York and London, 1965.

10) Putnam, F. W.: The plasma proteins, Vol. 1–2, Academic Press, New York and London, 1960.

11) Steiner, R. F. and Edelhoch, H.: Fluorescent protein conjugates, *Chem. Rev.*, **62**, 457–483, 1962.

REFERENCE

1) Chadwick, C. S., McEntegart, M. C. and Nairn, R. C.: Fluorescent protein tracers: A sample alternative to fluorescein, *Lancet*, **1**, 412–414, 1958.

2) Chaplin, H., Jr. and Cassel, M.: Studies on anti-eluate sera. I. The production of antiglobulin (Coombs) sera in rabbits by the use of antibodies eluted from sensitized red blood cells, *Vox Sang*, **5**, 32–42, 1960.

3) Cherry, W. B., Goldman, M. and Carski, T. R.: Fluorescent antibody techniques in the diagnosis of communicable diseases, U. S. Govt. Printing Office, Washington, D. C., 1960.

4) Clark, H. F. and Shepard, C. C.: A dialysis technique for preparing fluorescent antibody, *Virology*, **20**, 642–644, 1963.

5) Clayton, R. M.: Localization of embryonic antigens by antisera labeled with fluorescent dyes, *Nature*, **174**, 1059–1060, 1954.

6) Coons, A. H., Creech, H. J. and Jones, R. N.: Immunological properties of an antibody containing a fluorescent group, *Proc. Soc. Exper. Biol. & Med.* (N. Y.), **47**, 200–202, 1941.

7) Coons, A. H., Creech, H. J., Jones, R. N. and Berliner, E.: The demonstration of pneumococcal antigen in tissues by the use of fluorescent antibody, *J. Immunol.*, **45**, 159–170, 1942.

8) Coons, A. H. and Kaplan, M. M.: Localization of antigen in tissue cells. II. Improvements in a method for the detection of antigen by means of fluorescent antibody, *J. exper. Med.*, **91**, 1–13. 1950.

9) Coons, A. H.: Histochemistry with labeled antibody. (International Review of Cytology, Vol. 5, ed. by G. H. Bourne and J. F. Danielli) 1–23, Academic Press Inc., New York, 1956.

10) Creech, H. J. and Jones, R. N.: The conjugation of horse serum albumin with isocyanates of certain polynuclear aromatic hydrocarbons, *J. Am. Chem. Soc.*, **63**, 1661–1669, 1941.

11) Fieser, L. F. and Creech, H. J.: The conjugation of amino acids with isocyanates of the anthracene and 1, 2-benzanthracene series, *J. Am. Chem. Soc.*, **61**, 3502–3506, 1939.

12) Flodin, P., Gelotte, B. and Porath, J.: A method for concentrating solutes of high molecular weight, *Nature*, **188**, 493–494, 1960.

13) Goldstein, G., Slizys, I. S. and Chase, M. W.: Studies on fluorescent antibody staining. 1. Non-specific fluorescence with fluorescein-coupled, *J. exper. Med.*, **114**, 89–110, 1961.

14) Goldwasser, R. A. and Shepard, C. C.: Staining of complement and modifications of fluorescent antibody procedures, *J. Immunol.*, **80**, 122–131, 1958.

15) Heidelberger, M., Kendall, F. E. and Soo Hoo, C. H.: Quantitative studies on the precipitin reaction. Antibody production in rabbits injected with an azo-protein, *J. exper. Med.*, **58**, 137–152, 1933.

16) Hiramoto, R., Engel, K. and Pressman, D.: Tetramethylrhodamine as immunohistochemical fluorescent label in the study of chronic thyroiditis, *Proc. Soc. Exper. Biol. & Med.* (N. Y.), **97**, 611–614, 1958.

17) Hopkins, S. J. and Wormall, A.: Phenyl isocyanate protein compounds and their immunological reactions, *J. Biochem.*, **27**, 740–753, 1933.

18) Kawamura, A. Jr.: Fluorescent antibody methods, *Protein, Nucleic Acid & Enzyme*, **11**, 1621–1634, 1966 (in Japanese).

19) Marshall, J. D. Jr., Eveland, W. C. and Smith, C. W.: Superiority of fluorescein isothiocyanate (Riggs) for fluorescent antibody technique with a modification of its application, *Proc. Soc. Exper. Biol. & Med* (N. Y.), **98**, 898–900, 1958.

20) McDevitt, H. O., Peters, J. H., Pollard, L. W., Harter, J. G. and Coons, A. H.: Purification and analysis of fluorescein-labeled antisera by column chromatography, *J. Immunol.*, **90**, 634–642, 1963.

21) Mckinney, R. M., Spillane, J. T. and Pearce, G. W.: Factors affecting the rate of reaction of fluorescein isothiocyanate with serum proteins, *J. Immunol.*, **93**, 232–242, 1964.

22) Müller-Eberhard, H. J. and Nilson, U.: Relation of a glycoprotein of human sera to the complement system, *J. exper. Med.*, **111**, 217–234, 1960.

23) Peterson, E. A. and Sober, H. A.: Chromatography of proteins. I. Cellulose ion-exchange absorbents, *J. Am. Chem. Soc.*, **78**, 751–755, 1956.

24) Pressman, D., Yagi, Y. and Hiramoto, R.: A comparison of fluorescein and I^{131} as labels for determing the in vivo localization of antitissue antibodies, *Int. Arch. Allergy*, **12**, 125–136, 1958.

25) Reiner, L.: On the chemical alteration of purified antibody proteins, *Science*, **72**, 483–484, 1930.

26)   Riggs, J. L., Seiwald. R, J., Burckhalter, J., Downs, C. M., and Metcalf, T. G.: Isothiocyanate
      compounds as fluorescent labeling agents for immune serum, *Am. J. Path.*, **34**, 1081–1097,
      1958.
27)   Rinderknecht, H.: Ultra-rapid fluorescent labelling of proteins, *Nature*, **193**, 167–168, 1962.
28)   Saint-Marie, G.: A paraffin embedding technique for studies employing immunofluo-
      rescence, *J. Histochem. & Cytochem.*, **10**, 250–256, 1962.
29)   Singer, S. J.: Preparation of an electron-dense antibody conjugate, *Nature* (Lond.), **183**,
      1523–1524, 1959.
30)   Smith, C. W., Metzger, J. F., Zacks, S. I. and Kase, A.: Immune electron microscopy,
      Proc. Soc. Exper. Biol. & Med. (N. Y.), **104**, 336–338, 1960.
31)   Smith, C. W., Marshall, J. D. and Eveland, W. C.: Use of contrasting fluorescent dye as
      counterstain in fixed tissue preparations, *Proc. Soc. Exper. Biol. & Med.* (N. Y.), **102**, 179–
      181, 1959.
32)   Sober, H. A., Gutter, F. J., Wyckoff, M. M. and Peterson, E. A.: Chromatography of
      proteins, II, Fractionation of serum protein on amino-exchange cellulose, *J. Am. Chem. Soc.*,
      78, 756–763, 1956.
33)   Stanworth, D. R.: A rapid method of preparing pure serum γ-globulin, *Nature*, **188**,
      156–157, 1960.

PART II

CHAPTER VI

APPLICATION OF THE FLUORESCENT
ANTIBODY TECHNIQUES

1. Pox Virus

Antisera were prepared from rabbits previously infected with the LB Red strain of cowpox virus. The complement-fixing antibody titer of the serum was 256. The labeled antibody prepared by the ordinary method showed no cross reaction with varicella and other viruses except for pox viruses.

The chorioallantoic membranes of 10-day-old embryonated eggs were inoculated with the LB Red strain by Burnet's method. Twenty-four hours after inoculation, the ectodermal cells that proliferated in two to three layers, corresponding to a pock, showed an intense specific fluorescence in the cytoplasm (Fig. 1).

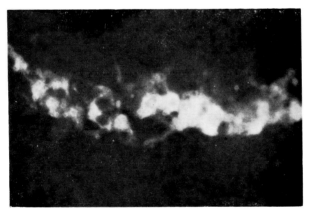

Fig. 1. The Chorioallantoic Membrane of a 10-Day-Old embryonated Egg Infected with the LB Red Strain

The FL cell monolayers were infected with the IHD strain of vaccinia virus. Specific fluorescence appeared first in the cytoplasm 5 to 6 hours after inoculation. Restaining with Giemsa solution indicated that the cytoplasmic fluorescence coincided with the site of a Guarnieri body. Nine hours after infection, fluorescence appeared diffusely in the cytoplasm as well as in Guarnieri bodies (Fig. 2).

Yuzo Aoyama

93

Fig. 2. FL Cell Infected with the IHD Strain.
9 Hours after Infection

2. ADENO VIRUS (Type 8)

Epidemic keratoconjunctivitis (EKC), one of the clinical types of infection caused by adenovirus, is generally diagnosed from clinical pictures and epidemiological characteristics. The direct fluorescent antibody technique is the most rapid diagnostic method for the confirmation of its etiology.

Antisera were prepared from the patients of EKC who had typical subepithelial punctate keratitis approximately one month after the onset of illness. Neutralizing antibody titers of the sera were 40 against adenovirus type 8. The virus used was a strain of adenovirus type 8 originally isolated from a patient with EKC.

Fig. 3 shows fluorescent nuclei in Hela cells infected 18 hours earlier with adenovirus type 8. A specific fluorescence first appears in the nucleus 6 to 8 hours after inoculation, becomes more intense, and 24 hours after inoculation most of the nuclei have a bright fluorescence. Thirty-six hours after inoculation, the cells assume a round shape and diffuse fluorescence also appears in the cytoplasms.

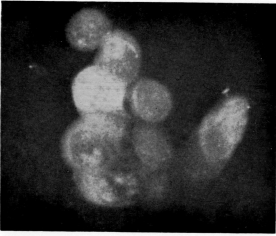

Fig. 3. Fluorescent Nuclei in Hela Cells Infected 18 Hours Earlier with Adenovirus Type 8

Color Plate I-1 shows the fluorescence in the nucleus of conjunctival epithelial cells scraped from a patient with clinical EKC.   A high percentage of antigen was usually found in conjunctival epithelial cells until the 7th day of illness. No positive results were obtained after two weeks.   Frequently, specific fluorescence was also found in corneal scrapings at an early stage of conjunctivitis prior to the onset of keratitis.   The duration of a positive reaction from the cornea was almost the same as that from conjunctiva.

Kozaburo Hayashi

3. HERPES GROUP VIRUSES

A. Herpes Simplex Virus

Preparation of antiserum: Rabbit serum was prepared by corneal inoculation of herpes simplex virus originally isolated from a patient with acute herpetic dendritic keratitis.   The complement-fixing antibody titer was 512 to 1024 against an HF strain of herpes simplex virus.

Case 1:   A 17-day-old boy. 8 days after birth, two exanthems, 0.5 cm in diameter, appeared on his mid-abdomen.   On the following day, there were several vesicular lesions in the right axilla and on the abdomen.   On the 15th day, exanthema appeared on both hands and on the forehead, and conjugated deviation was noted.   On the next day he was admitted to the Keio University Hospital because of loss of appetite, dyspnea, hematuria and the appearance of numerous petechiae.   The infant became weaker and died several hours after admission.

At autopsy, there were several vesicles on the trunk and extremities.   The liver was enlarged and rather firm in consistency.   It showed a reddish mottled appearance with many greyish-yellow spots, each about 1 mm in diameter. Similar necrotic foci were seen in the adrenal glands, especially in the cortex.

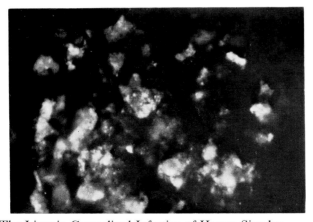

Fig. 4.   The Liver in Generalized Infection of Herpes Simplex
Specific fluorescence is seen both in the nuclei and cytoplasm of liver cells (autopsy case).

Microscopically, there were no typical intranuclear inclusion-bearing cells in the epidermis, liver and adrenals. Only atypical cells, such as faintly eosinophilic intranuclear inclusion bodies, were observed. However, frozen sections of the liver and adrenals, stained with fluorescent anti-herpes simplex virus antibody, showed specific fluorescence in the liver cells and in the cells of the adrenal cortex (Color Plate I-2, 3 and Fig. 4). Specific fluorescence was seen both in the nucleus and cytoplasm. The liver showed slightly cirrhotic changes, but there was no specific fluorescence in Glisson's area or in the interlobular connective tissue. This is characteristic and contrary to what is found in hepatitis caused by varicella-zoster virus (Color Plates I-5, 6).

The isolation of herpes simplex virus was performed by the inoculation of a 10% emulsion of liver tissue into a primary human embryonal fibroblast mono-layer. Two days after inoculation, specific fluorescence could be seen in the cells, forming many typical foci. The virus was identified by the neutralization test as herpes virus hominis.

Case 2: A 68-year-old male was admitted to the Clinical Department of Internal Medicine, The Institute of Medical Science, The University of Tokyo, on May 19, 1967. The first symptoms, dating back to 6 days before his admission, were occasional difficulty in speaking and a fever of 38 to 39°C. On May 18, the family noted tremor of the patient's right hand and foot. The patient was admitted the next day in an unconscious state. Over the course of the next few days he became comatose, and died on May 25, approximately 12 days after the onset of illness. On the 3rd day after admission, the herpes simplex and Japanese encephalitis virus complement-fixing antibody titers of the patient were 8 and <8, respectively.

At autopsy, performed 2 hours after death, there were numerous petechiae in the left temporal lobe, especially in the *gyrus temporalis medius, inferior, fusiformis* and *hippocampi.* Microscopically, in the necrotic foci, there were many nerve and glial cells with typical intranuclear inclusion bodies.

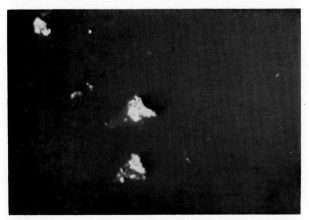

Fig. 5. Brain (Temporal Lobe) of a Herpetic Encephalitis Case
Two neuronal cells show a specific fluorescence in the cytoplasm (autopsy case).

Frozen materials taken at autopsy from the left temporal area and from other parts of the brain were sectioned and stained with various labeled antibodies, such as anti-herpes simplex, Japanese encephalitis, varicella-zoster, cytomegalo, influenza A and B, measles, Coxsackie A-9 and Coxsackie B-5 virus. Only specific fluorescence corresponding to herpes simplex virus was found in the neuron and glial cells in the necrotic foci and in the adjacent area of the left hemisphere; but this was not found in the midbrain and cerebellum.   A specific fluorescence was seen in the nuclei and cytoplasm, and sometimes only in the cytoplasm, of infected cells (Color Plate I-4 and Fig. 5).

Materials taken at necropsy from the left temporal cortex were prepared for inoculation by emulsifying the brain tissue in a virus culture medium.   This material was inoculated into a cell culture of primary human embryonal fibro-blasts ; it was also inoculated into several litters of new-born mice and hamsters intracerebrally.   Twenty-four hours after inoculation, when cytopathic changes were not obvious, a specific fluorescence was observed in the nuclei and cytoplasm of infected cells by staining with labeled anti-herpes simplex virus rabbit antibody (Fig. 6).   Three to four days after inoculation, cytopathic changes were clearly observable in the cell cultures, and the suckling mice and hamsters showed evidence of acute encephalitis.   Frozen sections of the brains taken from the infected animals were also stained with labeled antibody corresponding to herpes simplex virus.   Specific fluorescence was primarily seen in the meninges, ependymal cell lining and choroid plexus (Fig. 7, 8).   Two to three days after inoculation, it also appeared in the nerve cells and the glial cells of the hippocampi area.   Specific fluorescence was seen in the nuclei and cyto-plasm of infected cells (Color Plate I-7).

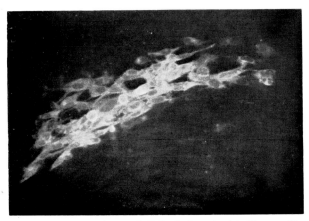

Fig. 6.   Primary Human Embryonal Cells Infected with Herpes Simplex Virus 24 Hours after Infection.

The serum taken at autopsy had a CF titer of 124 to herpes simplex virus. The virus isolated from cell culture and from the brain of infected rodents was neutralized with a specific herpes antiserum.

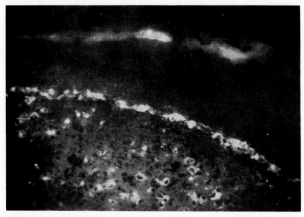

Fig. 7. Brain of a Suckling Mouse Infected with Herpes Simplex Virus Intracerebrally
Two days after infection, specific fluorescence was primarily seen in the meninges.

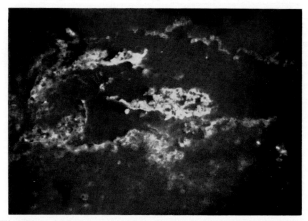

Fig. 8. The Choroid Plexus and Ependymal Cell Lining of the Same Mouse as in Fig. 7.

B. Varicella-Zoster Virus

Convalescent serum was obtained from a patient who suffered from severe herpes zoster. The varicella virus CF antibody titer was × 1024. Gamma globulin was purified and conjugated with FITC by the usual method. The staining titer of the conjugate was × 100. A diluted working solution showed no cross reaction with other herpes group viruses, or pox viruses.

A smear preparation of the patient's vesicular fluid was stained with the labeled antibody. Specific fluorescence was seen in the cytoplasm of infected epidermal cells (Fig. 9).

After the inoculation of vesicular fluid into primary human embryonal kidney cells, characteristic cytopathic changes were observed within 2 to 3 days. The

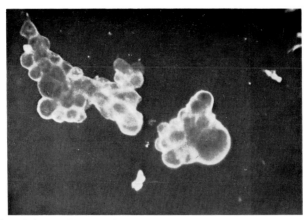

Fig. 9.   A Smear Preparation of Vesicular Fluid of a Varicella Patient

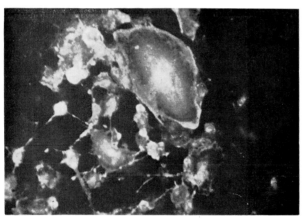

Fig. 10.   Primary Human Embryonal Kidney Cells Infected 2 Days Earlier with Varicella Virus

infected cells showed a specific fluorescence in the cytoplasm similar to that of the smear preparation (Fig. 10).

Autopsy cases of generalized chicken pox

Case 1:   A 4-year-old female.   Clinical diagnosis was acute leukemia with chicken pox.

Case 2:   A 67-year-old female.   Clinically diagnosed as myeloma with chicken pox.

The viscera taken at autopsy were examined by the fluorescent antibody technique.   The results are summarized in Table 1.

Skin: In Case 2, specific fluorescence was seen in the nuclei and cytoplasm of epidermal cells located in the vesicular or exanthematous lesions (Color Plate I-9).   In Case 1, a faint fluorescence was observed only in subcutaneous connective tissue.

Liver: In both cases, the connective tissue in Glisson's area showed specific

Table 1. Distribution of Viral Antigen in Two Autopsy Cases of
Generalized Chicken Pox

	Skin	Liver	Adrenal gland	Kidney	Lung	Spleen	Pancreas	Salivary gland	Thymus
Case 1	+	+	+	+	+	+	+	+	+
Case 2	+	+	n. t.	+	+	+	n. t.	n. t.	n. t.

staining, and a few liver cells in the peripheral zone of the lobule also showed
specific fluorescence (Color Plate I-5), in contrast to the results with herpetic
hepatitis.

Adrenal glands: In Case 1, there were many necrotic foci, each about 1 mm in
diameter, in the cortex.   Specific fluorescence was mainly seen in the cortical
connective tissue of the necrotic foci (Color Plate I-6).

Kidney: In both cases, specific fluorescence was found only in the interstitial
connective tissue (Color Plate I-8).   Epithelial cells in the renal tubule, which
are highly susceptible to infection with cytomegalovirus (Color Plate I-11),
showed no specific fluorescence.

The lung, spleen, pancreas, salivary gland and thymus were also stained
specifically (Figs. 11–15).   Specific fluorescence was observed mainly in the
connective tissue.   The epithelial cells of bronchioles and the reticular cells
near the trabecula in the spleen showed positive results, but the number of FA
positive cells was very small.

C. Cytomegalovirus

Convalescent sera taken from patients with cytomegalic inclusion disease
(CID), each having a CF antibody titer of over 32, were pooled and conjugated
with FITC.   The fractions which had an F/P molecular ratio of 1.5 to 2.0 were
collected and absorbed with acetone powder of human brain and liver.

Human embryonal fibroblasts (HEF) grown on coverslips were infected with

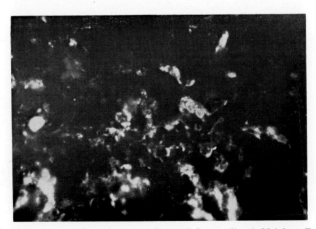

Fig. 11.   Lung of an Autopsy Case of Generalized Chicken Pox

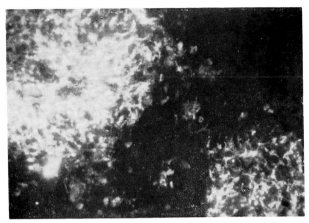

Fig. 12. Spleen of an Autopsy Case of Generalized Chicken Pox

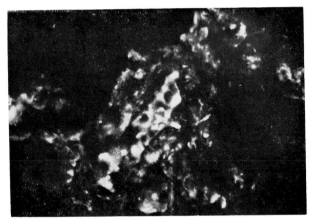

Fig. 13. Pancreas of an Autopsy Case of Generalized Chicken Pox

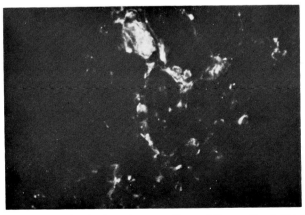

Fig. 14. Salivary Gland of an Autopsy Case of Generalized Chicken Pox

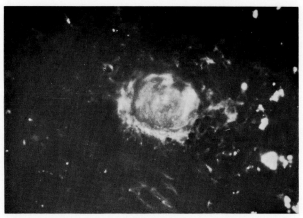

Fig. 15. Thymus of an Autopsy Case of Generalized Chicken Pox

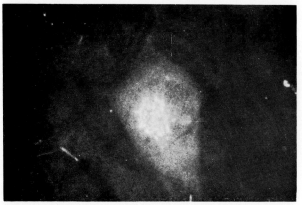

Fig. 16. Primary Human Embryonal Cells Infected with Cytomegalo Virus.
8 hours after infection, specific fluorescence appears only intranuclearly.

an AD 169 strain of cytomegalovirus. Eight hours after inoculation, specific fluorescence appeared in the nucleus (Fig. 16). Two to three hours later the cytoplasmic area corresponding to the site of a " cytoplasmic body " when stained with H and E showed a bright fluorescence (Fig. 17). Finally, 2 days after inoculation, intranuclear fluorescence disappeared and only cytoplasmic fluorescence remained until the cell became detached from the cover slip (Fig. 18).

Viruria of CID could be readily detected by inoculation of the patient's urine into HEF culture. Excretion of virus in the urine of a 20-day-old boy who was clinically diagnosed as a congenital hydrocephalus was confirmed using FAT (Color Plate I-12). The patient has been excreting the virus until now, approximately 2 years after the onset of illness.

Cytomegalic intranuclear inclusions have often been seen in salivary glands removed at autopsy. The viral antigen was clearly demonstrated by FAT in epithelial cells of the salivary duct (Color Plate I-10).

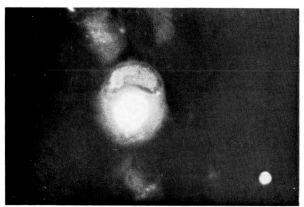

Fig. 17.   Primary Human Embryonal Cells Infected with Cytomegalo Virus. 10 hours after infection, specific fluorescence is seen both in the nucleus and cytoplasm.

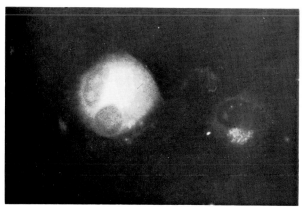

Fig. 18.   Primary Human Embryonal Cells Infected with Cytomegalo Virus. Two days after infection, the cytoplasmic fluorescence increases.   The right cell shows a condensed fluorescent area which corresponds to the cytoplasmic inclusion body.

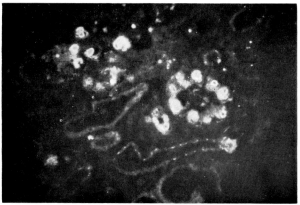

Fig. 19.   Fluorescent Tubular Kidney Epithelial Cells.
It is taken from an autopsy case of generalized cytomegalic inclusion disease.

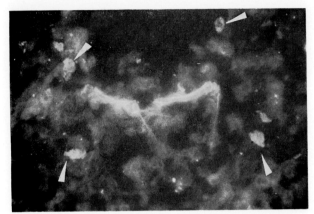

Fig. 20. Lung of the Same Patient as in Fig. 19.
The arrows show the desquamated fluorescent epithelial cells of bronchi and
bronchioli.

At autopsy, a 6-month-old girl who had been diagnosed as having acute
leukemia with CID at the age of 2 months, was studied with respect to the
localization of viral antigen in various organs. Exfoliated epithelial cells which
showed an intense fluorescence were found in the renal tubules (Color Plate
I-11 and Fig. 19). A faint fluorescence was also observed in desquamated
bronchial epithelial cells (Fig. 20). No fluorescence was seen in leukemic cells.

Yuzo Aoyama

4. INFLUENZA VIRUS*

A. Antibody

We employed guinea pigs in antibody preparation because high titered
CF(s) antibody is produced by intranasal inoculation of influenza virus,
without inducing the production of high titered antibody to normal egg material.
Antibody may be prepared in roosters and hens by intravenous inoculation of
crude allantoic fluid.

---

* Tateno, I., Suzuki, S., Kawamura, A., Jr., Kawashima, H., Kusano, N., Aoyama,
Y., Sugiura, A., Akao, Y., Oikawa, N., Homma, N. and Naito, M.: Diagnosis of influenza by means of fluorescent antibody technique, *Japan J. Exp. Med.*, **32**, 531–559,
1962.

Tateno, I., Suzuki, S., Nakamura, S. and Kawamura, A., Jr.: Diagnosis of in-
fluenza by means of fluorescent antibody technique, I. Some basic information; II.
Relation between immunocytologic, serological and clinical findings, *Japan J. Exp.
Med.*, **35**, 383–400, 401–410, 1965.

Ebisawa, I., Makino, M. and Takeuchi, Y.: Rapid diagnosis of influenza B with
fluorescent antibody, *Japan J. Exp. Med.*, **36**, 301–320, 1966.

Ebisawa, I., Takeuchi, Y. and Makino, M.: Immunocytology of nasal smears in
influenza A2, *Japan J. Exp. Med.*, in press.

Several inoculations of ether- or nembutal-anesthetized guinea pigs at 5–7 day intervals are required before the CF(s) titer rises to 1 in 32 or higher. Only immune sera with a homologous CF(s) titer of 1 in 32 or higher and a heterologous CF(s) titer of less than 1 in 4 are pooled. Antibody which is reactive with normal allantoic membrane is absorbed with uninfected allantoic membrane.

Fowl are inoculated with 10 m*l* of undiluted allantoic fluid on several occasions and are bled when the hemagglutination inhibition titer rises to 1 in 4096 or higher.

B. Examination of the Staining Titer and Specificity of the FITC-Conjugate

Immune sera are conjugated with FITC by a standard method and the conjugate is absorbed twice with acetone-treated human liver powder. Frozen sections of allantoic membrane infected with influenza virus are stained directly with serial two-fold dilutions of FITC-conjugate starting from 1 in 4. Allantoic membranes infected with both homologous and heterologous types of influenza viruses are stained with anti-A2 and -B conjugates to determine the staining titer and specificity. The staining titer of absorbed conjugates remains stable for at least 6 months if they are kept on dry ice.

C. Preparation of Nasal Smears and Other Clinical Materials

Nasal smears of patients with influenza or other acute respiratory diseases are obtained in the early stages of illness, preferably within 3 to 4 days of onset, although some patients yield positive smears as late as 7 to 8 days after the onset of illness. The patient is asked to clear his nose by blowing before the nasal smear is taken. The nasal cavity is examined carefully with a rhinoscope, and a cotton swab attached to a bamboo stick is inserted into the cavity. The swab is rotated along the surface of the nasal mucosa, usually between the medial and inferior nasal conchae or between the latter and the septum. The swab is pressed a little against the mucous membrane while it is rotated. Two smears, about 1 to 1.5 cm in diameter, can be prepared from one swabbing of the nasal epithelium. It is best to make the smears on separate slides.

Autopsy materials may be examined by preparing impression smears or frozen sections.

D. Results

(a) General Aspects of Fluorescent Cells in Nasal Smears.

Fluorescent antibody staining of nasal smears of influenza A2 and B patients has quite a dynamic aspect, in that the type of fluorescent cells and the localization of fluorescence within these cells show considerable variation with the chronological sequences of cellular infection with influenza virus.

(a-i) The types of fluorescent cells in nasal smears from influenza patients

The following types of cells are shown to fluorescence specifically in influenza.

Ciliated epithelial cells (cylindrical and slender or stout and short cells; Figs. 21 a-d).

The nucleus is usually at the base of the cell and occasionally a cytoplasmic tail protrudes from the base. The brush may be retained or detached. *Non-ciliated round and ovoid cells* (Figs. 21 e-f)

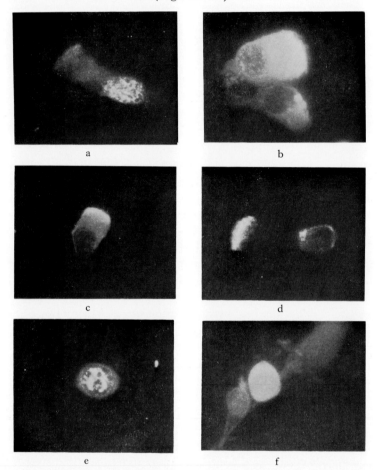

a

b

c

d

e

f

Fig. 21. Fluorescent Cells in Nasal Smears of Influenza A2 and B Patients

a. Ciliated cylindrical epithelial cell with predominantly nuclear fluorescence.

b. Ciliated cylindrical epithelial cell with both cytoplasmic and nuclear fluorescence. Note the presence of a fluorescent cytoplasmic "tail." The cell below is faintly and non-specifically fluorescent.

c. Ciliated cylindrical epithelial cell with predominantly cytoplasmic fluorescence.

d. Ciliated cylindrical epithelial cell with strong fluorescence in the periphery of the nucleus and at the ciliated border of the cell.

e. Ovoid and non-ciliated cell with strong nuclear fluorescence.

f. Round, non-ciliated cell with both cytoplasmic and nuclear fluorescence. The fluorescent cell is flanked by two non-fluorescent cells.

Some of these cells are deformed ciliated epithelial cells from which the tufts have been detached. However, small ovoid or round cells, which differ clearly from the ciliated epithelial cells, are found rather frequently, particularly in the later stage of influenza infection. These may be cells situated at the basal segment of the nasal epithelium.

Deformed or condensed cells including polygonal cells

It must be remembered that influenza virus-infected cells undergo rapid degeneration and deformation both in vitro and in vivo. The degenerated and shrunken epithelial cells often present a polygonal appearance.

Squamoid or squamous-like cells

This type of cell is characterized by a large amount of cytoplasm and small nucleus, and is found when the nasal swabbing is made near the vestibulum of the nose.

(a-ii)   Localization of antigen within cells

Fluorescent cells in nasal smears from influenza patients are divided into six types, according to the localization of intracellular fluorescence.

Type 1.   Only the nucleus is strongly fluorescent; the cytoplasm lacks any specific fluorescence. The nuclear fluorescence may be granular (rough or fine), but some cells show an accumulation of virus antigen at the periphery of the nucleus, and when the lens is not well focused, the whole nucleus appears homogeneously fluorescent.

Type 1'.   The nucleus is strongly fluorescent and the cytoplasm weakly or partially so (Fig. 21 a). Cytoplasmic fluorescence appears first near the nucleus or at the root area of the tufts.

Type 2.   Both cytoplasm and nucleus are fluorescent (Figs. 21 b & f). The cytoplasmic fluorescence is usually homogeneous and that of the nucleus is either homogeneous or granular.

Type 2'.   The cytoplasmic fluorescence is strong but the nuclear fluorescence is weak.

Type 3.   The fluorescence is strong in the cytoplasm but is absent in the nucleus (Fig. 21 c).

Type 3'.   Partial cytoplasmic fluorescence, usually in the area from which the brush sprouts (Fig. 21 d).

There are some cells that cannot be classified into any of the above types. One of these is the ciliated cell, in which the perinuclear region and the apical portion of the cell from which ciliae sprout are strongly fluorescent (Fig. 21 d).

The presence of degenerated, shrunken or condensed cells often makes classification very difficult.

(b)   Relation Between Immunocytologic and Serological Findings.

The immunocytologic study of nasal smears agreed well with the results of serological tests in the case of influenza B. All 33 patients with positive immunocytologic findings were confirmed to have influenza B by a conventional method, although there were 10 patients with positive serologic but negative immunocytologic tests. Nine patients yielded negative results in both serologic and immunocytologic tests (Table 2-a).

Table 2. Relation between Immunocytologic and Serologic Tests

2-a.　Influenza B (1966).

Serologically or by virus isolation	Immunocytologically		Total
	Positive	Negative	
Positive	33	10	43
Negative	0	9	9
Total	33	19	52

2-b.　Influenza A2 (1967–1968).

Serologically	Immunocytologically		Total
	Positive	Negative	
Positive	69	5	74
Negative	6	30	36
Total	75	35	110

There was a significant correlation between the immunocytologic and serologic tests in the case of influenza A2, although there were some contradictory findings. Sixty-nine out of 74 serologically confirmed influenza A2 patients yielded positive immunocytologic findings of nasal smears. On the other hand, there were 6 patients with positive immunocytologic findings out of 36 patients who could not be confirmed to be suffering from influenza A2 by means of conventional serologic methods (Table 2-b). These patients were all seen during the 1967–1968 epidemic of influenza A2. Positively fluorescing cells of these patients were photographed, and their appearance was indistinguishable from those seen in the serologically positive patients. It is probable that in the case of influenza A2, there are some patients in whom there is a definite infection of the nasal epithelium without significant antibody response.

(c)　The Day of Illness on which Positive Smears were Obtained.

The majority of positive nasal smears were obtained during the first to fourth days of illness, and rarely in the second week (Table 3). However, some influenza A2 patients yielded positive smears as late as the 12th and 25th days of illness when they had recrudescence of fever or pneumonia after recovery from the initial attack of influenza. Details of these cases are reported elsewhere.

Table 3.   The Days of Illness on Which Positive Nasal Smears were Obtained.

Day of illness / Influenza	1	2	3	4	5	6	7	8	12	25	29	Total
B		7	13	6	2	2	1	2				33
A2	5	17	20	8	4	2	4		(1)*	1	(1)**	61

* This patient also yielded a positive nasal smear on the 2nd day.
** This patient also yielded a positive nasal smear on the 25th day.

Isao Ebisawa

Experimental Study of Influenza Virus Infection

Experimentally, young mice of DD strain can be infected with an NWS strain of influenza A virus by intra-cerebral inoculation.   Ependymal cells show a specific fluorescence 20 hours after infection (Color Plate II-1).   The virus then multiplies and spreads into the brain parenchyma, especially the neuronal cells in the hippocampus area (Color Plate II-2).

Yuzo Aoyama

5. HVJ

Sendai virus agglutinates the erythrocytes of several species of animals and causes a pneumonic lesion in laboratory mice (Color Plate II-3).   This indigenous infection is demonstrable in a wide range of breeder mouse colonies in Japan, and there is some thought that it may be persistent in their populations.   Consequently, this viral contamination is a great hindrance in isolating viruses from cases of respiratory disease or in studying the histogenesis of pneumonic lesions by intranasal inoculation of test materials into mice.   Since it is not easy to obtain a mouse colony free from Sendai virus infection, viral contamination must be checked for in the pneumonic lesion, and for such a test the immunofluorescence technique is very useful.   The mode of infection and/or epizootic factor for the viral spread is still obscure.   While younger mice appear more susceptible to infection than adult mice, the actual tropism of the virus to organs and tissues other than the lungs of mice is not fully understood.   In frozen sections obtained from suckling mice inoculated with the virus through different routes, multiplication of virus was examined in the main organs by the direct immunofluorescence technique.

An MN strain passaged in allantoic fluid of chick embryos was used; its hemagglutinin titer and EID50 value were 320 and $10^{7.5}/0.1$ ml of fluid, respectively. Animals used were 24 or 48-hour-old suckling mice and 3 or 4-week-old mice, reared in an isolated breeding room of the Institute of Medical Science, University of Tokyo.   The parents were obtained from a mouse colony free from Sendai virus, at Tohoku University, Sendai, through the courtesy of Prof. Nakao Ishida,

Color Plate I

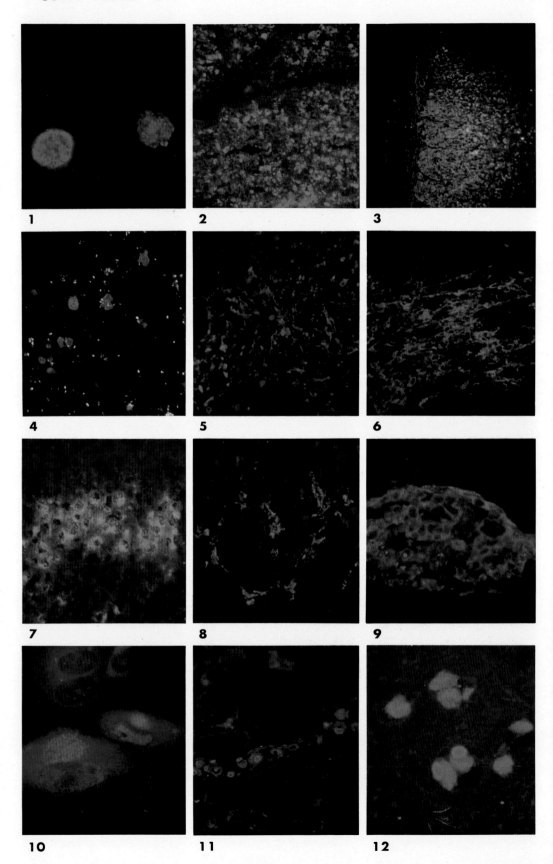

Department of Bacteriology, the School of Medicine.   A number of adult mice were intraperitoneally immunized with 0.2 m*l* of 20% lung emulsion from mice infected intranasally with the stock virus suspension 5 times at weekly intervals. A pool of sera showing a hemagglutination inhibiting antibody titer of more than 640 was subjected to fractionation and the crude γ-globulin obtained by salting-out was conjugated with fluorescein isothiocyanate according to the usual procedures.   For use, the labeled antibody solution was diluted 1: 16 so as to give 2 units of the staining titer.

A. Intraperitoneal Inoculation

Suckling and 1-week-old mice succumbed to intraperitoneal infection, and the LD 50 was calculated as $10^{-0.84}/0.05$ m*l* of the viral suspension in both cases, whereas no deaths were observed among adult mice thus inoculated.   Even with a lesser dose of the virus, such as a 10^{-3} dilution, a markedly supressed weight gain was observed in the suckling mice and there was a greater amount of hemorrhagic

---

$\Leftarrow$

Explanation of Color Plate I

I-1.   Smear preparation of conjunctival epithelial cells scraped from a patient with clinical E. K. C.   Specific fluorescence of adenovirus antigen is seen only in the nuclei.

I-2.   Liver of a generalized herpes simplex case.   Almost all hepatic cells show specific fluorescence.   Note the lack of fluorescence in Glisson's capsule and the interlobular connective tissue (Case 1).

I-3.   Adrenal gland of a generalized herpes simplex case.   A wedge-shaped necrotic focus in the cortical area shows intense fluorescence (Case 1).

I-4.   Temporal area of a herpetic encephalitis case.   Many neurons and glial cells show specific fluorescence.   Bright yellow spots are due to the autofluorescence of lipofuscin (Case 2).

I-5.   Liver of a generalized chicken pox case.   Specific fluorescence is seen in the connective tissue of Glisson's sheath.   A few liver cells in the peripheral zone of the lobule show specific fluorescence (Case 2).

I-6.   Adrenal gland of a generalized chicken pox case.   Specific fluorescence is seen in the cortical connective tissue of the necrotic lesion (Case 1).

I-7.   Ammon's horn of a suckling mouse infected 3 days previously with herpes simplex virus.

I-8.   Kidney of a generalized chicken pox case.   Specific fluorescence is seen in the interstitial connective tissue (Case 1).

I-9.   Skin of a generalized chicken pox case.   Marked fluorescence is seen in the nuclei and cytoplasm of epidermal cells (Case 2).

I-10.   Human embryonal fibroblasts inoculated 2 days previously with urine from a child with cytomegalic inclusion disease (CID).   Specific fluorescence is clearly demonstrated in the nuclei and cytoplasm.   Nucleoli have no fluorescence.

I-11.   Kidney of CID patient.   Numerous exfoliated epithelial cells showing intense fluorescence are seen in a renal tubule.

I-12.   Parotid gland of CID patient.   Enlarged fluorescent epithelial cells are seen in the salivary ducts.

exudate in their peritoneal cavities.   Fluorescence microscopic observations of frozen sections of the abdomen, prepared 4 days after infection with 0.05 m*l* of a 1 : 10 dilution of the virus fluid, revealed a marked degree of specific fluorescence along the cell lining of the peritoneum (Fig. 22), but no definite fluorescence could be observed either in the peritoneum of adult mice or in the parenchyma of such organs as the liver, spleen and lungs of suckling mice.

Fig. 22.   Fluorescent Peritoneal Cells of Small Interstines of Suckling Mice 4 Days after Intraperitoneal Injection with 0.05 m*l* of a 1 :10 Dilution of the Viral Inoculum

B. Intracerebral Inoculation

In this procedure, the LD 50 was calculated as $10^{-1.0}/0.01$ m*l* of virus suspension against suckling and 1-week-old mice.   However, all adult mice survived infection with undiluted inoculum.   In frozen sections of brains of mice killed 4 days after inoculation with 0.01 m*l* of a 1 : 10 dilution of virus suspension, specific fluorescence was observed in the choroidal plexus and ventricular epithelium of the lateral and third ventricles of suckling and adult mice.   It was

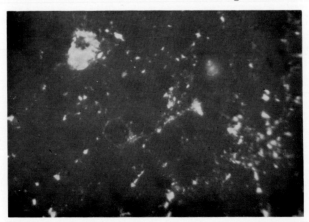

Fig. 23.   Fluorescent Granules in Brain Parenchyma of Suckling Mice 4 Days after Inoculation with 0.01 m*l* of a 1 :10 Dilution of the Viral Inoculum

mostly noticeable in suckling mice, and the fluorescent cells were distributed in the nasal tissues and in brain parenchyma where, although intracellular localization was not clear, a number of fluorescent granules existed (Fig. 23).

C. Intranasal Inoculation

The LD 50 values calculated were $10^{-5.6}$ and $10^{-3.0}$ per 0.01 ml in suckling and 1-week-old mice, respectively. No deaths were observed among 4-week-old mice.

When groups of suckling mice were intranasally infected with various doses of virus and killed at weekly intervals to prepare vertical frozen sections of respiratory tissue for titrating the infectivity by immunofluorescence, it was demonstrated that almost all mice could be infected even with 0.01 ml of a 10^{-7} dilution of the virus suspension in 2 weeks. Also many typical fluorescent cells existed in nasal, tracheal, bronchial and alveolar epithelium (Figs. 24–26), but none in abdominal organs and tissues. Later, and even after treatment of these mice with cortisone, fluorescent cells became difficult to find in the tissues, suggesting that persistent infection might fail in mice under these circumstances. Ascending spread of the infection to brain tissues has been reported in chicks intranasally infected with Newcastle disease virus, but this was not the case in the suckling mice infected with Sendai virus.

Both hemagglutination inhibition and complement fixation tests can frequently detect antibody to Sendai virus in laboratory mouse populations. In an attempt to observe how frequently the mice are actually infected a number of groups of adult mice from several commercial breeders were subcutaneously injected with 5 mg of cortisone acetate and killed 10 days later. In order to detect infected cells by immunofluorescence, frozen sections of several organs were prepared, and in some cases, smears of nasal tissues, tracheae and lungs were taken. This work was done in cooperation with Assistant Prof. Kosaku Fujiwara of the Institute of Medical Science, the University of Tokyo.

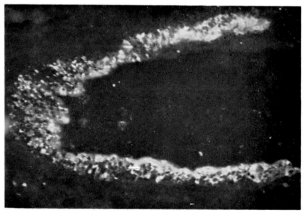

Fig. 24. Fluorescent Nasal Epithelium of Suckling Mice 4 Days after Intranasal Application of 0.01 ml of a 10^{-7} Dilution of Virus

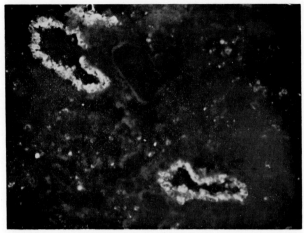

Fig. 25.   Fluorescent Bronchiolar and Alveolar Epithelium of Suckling Mice 4 Days after Intranasal Application of 0.01 m*l* of a 10^{-7} Dilution of Virus

Fig. 26.   Magnification of a Fluorescent Bronchiole of a Suckling Mouse 4 Days after Intranasal Application of 0.01 m*l* of a 10^{-7} Dilution of Virus

In a total number of 265 mice, 15% showed pneumonic lesions; positive immunofluorescence was observed in 20, 8 and 5% of the nasal tissues, tracheae and lungs, respectively.

It was suggested that natural infection in mice might be limited to the respiratory tract and might be a type of upper respiratory disease.   However, it was not clear whether or not cortisone enhanced the spread and intensity of viral infection.

Yuriko Murata and Tsuyoshi Iida

6. Mumps Virus

The immune serum was obtained from guinea pigs infected intranasally with the Enders strain of mumps virus.   The pooled immune serum used had a CF titer of

1/64 to 1/128.   Suckling mice can be infected with the Enders strain intracerebrally.   The initial site of virus multiplication seems to be the ependymal cells
(Color Plate II-4a).

Specific fluorescence appeared only in the cytoplasm of these cells.   Two to
three days after inoculation, specific fluorescence was found in the neuronal cells
of the subependymal area.   The fluorescence takes a droplet-like shape that
seems to be characteristic of mumps infection (Color Plate II-4b).

Yuzo Aoyama

7. MEASLES VIRUS

Fluorescent antibody was prepared with convalescent serum from a Japanese
monkey infected subcutaneously with the Sugiyama strain* of measles virus
grown in FL cell cultures.   The immune serum used had a CF titer of 1/256 and
a neutralizing titer of $1/2^{9.5}$ with 100 $TCID_{50}$ of virus.   The fraction of conjugate
with an F/P molecular ratio of 1.0 to 2.0 was then collected.   The preparation
was found to have staining activity at dilutions up to 1: 16 when tested with FL
and Hep-2 cell cultures infected with the Sugiyama strain.   The conjugated
globulin solution was absorbed with acetone powder of human liver and brain
and mouse liver and brain to remove non-specific staining activity.

The specificity of the conjugated globulin was carefully tested with FL cells,
both normal and infected, with Sugiyama strain and with sections of normal mice
and mice infected with herpes and Japanese encephalitis viruses.   The smear
preparations and infected culture cells were pretreated with acetone at $-20°C$ for
30 minutes.

A. FL Cells Infected with Sugiyama Strain

Specific fluorescence appeared in the cytoplasm 18 hours after infection.   The
intensity of the fluorescence then increased, and finally occupied almost the entire
cytoplasm.   Fusion of infected cells occurred 24 hours after infection and the
central area of multinucleated giant cells showed a bright fluorescence (Color
Plate II-5).

B. Smear Preparations from Measles Patients

Specific fluorescence was clearly found in nasal, throat and conjunctival smear
preparations (Color Plate II-6, a-c), and in urine sediment from measles
patients (Color Plate II-6d, Tables 4, 5).   Nasal smears prepared between 4 days
before and 3 days after the appearance of exanthema showed a positive fluores-

---

*   Matsumoto, M., Mutai, M., Ogiwara, H., Nishi, I., Kusano, N., and Aoyama, Y.:
Isolement du virus de la rougeole en culture du tissue renal du singe, *C. R. Soc. Biol.*,
153, 879–883, 1959.

Matsumoto, M., Mutai, M., and Ogiwara, M.: Proliferation du virus rougeoleux en
culture de cellules renales bovines, *C. R. Soc. Biol.*, **155**, 1192–1195, 1961.

Color Plate II

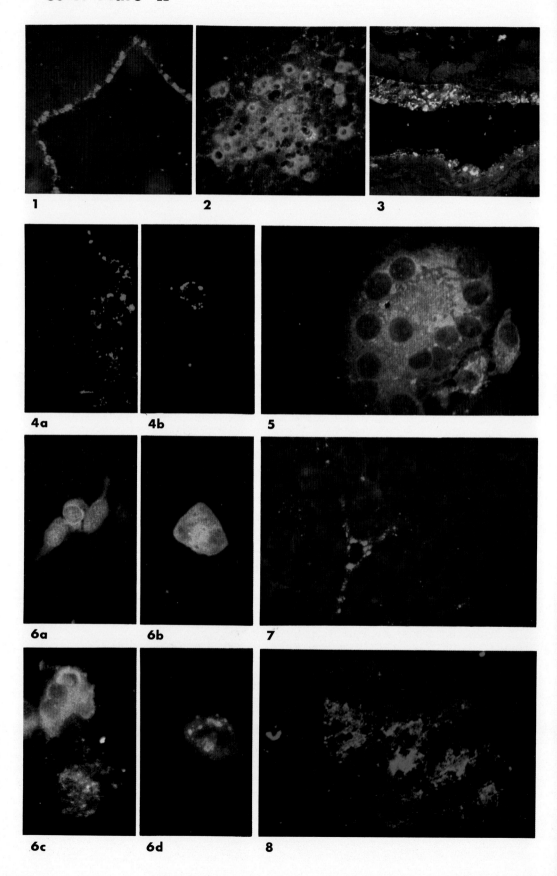

cence in more than 80% of the specimens tested.   Preparations from normal children showed no fluorescence.   Nasal, throat and conjunctival smears of children after the administration of measles live vaccine also showed no specific fluorescence.

C. A Neurotropic Variant of Measles Virus in the Suckling Mouse Brain

The Sugiyama strain, adapted to FL cells after 6 passages in primary monkey renal cells, acquired the ability to propagate serially in the brain of suckling mice somewhere between the 49th and 76th FL passage.   The virus produced a lethal spastic paralysis in about half of the mice in the early passages and in almost all of the mice from the 9th passage on.   Mice were nearly 100% susceptible within 5 days after birth and almost 100% resistant at the age of 7 days or more. Extraneural routes of inoculation were ineffective for infection.

Histologic changes were found only in the cerebrum and not in the cerebellum or spinal cord, or in other visceral organs.   They consisted of the degeneration of nerve cells with or without the formation of inclusions characteristic of measles, multinuclear giant cells formed by the fusion of nerve cells (see Fig. 27), and the proliferation of glial cells.   The fluorescent antibody study revealed a remarkable specificity of nerve cell involvement.   Specific measles antigens were found predominantly in nerve cells (Color Plate II-7, 8), only rarely in glial cells, and not

⇐

Explanation of Color Plate II

II–1.   Ependymal cells of young mice (DD strain) show specific fluorescence 20 hours after intracerebral inoculation with influenza A virus (NWS strain).

II–2.   Influenza A virus (NWS strain) spreading into the ganglion cells in the hippocampus area of young mice (DD strain).

II–3.   Lung of mice spontaneously infected with HVJ, stained with FITC conjugated pooled sera of untreated mice.

II–4a.   Ependymal cells of suckling mice, infected with Enders strain of mumps virus intracerebrally, are the initial site of the appearance of specific fluorescence.

II–4b.   Two days after mumps virus infection.   The droplet-like shape of specific fluorescence was found in the ganglion cell in the subependymal area of suckling mice.

II–5.   Tissue culture cells (FL cell) fused 24 hours after infection with measles virus (Sugiyama strain).   The central area of a multinucleated cell shows bright fluorescence.

II–6a.   Nasal smear preparation of measles patient.

II–6b.   Throat smear preparation of measles patient.

II–6c.   Conjunctival smear preparation of measles patient.

II–6d.   Urine sediment of measles patient.

II–7.   Specific fluorescence of measles virus antigen is shown in the cytoplasm of a nerve cell.

II–8.   Hippocampus of suckling mice infected with measles virus intracerebrally 10 days earlier.   Note the cytoplasmic bright fluorescence of nerve cells.

Table 4. Summary of Fluorescent Antibody Study in the Diagnosis of Measles Infection

Materials	>6	6	5	4	3	2	1	Eruption of Exanthem	1	2	3	4	5	6	6<	Total No. of specimens	No. of specimens	Control No of specimens
Nasal smear	0/4	0/2	(★1) 1/3	(★1) 3/6	5/5	8/10	(☆1) 9/10	(☆1) 15/17	(☆3) 10/15	6/7	6/8	0/5	0/2	0/4	0/2	102	54	21
Urine sediment				0/3	0/2	(★1) 3/6	4/8	(☆1) 6/10	6/9	(★1) 1/4	0/3		0/2		0/1	48	25	9
Throat smear			0/1	0/2	(★1) 1/2	0/4	1/3	3/6	0/4	0/1			0/1			24	18	7
Conjunctival smear				0/2	0/2	2/3	7/10	(★1) 1/4		0/3	0/1		0/1			26	23	5
Koplik spots						0/1	0/5	0/5	0/1							12	11	
Blood smear						0/2	0/2	0/3	0/5	0/2	0/1					15	12	4

No. of positive / No. of specimens ★ No. of questionable specimens ☆ No. of unsatisfactory specimens.*

in other types of cells. Specific fluorescence was always found in the cytoplasm and not in the nucleus, as in infected FL cells.*

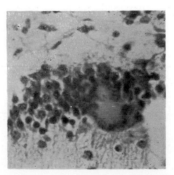

Fig. 27. Giant Cells Formed by Fusion of the Pyramidal Cell Layer in Ammon's Horn, 9 days after Infection (Gallocyanin staining)

Yuzo Aoyama and Hitoshi Nagahama

* Matsumoto, M., Saburi, Y., Aoyama, Y., and Mutai, M.: A neurotropic variant of measles virus in suckling mice, *Arch. ges. Virus.*, **14**, 683–696, 1964.

Table 5.   Clinical Course of Cases of Measles Infection

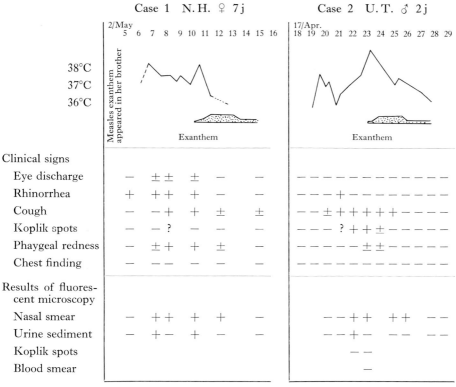

Clinical signs														
Eye discharge	−	±	±	±	−		−		−	−	−	−	−	−
Rhinorrhea	+	+	+	+	−		−		−	−	+	−	−	−
Cough	−	−	+	+	±	±	−	−	±	+	+	+	+	−
Koplik spots	−	−	?	−	−	−	−	−	−	?	+	+	±	−
Phaygeal redness	−	±	+	+	±	−	−	−	−	−	−	±	±	−
Chest finding	−	−	−	−	−	−	−	−	−	−	−	−	−	−
Results of fluorescent microscopy														
Nasal smear	−	+	+	+	+	−		−	−	+	+	+	+	−
Urine sediment	−	+	−	+	−	−		−	−	+	−	−	−	−
Koplik spots										−	−			
Blood smear										−				

Nagahama et al., 1964

8. CANINE DISTEMPER VIRUS*

Labeled antibodies were made with sera obtained from hamsters, minks and dogs immunized with viral material originating from their respective species. No essential difference was recognized, however, among these serum donors when they were tested with cultured chicken embryo fibroblasts and tissue sections or smears obtained from diseased dogs infected with various strains of distemper virus. The best results were obtained by pretreatment of the antigen with acetone kept at −20°C for 30 minutes.

Following an aerosol exposure to virulent distemper virus, dogs manifested a series of clinical signs which showed two peaks in depression, inappetence, fever and nasal and/or ocular discharges. At the second peak of symptoms, for about one to two weeks, fluorescent cells were detected in smears prepared from leucocytes, conjunctiva, nasal mucosa and urine sediments. Distribution of the

---

*   Nakagawa, H.: Studies on canine distemper infection by means of the fluorescent antibody technique, Thesis, Nippon Vet. and Zootech. Coll., Tokyo, 1968 (in Japanese).

antigen in the bodies of the affected dogs was similar to that reported by previous workers (see Color Plate III-2, Fig. 28). For rapid specific diagnosis of canine distemper during the acute stage of illness, it was found that the fluorescent antibody technique could be easily applied to any of the smears described above (see Color Plate III-1) when the animal was brought to a veterinarian after they became ill.

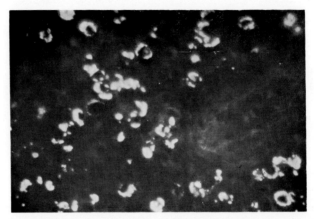

Fig. 28. Section of Dog Spleen, 32 Days after Infection with Canine Distemper Virus
Pretreatment with acetone at −20°C for 30 min.

Hidetsugu Nakagawa and Tsunemasa Motohashi

9. Rinderpest Virus*

The relationship between measles, canine distemper and rinderpest viruses has been demonstrated by investigators, and the fluorescent antibody technique has been successfully applied to studies on the first two viruses. With respect to the rinderpest virus, however, only a brief report on the use of the indirect method with cultured cells has been made and no further details have yet been published.

A series of experiments was performed to investigate the appearance and localization of antigen in cells infected with rinderpest virus. The relationship between these phenomena and the occurrence of pathological changes was another subject of study. Cultured bovine kidney cells were infected with a strain of rinderpest virus which was adapted to the cultured cells, and a sequential study

---

* Ushizima, T., Tajima, M. and Kishi, S.: Pathological study on rabbits and cultured cells infected with rinderpest virus by means of the fluorescent antibody technique, *Jap. J. Vet. Sci.*, **28**, Supplement, 388, 1966 (in Japanese).

Ushizima, T., Tajima, M. and Kishi, S.: Observations on cultured cells infected with rinderpest virus by means of the fluorescent antibody technique, *NIBS Bull. Biol. Res.*, in press.

was made by means of hematoxylin-eosin and fluorescent antibody staining. Similar observations were made with rabbits inoculated with a lapinized strain of rinderpest virus.

In cultured cells, the antigen was found in the cytoplasm within 24 hours of infection, although the infective titer began to increase two days after virus inoculation. Specific fluorescence was first seen near the nucleus as fine granules which increased in size and number with the passage of time (Fig. 29), eventually filling

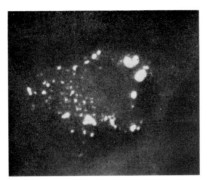

Fig. 29. An Infected Culture Cell on the Second Day after Inoculation with Rinderpest Virus
A number of fine fluorescent granules are seen around the nucleus of the cell. Pretreatment with acetone at $-20°C$ for 30 min.

the cytoplasm. In some of the infected cells, granules with slight fluorescence began to appear in the nucleus three days after infection. Conventional light microscopy of cultured cells three days after virus inoculation revealed the occurrence of a cytopathic effect, the formation of multinucleated giant cells and the appearance of cytoplasmic and intranuclear inclusion bodies. It was confirmed that the location and size of the large cytoplasmic inclusion bodies were identical with those of the fluorescent mass (Color Plate III-3).

In rabbits, the specific antigen was found 20 hours after infection, mostly in the cytoplasm of cells in the lymph nodes and lymphoid tissues of the alimentary tract (Color Plate III-4). It was first recognized as fine granules which increased in size and number. The distribution of the antigen was identical with the location of morphological changes seen under a conventional light microscope.

On the basis of the results described above, it has been suggested that the cytoplasm may be the principal site of synthesis of rinderpest virus and that the cytoplasmic inclusion bodies may be closely connected with virus synthesis.

Cytoplasmic inclusion bodies to which ferritin-conjugated antibody was attached were also visible with an electron microscope.

Takeshi Ushizima and Tsunemasa Motohashi

10. Hog Cholera Virus

Immune serum was prepared from a pig previously inoculated with inactivated vaccine after a booster injection with virulent virus (peripheral blood of the infected pig). The neutralizing titer was over $16,000 \times$ (by the END method). After labeling with FITC, the conjugate was absorbed with acetone powder from normal pig spleen and lymph node.

Pigs were inoculated subcutaneously in the neck with virulent hog cholera virus. Two days after inoculation, virus antigen appeared in the regional lymph node and tonsils, spreading to the lymph nodes of the body and spleen after 3 days.

In the early phase of infection, fluorescent antigen was seen in the lacunar epithelium of the tonsils and the cells of the reticuloendothelial system. In the middle phase of infection they were found in the mucous epithelium of the digestive canal, acinous cells of the pancreas, glandular epithelium of the salivary glands and the adrenal cortical epithelium. Finally, they appeared in the glial cells of the central nervous system and connective tissues throughout the body. Liver cells, muscle and nerve cells showed no fluorescence at any phase.

Color Plate III, 5a, b shows a tonsil three days after inoculation. The lacunar epithelium reveals a bright fluorescence and the reticulum cells of the lymphoid tissues are weakly fluorescent. Color Plate III, 6a, b shows the spleen 5 days after inoculation. Fluorescent antigen is found in the cytoplasm of reticulum cells of the lymphoid follicles but not in the vascular endothelia. Two days after infection with the attenuated virus (through tissue culture passages), a small amount of virus antigen appears in the reticulum cells of the lymph nodes throughout the body, diminishing gradually on the 7th day.

The early appearance of a bright fluorescence in the lacunar epithelium of tonsils led us to apply this technique to the diagnosis of hog cholera. Fig. 30 shows the cytoplasmic fluorescence of the lacunar epithelium in a smear preparation of tonsils obtained from a naturally infected pig. This method is superior to

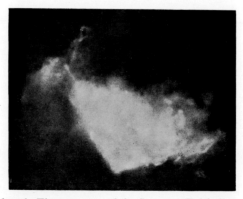

Fig. 30. Cytoplasmic Fluorescence of the Lacunar Epithelium in a Smear Preparation of Tonsils Obtained from Pig a Naturally Infected with Hog Cholera Virus

Aiken's method (smear preparation of peripheral lymph node or spleen for FAT—1964) in its specificity, higher percentage and earlier detection.

Minoru Sawada

11. Rabies Virus

Many questions remain to be solved concerning the pathogenesis of rabies infection. It is still unknown whether rabies virus multiplies at the point of entry or not. According to present knowledge, cells in which rabies virus multiplies outside the nervous system are salivary gland cells, brown fat cells and perhaps muscle fibers. However, we cannot come to any conclusion as to whether multiplication in extra-neural cells is the essential primary step for the invasion of rabies virus into the central nervous system or not. Without multiplication at the point of entry, the agent causing this disease cannot reach the central nervous system through the blood stream, because the amount of rabies virus contained in the saliva of rabid animals is not sufficient to cause viremia. The observations of Dean et al. (1960) point to the neural route; on the other hand, the outcome of Zunker's experiment (1963) can be explained only by blood-borne transmission of the virus.

This confusing situation probably arises from the following circumstances: (1) Underestimation of the difference in biological characteristics between rabies street virus and the fixed virus. When carrying out experiments on the pathogenesis of rabies infection, we must remember that these two viruses are very different in character. (2) The introduction of over-artificial techniques, e.g. neurectomy or parabiosis, in animal experiments on the pathogenesis of rabies infection. These operations have undefined effects on experimental animals and their introduction obscures the experimental results.

We have generally used an AY-163 strain of virus isolated from a rabid dog brain in Ayudhaya (Thailand) on Dec. 18, 1963. The dog brain emulsion was inoculated intraperitoneally into suckling mice and their salivary glands were harvested when they developed the complete symptoms. An emulsion of these salivary glands was again inoculated into other mice intraperitoneally. By repeating this method, we believe that it is possible to keep the virus strain from losing the characteristics of street rabies virus for the following reasons : (1) This method does not decrease the peripheral infectivity and the Negri body producing activity of the virus strain. (2) It does not modify the incubation period.

Antirabies virus serum was obtained from rabbits hyperimmunized by injecting one-day-egg rabies vaccine with Freund's incomplete adjuvant intramuscularly once a month for one year. The last inoculum comprised only rabies vaccine. Three weeks after the last injection, rabbits were bled to death and the serum was separated. γ-Globulin, which was salted-out from the serum by adding a saturated aqueous solution of ammonium sulfate, was conjugated with fluorescein isothiocyanate.

Color Plate III

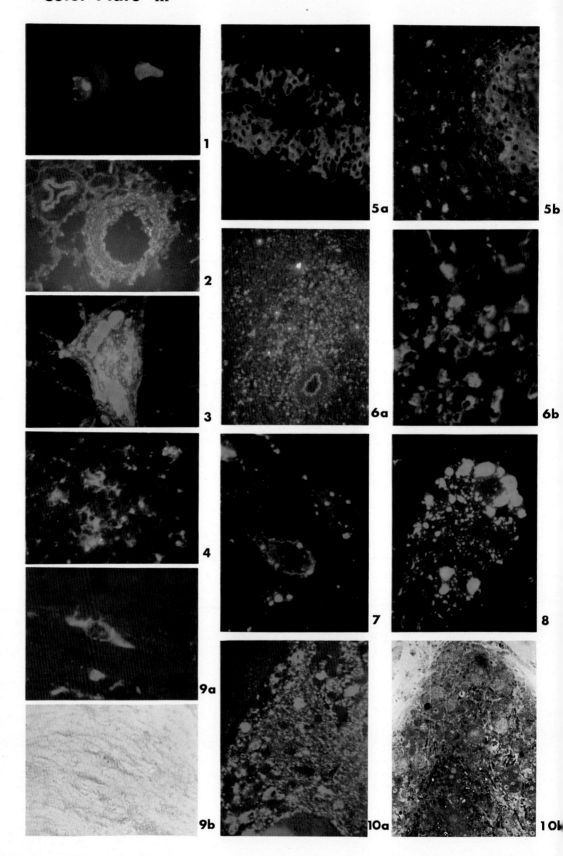

When sections infected with rabies street virus were examined under a fluorescent microscope, a number of fluorescent cells were found. Neuronal cells in the hippocampus have a few large round or oval intracytoplasmic inclusion bodies which fluoresce weakly (Color Plate III-7), while cells in the sympathetic ganglia and dorsal root ganglia contain numerous brilliantly fluorescing coarse granules (Color Plate III-8). For photographing the dorsal root ganglia, a 20 to 40-fold diluted conjugated serum may be used, but for a good photomicrograph of Negri bodies one must use a 5 to 10-fold diluted conjugate. Elimination of non-specific staining, which forms with rather heavy conjugates, requires adsorption by fresh homogenates of the tissues. An emulsion of whole body tissue from control mice was generally used for the purpose. The choice of absorbing material depends on immunological and virological considerations. However, this method has a disadvantage in that it is difficult to stain tissue sections by ordinary staining methods, such as hematoxylin and eosin staining, because of the enzymatic acitivity of the homogenate. In order to avoid these side effects, a

---

⇐

Explanation of Color Plate III

III–1. Smear of conjunctiva from dog, 15 days after infection with canine distemper virus.

III–2. Section of lung from dog, 32 days after infection with canine distemper virus.

III–3. An infected culture cell 12 days after inoculation with rinderpest virus. Larger fluorescent areas correspond to eosinophilic cytoplasmic inclusions in size and shape.

III–4. Mesenteric lymph node of a rabbit 20 hours after inoculation with Granular specific fluorescence is found in the cytoplasm of reticulum cells.

III–5a. 3 days after inoculation with hog cholera virus. Brilliant fluorescence is seen in the lacunar epithelium.

III–5b. 3 days after inoculation with hog cholera virus. Reticulum cells of tonsillar lymphoid tissue are also weakly fluorescent.

III–6a. Fluorescent antigen is seen in the spleen 5 days after inoculation with hog cholera virus.

III–6b. Cytoplasmic fluorescence of numerous reticulum cells of lymphoid follicles is seen, but not in the vascular cells.

III–7. Negri bodies in Purkinje cells of a puppy experimentally infected with AY-163 strain of rabies street virus. Exptl. duration 7 days.

III–8. Sympathetic ganglion cells of suckling hamster infected with rabies street virus AY-163 strain. Exptl. duration 8 days.

III–9a. Schwann cells in peripheral nerve tract of a suckling mouse infected with rabies street virus SIM strain. Exptl. duration 13 days.

III–9b. Schwann-cells in peripheral nerve tract of a suckling mouse infected with rabies street virus SIM strain. Exptl. duration 13 days. H. E. stain.

III–10a. Dorsal root ganglion of suckling mouse infected with rabies street virus of SIM strain. Exptl. duration 13 days.

III–10b. Dorsal root ganglion of suckling mouse infected with rabies street virus SIM strain. Exptl. duration 13 days. (Electron micrograph)

heavy metal preparation such as merthiolate solution is added at staining. By this method, we can restain tissue sections with hematoxylin and eosin well enough to identify the cells (Color Plate III-9 a, b).

An FITC positive result indicates the presence of an antigenic component connected with rabies virus infection, but it does not always indicate the presence of complete or infective particles of rabies virus. On the basis of fluorescent microscope and electron microscope photographs of various cells infected with rabies virus, it is suggested that the fluorescent coarse granules seen under a fluorescent microscope may be identical to the so-called matrix in electron microscope photographs (Color Plate III-10 a, b).* Some matrices contain abundant rod-like particles, which Prof. Matsumoto has identified as rabies virus particles; on the other hand, electron microscopic investigations show that the formation of a matrix is not always followed by the production of rod-like particles. The next step is to clarify the immunological properties and characteristics of the matrix and the virus particles in pathogenesis by the fluorescent antibody staining method.

By means of precipitin and complement fixation tests, it was found that crude material from infected cerebra contains at least two different antigens. In order to study the pathogenesis of rabies infection by the fluorescent antibody staining method, it is essential first to separate the virus from the soluble antigen. Once this is achieved, it should be possible to obtain a potent, specific anti-S and anti-V serum, and then antibody globulin from such serum, labeled with fluorescein isothiocyanate, can be used to provide answers to many important questions. Until this is achieved, however, the fluorescent antibody staining method must be used together with ordinary staining methods and electron microscope techniques in morphological investigations of the pathogenesis of rabies infection.

Sugito Otani

12. Coxsackie Viruses

A. Materials and Methods

Viruses: Coxsackie Virus Group A Type 9, Bozek strain, and Group B Type 5, Faulkner and Kurano strain, were used. The former two were from C. D. C. and were passaged through monkey kidney cells, whereas the latter was a prototype and was passaged through newborn mouse brain. The LD_{50} for newborn mice was $10^{7.1}$, $10^{1.7}$ and $10^{7.3}$/ml/mouse intracerebrally, respectively.

Labeled antisera: The γ-globulin fraction of vaccinated rabbit sera was conjugated with FITC and the fraction of F/P 1.5 to 2 was used at optimal dilution.

Mouse: DD-strain mice, 0 to 9 days old, were used, usually one litter as a group.

---

* Yamamoto, T., Otani, S. and Shiraki, H.: A study of the evolution of viral infection in experimental herpes simplex encephalitis and rabies by means of fluorescent antibody, *Acta neuropathologica*, **5**, 288–306, 1965.

Experimental design: The viruses were inoculated intraperitoneally (i.p., 0.2 ml) or intracerebrally (i.c., 0.1 ml). Mice were sacrificed by freezing in toto in cooled *n*-hexane, and cut in a cryostat at 4 μ thick. The sections were fixed with acetone for 10 min and stained with flurorescent antibody by the direct method. Serial sections were stained with hematoxylin and eosin.

B. Findings

(a) Coxsackie Virus Group A Type 9 Infection:

With i.p. and i.c. administration of A-9 virus, the skeletal musculature and the liver were affected, but in the latter only scattered hepatocytes showed positive fluorescence without histological changes. The skeletal muscles were ubiquitously affected as early as the first day. As shown in Fig. 31, a specific fluorescence was present in the cytoplasm of muscle cells, often perinuclearly and not in the nuclei. The lesion began in the muscle cells located around the interstitium. The infected muscle cells underwent coagulation necrosis showing a bright fluorescence, followed by histiocytic reaction and sarcolemmal cell proliferation.

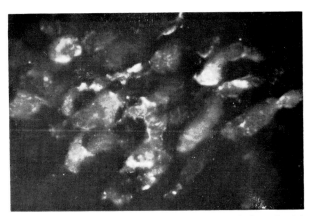

Fig. 31. Intercostal Muscle of a Newborn Mouse Infected with 10^{-1} A–9 Coxsackie Virus
i.p., 3 days after injection

The myocardium, after 4 weeks, showed scattered calcification of the necrotic muscle cells, with some specific fluorescence still present.

(b) Coxsackie Virus Group B Type 5 Infection:

Two strains of B-5 were examined to compare their virulence. Both strains affected various organs (Table 6). Of note is that the prototype, mouse brain passed Kurano strain, was by far more virulent than the standard MK cell passed Faulkner strain.

In the brown fat (Fig. 32), a specific fluorescence appeared from the first day in every mouse injected by any route. It began in the peripheral portion of the lobule, diffuse or granular in the cytoplasm, followed by necrosis with loss of specific fluorescence, mononuclear cell infiltration and calcification in 3 to 5 days.

Table 6. Distribution of Specific Fluorescence in Baby Mice

	A-9 BOZEK	B-5 FAULKNER	B-5 KURANO
Muscle	++ cal.	−	−
Liver	+	+	+
Brown fat	−	++ cal.	++ cal.
Heart	−	−	+ cal.
Brain	−	−	+
Skin	−	+	+

A difference in organ affinity between group A and B and strain Faulkner and Kurano is apparent.

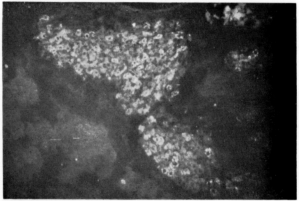

Fig. 32. Brown Fat of 1-Day-Old Mouse Infected with 10^{-1} B-5 Coxsackie Virus (Faulkner) i.p., 2 days after injection

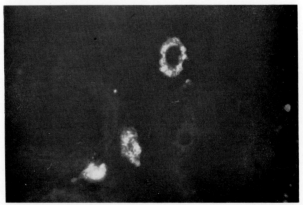

Fig. 33. Skin of 0–Day-Old Mouse 5 Days after Intranasal Injection with Kurano Strain of Coxsackie B–5 Virus

Interestingly enough, large round cells in the corium, unidentified in origin, showed positive specific fluorescence in the cytoplasm (Fig. 33).

In the case of intraperitoneal injection a specific fluorescence appeared first in the liver cells, which were scattered singly or focally throughout the lobule.

In the 7-day-old mice, myocarditis was observed 5 days after innoculation of the Kurano strain, showing specific fluorescence, necrosis of myocardial cells and calcification.

Intracerebral injection of the Kurano strain caused encephalomeningitis. Twenty hours after injection, ependymal cells showed a specific fluorescence (Color Plate IV-1). On the following days specific fluorescence spread in the brain substance, beginning from the subependymal areas. Only the cytoplasm of nerve cells showed fluorescence.

Koichiro Otsubo

13. POLIOMYELITIS VIRUS

Despite extensive investigations, the site of initial multiplication of polio-virus administered orally has yet to be determined. The present study has been carried out in order to determine the site of multiplication at the cellular level, using the immunofluorescent antibody method. Monkeys were fed with a virulent Mahoney strain of type 1 poliovirus cynomolgus. The same virus was instilled through a rubber tube inserted from the anus into the transverse colon of other monkeys. A few monkeys of the latter group were further smeared with the virus on the oropharyngeal wall one day after the per-anal instillation of virus. One or two monkeys thus infected were autopsied daily, starting 24 hours after the infection until the day of onset of paralysis. Frozen sections at 4 μ thickness were cut in a cryostat and stained with fluorescent antibody prepared from hyper-immune monkey and rabbit antesera to the Mahoney virus.

A. Results

Oropharynx: Epithelial cells with specific fluorescence appeared in smears from the pharyngeal swabs collected 24 hours after virus feeding (Fig. 34). Mononuclear cells in the submucosa of the posterior pharyngeal wall of the same monkey also contained the virus antigen. Fluorescent flecks were clustered in the squamous epithelium covering the crypt of the posterior pharyngeal wall 4 days after virus feeding. Mononuclear cells with the virus antigen were found in the lymphoid tissue of the tonsils as early as 24 hours after the smearing of virus on the oropharyngeal wall (Fig. 35). Infected cells were sparse in the tissues of the esophagus and the stomach.

Small intestine: Infected cells were rarely found in the duodenum and the jejunum throughout all stages of infection. Cells containing virus antigen were detectable more frequently in the ileum, particularly in its terminal segment at the early stage of infection. Infected mononuclear cells were scattered in the lam-ina propria, located beneath the basement membrane of the epithelium or along the blood capillaries of the villi (Fig. 36). At a later stage of infection, similar

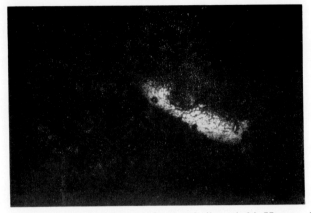

Fig. 34.   Smear of the Pharyngeal Swabs Collected 24 Hours after Virus Feeding
The cytoplasm of the epithelial cell is filled with fine fluorescent granules, while the nucleus and vacuoles do not contain the virus antigen.

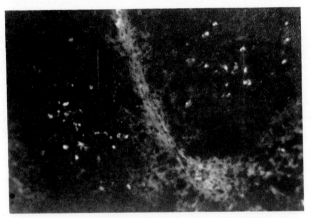

Fig. 35.   Palatine Tonsil 24 Hours after Smearing of Virus
Infected cells are scattered in the lymphoid tissue.

cells appeared also in the lymphatic tissue of the Peyer's patch.   However, no specific fluorescence was detected in the mucosal epithelium stage of infection.

Large intestine: Bright fluorescence was detectable occasionally in the epithelial layer of the large intestine (Color Plate IV-2).

The fluorescence could be reduced by the inhibition test using homologous antiserum, indicating that the fluorescence is specific to poliovirus antigen. However, the authors* later found that the cell layer occasionally lost its fluorescence when the section was stained with the fluorescent antibody absorbed

---

* Kanamitsu, M., Kasamaki, A., Ogawa, M., Kasahara, S. and Imamura, M.: Immunofluorescent study on the pathogenesis of oral infection of poliovirus in monkey, *Japan J. Med. Sci. Biol.*, **20**, 175–194, 1967.

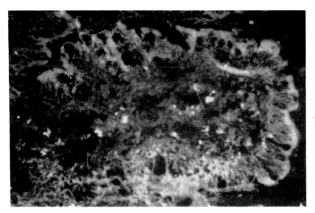

Fig. 36.   Ileum 2 Days after Virus Feeding
Infected cells are located in the lamina propria of the villus.   No specific fluorescence is seen in the mucosal epithelium.

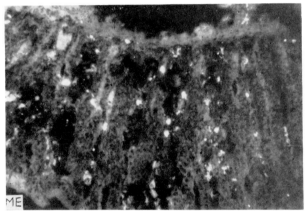

Fig. 37.   The Same Tissue as Shown in Color Plate IV–2
Only the mononuclear cells in the lamina propria contain virus antigen.   The
section was stained with the labeled antibody absorbed doubly with the monkey
spleen and with the intestinal mucosa.
ME: mucosal epithelium

with acetone powder of monkey intestinal mucosa.   Moreover, a similar fluorescence could sometimes be seen on the surface of the mucosal epithelium of
the large intestine of normal monkeys.   These findings indicate that great
caution should be exercised in determining the specificity of fluorescence of the
cell layer.   In contrast to this, the intracytoplasmic fluorescence of mononuclear
cells located along the blood capillaries in the submucosa was proven to be specific
to the virus antigen (Fig. 37).

Nervous tissue: Although no specific fluorescence was found in the peripheral nervous tissues including nerve ganglia, fluorescent cells were readily found
in the spinal cord after onset of paralysis, and virus antigen was seen in the

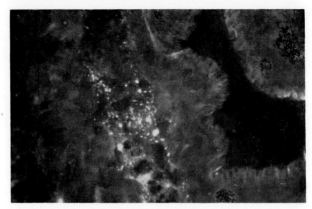

Fig. 38.   Medulla Oblongata 12 Hours after the Onset of Paralysis
Fine fluorescent granules are distributed in the endothelial cells of an arteriolar
blood vessel.

cytoplasm of nerve cells undergoing necrosis.   The antigen was distributed at
the highest concentration in the motor nerve cells of the anterior horn.   The
endothelial cells lining the arteriole of the medulla oblongata contained the virus
antigen (Fig. 38).   This finding suggests that poliovirus in blood may reach the
nerve cells of the CNS after multiplying in the local vascular endothelium.

Masatsugu Kanamitsu, Akiko Kasamaki and Mikio Ogawa

14. Japanese Encephalitis Virus (JEV)

Anti-JEV serum was prepared from rabbits vaccinated with formol-killed
purified JEV (Nakayama strain) from infected mouse brain.*   After conjugation
with FITC the antibody was absorbed with liver and brain powder of mice or
humans according to the materials to be examined.

This fluorescent antibody showed a high staining titer,   and non-specific
staining could be reduced to such a degree that in the stained section no cellular
structures could be distinguished except for specific and natural fluorescence.

Frozen sections of brain were treated with CCl_4 before staining, and those of
other organs with acetone.

For infecting virus, the JaTH 160 strain was chiefly used.

A. Multiplication in Cultured Cells

In PS (Y-15) cells the viral antigen appeared 5 to 6 hours after infection in

---

* Nozima, T., Mori, H., Minobe, Y. and Yamamoto, S.: Some properties of Japanese
encephalitis virus, *Acta virol.*, **8**, 97–103, 1964.

   Kusano, N., Aoyama, Y., Kawamura, A., Jr. and Kawashima, H.: The diagnosis
of Japanese encephalitis by means of fluorescent antibody technique in autopsy cases,
Neuropatologia Polska, IV, 3–4, 449–456, 1966.

fine granules in the perinuclear regions (Color Plate IV-3). The granules increased in number, and became confluent and occupied the entire cytoplasm of almost all cells within 10 hours. The nuclei showed no fluorescence throughout the course of infection. The cytopathic effects were relatively mild. No inclusion bodies, either nuclear or cytoplasmic, were formed.

Frequently, the fluorescence appeared in pairs in the neighboring cells, seemingly in the stage shortly after mitosis, suggesting some correlation between the multiplication of virus and certain stages of growth of the cells, at least in growing cells (Fig. 39).

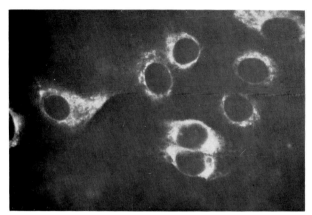

Fig. 39.

B. Experimental Infection in Mice

(a) Brain

The findings for encephalitis in mice in the cases of peripheral (subcutaneous, intravenous or intraperitoneal) infections were essentially the same as those in intracerebral infection, after the infection in the brain tissue was established. Little difference was observed between suckling and adult mice.

About one day before the appearance of clinical symptoms, more than 50% of the neuronal cells of the cerebrum showed a bright fluorescence. The brain cortex and hypocampus were most strongly affected. The fluorescence spread to the brain stem, cerebellum, and then to the spinal cord, and at the time of death, one or two days after the appearance of clinical symptoms, about 80 to 90% of the neuronal cells of the brain were affected (Color Plate IV-4).

The meningeal cells, choroidal plexus, ependym, glia cells, blood vessels and cuffing cells showed no fluorescence.

The viral antigen filled the entire cytoplasm of neuronal cells densely, in the form of fine granules reaching continuously to the fine dendrites. Frequently, connection of the fluorescent dentrites of two cells could be observed (Fig. 40).

Under low magnification the gray matter of the infected brain showed diffuse fluorescence in the background, as if caused by non-specific staining, but under higher magnification it became clear that it was due to specific staining of the fine

Fig. 40.

dendrites.   The white matter always remained unstained.   These findings suggest that the virus spreads in the brain tissue from neuron to neuron through the
dendrites.

In the case of intraperitoneal infection or other peripheral infections, in which
the symptoms of encephalitis appeared 7 to 10 days after infection, the viral
antigen was detected first in a few neuronal cells of the brain cortex, showing no
definite predilection for any particular site.   The infection spread rapidly and
rather diffusely to the whole brain without forming any localized foci.

(b)   Extracerebral site of virus multiplication

The titration of virus in peripheral infection of adult mice, especially in viremia,
1 to 3 days after infection indicates that the virus multiplies in the early phase of
infection in tissue or organs other than the brain.   Nevertheless, no fluorescence
strong enough to conclude that multiplication of virus occurred was detected in
any tissue or organ.

In suckling mice, however, extracerebral multiplication of virus was clearly
demonstrated.   Beginning from about ten hours after intraperitoneal infection
a bright fluorescence was observed in the cells of plexus Auerbachi of the digestive
tract, spindle-shaped cells of the perichondrium and periostium (Color Plate IV-
10), spindle-shaped cells of undefined origin in cutaneous tissue and teeth roots,
etc.   Fluorescent cells in the brain appeared later, about two days after infection.
Frequently, the smooth muscles showed fluorescence together with the nerve
plexus, less frequently the epidermal cells, small groups of cells in the hair follicles,
rarely tubular epithelium of the kidney and endothelial cells of the venous
capillaries in deep parts of the body.   With increase in age of the mice, the
affinity of these cells diminished rapidly.   In 2-week-old mice only the cells of
the cutis, periostium and nerve plexus showed fluorescence, and in 3-week-old
mice no fluorescent cells were detected in extracerebral tissues as in the case of
adult mice.

No cells in the spleen and lymph nodes showed clear enough fluorescence to
conclude that multiplication of the virus occurred.

C. Experiments with Other Animals

(a) Hamster

The findings for the brain were almost the same as those for mice. The affinity of the nerve plexus and other cells to JEV seemed to be the same in the case of peripheral infection in suckling hamsters as suckling mice.

(b) Monkey

The most conspicuous difference compared with mice was that in the monkey the spinal cord (anterior horns) was affected earlier and more severely than the brain (Color Plate IV-8).

(c) Embryonated egg

Ten-day eggs were infected. The extracerebral nerve cells, striated and non-striated muscle cells, and cells of the perichondrium and periostium showed a brighter and more extensive fluorescence than in suckling mice, and the cells in the cutis and subcutaneous tissues were diffusely fluorescent. Nerve tissue of the brain and spinal cord adjacent to bone or chondrium with surrounding fluorescent cells was negative or far less fluorescent. This corresponded well to the titration data for virus obtained by Dr. J. Nakamura, in which the titer of the brain was far lower than that of the rest of the body.

D. Diagnosis of JE Using the FAT in Autopsy Cases.

Sixty-four cases of patients diagnosed or suspected as JE during 1963 and 1967 were examined. Thirty-one cases showed positive fluorescence. This corresponded well with the available data on virus isolation, titers of antibody in blood and histological findings. As is well known, the virus can rarely be isolated from the brain beyond the 8th day of illness, and the titer of antibody in blood does not increase significantly before the third week of illness. The FAT reveals a constant positive finding from the early to late stage (the latest case examined by us was on the 21st day of illness) without such a gap for diagnosis.

Viral antigen was almost invariably detected in the thalamus, substantia nigra, and less frequently in the cortex and cerebellum. Fluorescent cells in autopsy cases were usually scanty and less bright compared to those in infected mice. Often careful search was needed to detect a few positive cells in a section ; however, the diagnosis is reliable once they are detected. The fluorescent cells showed more or less strong degeneration and often only fluorescent debris of cytoplasm or dendrites could be detected (Color Plate IV-5–7). However, even in the late stages of illness, for example on the 21st day, one could find relatively intact bright fluorescent cells as in the case of mice, although only very few. This finding suggests that the multiplication of virus continues till the late stage, but without reaching a level of titer at which attempts to isolate active virus can succeed. Only neuronal cells became positive and all other cells showed no fluorescence, as in mice.

The degeneration of cells due to virus was always accompanied by an increase of lipid-containing pigment having the same orange autofluorescence as lipofuscin, which is normally found in neuronal cells and increases with age. A

Color Plate IV

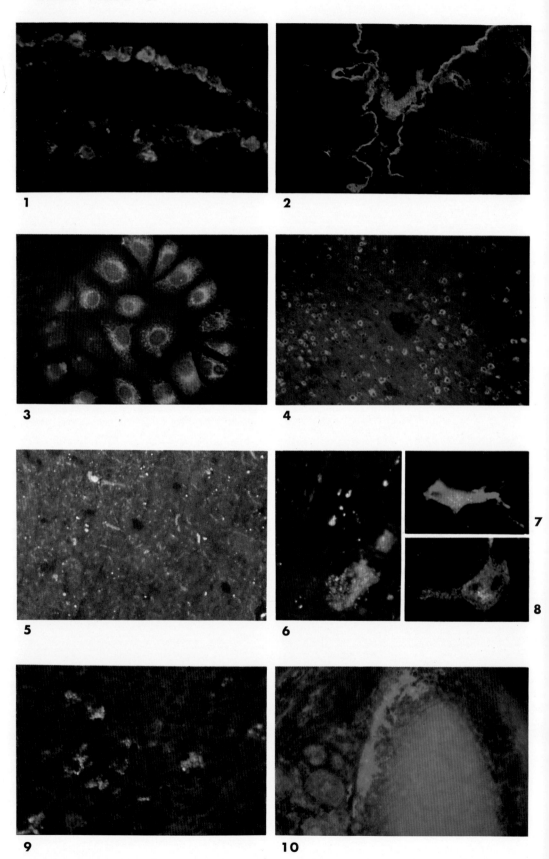

similar phenomenon was observed in mice once infected and examined after clinical healing (Color Plate IV-9).

As for the meaning of negative fluorescence in the cortex where typical histologic changes of encephalitis were observed, it seems reasonable to consider that the cortex was affected earlier than the brain stem and that the viral antigen had already disappeared at the time of death.

E. Examination of Spinal Fluid and Blood

Spinal fluid taken from patients was negative throughout the course of illness. This corresponds with the negative data for the ependyma and choroidal plexus, in contrast with Coxsackie virus infection, in which the ependyma is affected and the virus can frequently be isolated from the spinal fluid. Blood smears from the patients were always negative.

Nobuo Kusano and Yuzo Aoyama

15. TUMOR ANTIGEN

Adenovirus 12T Antigen in Cells

Adenovirus 12 induces tumors in hamsters.   Although no infectious virus can be recovered from the tumor, the T (tumor) antigen specific to adenovirus 12 can be detected.   The existence of the T antigen suggests the existence of viral genetic material in tumor cells.   The T antigen is also found in cells infected with adenovirus 12,* but is rarely found in virions synthesized in the cells.   Thus,

---

⇦

Explanation of Color Plate IV

IV-1.   Coxsachie virus B-5 (Kurano strain).   Brain of mouse 20 hours after intracranial infection.   Ependymal cells show a bright fluorescence.
IV-2.   Poliomyelitis.   Transverse colon of monkey 2 days after per-anal instillation of virus.   The epithelial cell layer is lined with bright fluorescence.
IV-3.   Japanese Encephalitis (JE).   PS (Y-15) cells 9 hours after infection.
IV-4.   JE. Brain of adult mouse 8 days after intracranial infection.   Only neuronal cells are fluorescent.   Cell cuffing in the center of figure is negative.
IV-5,6,7.   JE. Autopsy case, brain of T. F., 20 yr. male, died on the 11th day of illness.   Orange yellow fluorescence is natural for lipofuscin.
IV-8.   JE. Cervical cord of monkey 10 days after intracerebral infection.
IV-9.   JE. Brain of recovering mouse 15 days after intracranial infection. Six mice among 21 infected survived over two weeks, four of which showed fluorescence when examined after 15–20 days.   Note orange yellow pigment similar to that seen in human cases.
IV-10.   JE. Suckling mice 1 day after intraperitoneal infection.   Perichondral cells are fluorescent.   The blue is the natural fluorescence of cartilage tissue.

the T antigen is not capsid antigen and is synthesized in cells after infection.*
These observations indicate that an investigation of the T antigen may be
useful for analyzing the replication of adenovirus 12 in cells and the mechanism of
the transformation of cells by adenovirus 12.

The T antigen was first detected through a complement-fixation test (CFT)
between the tumor extract and the tumor-bearing hamster serum.*   In order to
investigate in greater detail the nature of the T antigen in infected or tumor cells
and to analyze the relationship between the T antigen and the virion antigens, the
fluorescent antibody technique was applied.   The following is a description of
the method used and the results obtained.**

Secondary cultures of human embryonic kidney cells (HEK), hamster embryonic cells (Ham E) and hamster tumor cells (Ham T), prepared on coverslips,
were used.   The growth medium used was Eagle's MEM supplemented with
10% bovine serum.   After infection with the virus, the cultures were maintained
in Eagle's MEM without serum.   Adenovirus 12 prototype Huie strain was used.
Cells were infected at an input multiplicity of 30 TCID per cell.

Many sera from tumor-bearing hamsters, either transplanted or virus induced,
were examined through CFT, using a tumor extract as T antigen and the virus
stock as virion antigen.   They were grouped into narrow anti-T sera (reactive
only to T and not to virion antigen) and broad anti-T sera (reactive to both T
and not virion antigen).   Sera with high CF titers (anti-T 1:64 or higher),
were selected for conjugation with fluorescent dye.   Anti-adenovirus 12 rabbit
and guinea pig serum was used without absorption, but the rabbit serum showed
the presence of some anticellular antibodies when tested through CFT against
HEK extract and was used after absorption with dried human liver powder.   Anti-
adenovirus 16 rabbit serum was used to detect group-specific A antigen (anti-A
serum).

γ-Globulin fractions prepared from the above sera were labeled with FITC
and conjugates were purified by Sephadex gel-filtration and DEAE-cellulose
column chromatography.   The staining titer of the conjugate was determined by
test staining of HEK infected with adenovirus 12 (24 hours post-infection)
with serial two-fold dilutions of the conjugate.   The conjugate, diluted so as to
contain 4–8 units of the staining titer, was used to detect the antigen.   Only the
direct method of staining was used to avoid nonspecific fluorescence.   The
coverslip was pretreated with carbon tetrachloride at 4°C for 30 minutes.

HEK monolayers formed on coverslips were infected with adenovirus 12.
Coverslips were taken out at hourly intervals for staining with the conjugates.
Up to 5 hours post-infection (p.i.), no specific fluorescence could be detected.

---

* Shimojo, H., Yamamoto, H., Yoshikawa, E. and Yamashita, T.: The nature of tumor
antigen of adenovirus type 12 and its formation in cultured cells after infection, *Japan
J. Med. Sci. Biol.*, **19**, 9–22, 1966.

** Shimojo, H., Yamamoto, J. and Abe, C.: Differentiation of adenovirus 12 antigens
in cultured cells with immunofluorescent analysis, *Virology*, **31**, 748–752, 1967.

Cells showing slender threads of fluorescence were detected with anti-T con-jugate (broad and narrow) at 6 hours p.i. At first the slender threads seemed confined to the nucleus, but soon a similar fluorescence appeared in both nucleus and cytoplasm. The number of cells with fluorescence, as well as the intensity of fluorescence, increased gradually with time. Some of the slender threads aggregated and formed fluorescent flecks (Color Plate V-1). Fluorescent flecks and slender threads were not stained by the antiviral conjugate. The mor-phology, time of appearance and stainability indicated that the fluorescent flecks and slender threads might be of the same antigen, and might be grouped together as fluorescent flecks (FF). FF could be differentiated into nuclear and cyto-plasmic FF by the localization in cells.

With the broad anti-T conjugate, fluorescent dots, morphologically different from FF, were detected in the nucleus at 14–16 hours p.i. Sometimes the fluorescence took the form of doughnuts with unstained centers, or of fine granules with a ground glass appearance. The number of cells with fluorescent dots and the intensity of fluorescence increased with time (Color Plate V-2). Fluorescent dots, doughnuts, or granules could not be stained with the narrow anti-T conjugate. The broad anti-T serum showed CF antibodies against T and virion antigens, but the anti-T titer was higher than the antiviral titer. As with the CF titers, the staining titer of FF was higher than that of the fluorescent dots, doughnuts and granules. These observations suggested that the latter might be of the same antigen and might be grouped as fluorescent dots (FD).

The C antigen was detected in the nucleus with anti-C conjugate at 15–20 hours p.i. At first, the fluorescence took the form of granules distributed evenly throughout the nucleus. The number of cells with fluorescent granules and the intensity of fluorescence increased with time (Color Plate V-3a). The A antigen was detected in the nucleus with anti-A conjugate at about 20 hours p.i. The appearance and progress of A antigen followed those of the C antigen (Color Plate V-3b). No morphological difference could be observed between the C and A antigens. The appearance and progress of antigens in infected HEK are summarized in Table 7.

To confirm the specificity of staining, serum blocking tests were carried out (Table 8). From the table, it can be said that the FF are quite distinct from virion antigen since they were not blocked by the antiviral sera. The FD may be virion antigen since they were not blocked by the narrow anti-T serum but were blocked by the anti-C serum. They may, however, be distinct from C antigen, because they were not stained by the anti-C conjugate.

The nonvirion nature of the FF and the virion nature of the FD were also confirmed by absorption of the broad anti-T conjugate with a partially purified virus. The virus stock was treated with a fluorocarbon and then precipitated on a cushion of cesium chloride solution (density 1.43) by centrifugation at 30,000 rpm for 60 minutes. The resulting partially purified virus (about 10^8 TCID$_{50}$) was then added to the broad anti-T conjugate containing 8 staining units of anti-T antibody. The mixture was kept at 36° for 2 hours and then in a refrigerator

Table 7. Development of Antigens in HEK Infected with Adenovirus 12*

Time p.i. (hours)	Nuclear FF		Cytoplasmic FF		Nuclear FD		Type specific C antigen		Group specific A antigen	
1	−**		−		−		−		−	
2	−		−		−		−		−	
3	−		−		−		−		−	
4	−		−		−		−		−	
5	±	0.2***	±	0.1	−		−		−	
6	+	2	±	0.2	−		−		−	
7	+	50	+	10	−		−		−	
8	++	70	+	35	−		−		−	
9	++	80	++	65	−		−		−	
10	++	80–100	++	70	−		−		−	
11	++	,,	++	80	−		−		−	
12	++	,,	++	80–100	−		−		−	
13	++	,,	++	,,	−		−		−	
14	++	,,	++	,,	±	0.1	−		−	
15	++	,,	++	,,	+	4	+	2	+	0.2
16	++	,,	++	,,	+	20				
17	++	,,	++	,,	+	30				
18	++	,,	++	,,	+	40	++	20	++	2
20	++	,,	++	,,	++	80	++	30	++	10
22	++	,,	++	,,	++	,,				
24	++	,,	++	,,	++	,,	++	40	++	30
26	++	,,	++	,,	++	,,				
28	++	,,	++	,,	++	,,	++	70–80	++	70–80
30	++	,,	++	,,	++	,,	++	100	++	100

 * HEK was infected with adenovirus 12 (input multiplicity 30 $TCID_{50}$ per cell) and the cells stained at the time indicated.

 ** − indicates no specific fluorescence, ± faint fluorescence, + distinct fluorescence and ++ intense fluorescence.

*** Figures show the percentage of fluorescent cells present.

overnight, after which it was centrifuged at 30,000 rpm for 60 minutes. The supernatant material showed no reduction in FF stainability despite the marked reduction in FD stainability.

Actinomycin D (0.25 and 1.0 μg/ml) and cytosine arabinoside (2.5, 10, and 40 μg/ml) were added to the HEK culture immediately and 8 hours after infection with adenovirus 12, and the cells were stained at 29 hours p.i. Actinomycin D completely inhibited the formation of all types of antigen. Cytosine arabinoside inhibited the formation of the FD, C and A antigens, but not of FF.

Table 8. Blocking of Specific Fluorescence by Unlabeled Sera*

Stained with	Blocking serum**	Specific FF	Fluorescence FD	Stained C or A	Antigen detected
Anti-C conjugate (guinea pig)	non-treated	—***	—	++	C
	anti-T narrow	—	—	++	C
	anti-C gp	—	—	—	none
	anti-C r	—	—	—	none
	anti-A	—	—	++	C
Anti-C conjugate (rabbit)	non-treated	—	—	++	C
	anti-T narrow	—	—	++	C
	anti-C gp	—	—	—	none
	anti-C r	—	—	—	none
	anti-A	—	—	++	C
Anti-A conjugate	non-treated	—	—	++	A
	anti-T narrow	—	—	++	A
	anti-C gp	—	—	++	A
	anti-C r	—	—	++	A
	anti-A	—	—	—	none
Anti-T broad conjugate	non-treated	++	++		FF, FD
	anti-T narrow	—	++		FD
	anti-C gp	++	±		FF, (FD ?)****
	anti-C r	++	+		FF, (FD ?)
	anti-A	++	++		FF, FD

* HEK was infected with adenovirus 12 (input multiplicity 30 TCID$_{50}$ per cell) and the coverslips taken out at 26 hours p.i. After treatment with carbon tetrachloride, the coverslips were covered with blocking sera and kept at 4°C overnight. They were then stained with the conjugates (4°C overnight).

** Sera used for blocking were :
Anti-T narrow: serum from a tumor bearing hamster (undiluted, 128 CF units).
Anti-C gp: serum from an immunized guinea pig (diluted to 1 : 4, 64 CF units).
Anti-C r: serum from an immunized rabbit (diluted to 1 : 4, 64 CF units).
Anti-A: anti-adenovirus 16 rabbit serum (diluted to 1 : 2, 64 CF units).

*** —, ± and ++ indicate the intensity of fluorescence as in Table 7.

**** Although the intensity of fluorescence was markedly reduced and the number of cells with FD became very small, complete blocking could not be attained.

In Ham E, the appearance and progress of the FF were similar to those observed in HEK (Table 9, Color Plate V-4a). The FF appeared at 6–7 hours p.i. and increased gradually. They were detected either with the narrow or the broad anti-T conjugate. The FD appeared at about 20 hours p.i., and were stained with the broad but not the narrow anti-T conjugate (Color Plate V-4b).

Table 9.　Development of Antigens in Ham E Infected with Adenovirus 12*

Time p.i. (hours)	Nuclear FF		Cytoplasmic FF		Nuclear FD		Type specific C antigen
1	−**		−		−		−
2	−		−		−		−
3	−		−		−		−
4	−		−		−		−
5	±	5***	−		−		−
6	±	10	±	1.2	−		
7	±	20	±	15	−		
8	+	30	±	20	−		
10	+	30	+	25	−		
12	+	34	+	26	−		
14	++	48	++	36	−		
16	++	35	++	20	−		
18	++	39	++	31	−		
20	++	53	++	40	+	0.2	−
24	++	57	++	27	++	0.4	−
26	++	56	++	45	++	0.75	−
30	++	55	++	50	++	1.6	−

* Ham E was infected with adenovirus 12 (input multiplicity 30 $TCID_{50}$ per cell) and the cells stained at the time indicated.

** −, ±, + and ++ denote the intensity of the specific fluorescence as in Table 7.

*** Figures show the percentage of fluorescent cells present.

Neither A nor C antigen was detected with the antiviral conjugates, even in later stages of infection.

In Ham T, FF and FD were detected with anti-T conjugate. The cultured cells of Ham T were thick, making it rather difficult to take sharp pictures, although observation of the FF and FD was not impaired under direct microscopic examination (Color Plate V-5). Neither C nor A antigen could be detected with the antiviral conjugate. The number of cells with FF and the intensity of fluorescence differed from one tumor to another. In some tumors, most cells showed many FF with distinct fluorescence, but in other tumors a small number of cells were found to have a few short rods exhibiting a weak fluorescence. The number of cells with FD and the intensity of fluorescence of FD also differed markedly from one tumor to another. FD could easily be detected in some tumors, although the number of cells with FD was very small. In other tumors, FD were rarely found, and were confined to the nucleus.

Thus four antigens, fluorescent flecks (FF), fluorescent dots (FD), type-specific C and group-specific A antigens were differentiated on the basis of the kind of staining serum used, differences in morphology, localization and time of appearance of fluorescence.   The FF seemed to be a major part of the T antigen and distinct from the virion antigen.   The FD may be a minor part of the T antigen and of the nature of a virion antigen.   If the FD are virion antigen, it may be distinct from C antigen.

Using the technique described above, further investigations into the nature of T antigen and its role in the transformation of cells have been carried out.   Some preliminary results are outlined below.

One problem is the localization of T antigen in a cell.   The T antigen of SV40 is found only in the nucleus and not in the cytoplasm, either in SV40 tumor cells or in SV40-infected cells (early stage of infection) (Color Plate V-6).   The T antigen of polyoma virus is also found only in the nucleus.   By contrast, T antigen of adenovirus 12 is found both in the nucleus and in the cytoplasm.   In order to investigate this difference further, the localization of adenovirus 12-T antigen was examined in infected cells and in tumor cells.   In infected cells (HEK and Ham E), T antigen (FF) was first detected in the nucleus, but soon was also found in the cytoplasm.   The time between the appearance of T antigen first in the nucleus and then in the cytoplasm was too short to arrive at any conclusion about the localization of T antigen synthesis.

In later stages of infection, most cells showed both nuclear and cytoplasmic FF.   Cells with only nuclear FF were also found, but cells with only cytoplasmic FF were very rare or absent.   When cytosine arabinoside was added to the infected culture $(20\mu g/ml)$, the appearance of nuclear FF was not affected and the appearance of cytoplasmic FF was inhibited.   In later stages of infection, many cells treated with cytosine arabinoside showed only nuclear FF.*   It is reported that T antigen was confined to nuclei in cells derived from human amnion cells after infection with adenovirus 12.   The above observations indicate that T antigen of adenovirus 12 is synthesized in the nucleus, as is that of SV40 or polyoma virus, and that it migrates rapidly to the cytoplasm in HEK and Ham E, contrary to that of SV40 or polyoma virus, which remains in the nucleus.

In contrast to the infected cells, T antigen (FF) was found only in the cytoplasm in most tumor cells, although some tumor cells contained T antigen both in the cytoplasm and nucleus.   Tumor cells with only nuclear FF, lacking cytoplasmic FF, were not found in this examination.   This observation can be understood by supposing that T antigen may be synthesized in the nucleus during a special phase in the growth cycle of cells, and may disperse into the cytoplasm during another phase (possibly during mitosis).   Therefore, in cells following mitosis only cytoplasmic FF may be found and in cells following the phase of FF formation in the nucleus, both cytoplasmic and nuclear FF may be found (Fig. 41).**

---

* Yamamoto, H.: unpublished observation.

** Shimojo, H., Yamamoto, H. and Tsuchiya, Y.: Further studies on the nature of tumor antigen induced by adenovirus 12.   Presented at the 9th International Congress of Cancer, Tokyo, 1966.

Infected cells

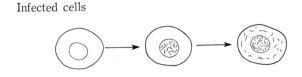

Tumor cells

After phase of
FF formation

Mitosis?

Fig. 41. FF Formation in Cells

In order to confirm this supposition, an examination of T antigen in a synchronized culture of Ham T was carried out. Ham T was synchronized by treatment of cells with excess thymidine for 24 hours at 35°C. After removal of thymidine, the cultures were incubated at 35°C and the coverslips stained with anti-T conjugate at hourly intervals. The examination of DNA synthesis through autoradiography and the examination of mitosis with stained preparations were carried out simultaneously. Contrary to the above supposition, many cells in the G 1 phase showed both nuclear and cytoplasmic FF. During the S phase, the number of cells with both nuclear and cytoplasmic FF decreased. At the end of the S phase and during the G 2 phase, most cells showed only cytoplasmic FF and the number of cells with both cytoplasmic and nuclear FF were at a minimum.* The explanation of this preliminary observation is that T antigen may be synthesized in the nucleus in the G 1 phase and may migrate into the cytoplasm during the S phase, where cellular DNA is actively synthesized. The formation of T antigen during the G 1 phase, its migration from nucleus into cytoplasm during the S phase and the inhibition of T antigen migration into the cytoplasm by cytosine arabinoside, an inhibitor of DNA synthesis, suggest the close connection between T antigen and cellular DNA synthesis.

* Yamamoto, H. and Shimojo, H.: unpublished observation.

Another problem that has been studied through the fluorescent antibody technique concerns the nature of the genetic information necessary for the induction of T antigen.   For this study, adenovirus 12 was inactivated either with ultraviolet (UV) or X irradiation, and the decrease in its capacity to replicate (infectivity) and to induce T antigen was measured.   The infectivity was titrated with plaque forming unit (PFU) in HEK.   The capacity to induce T antigen in a single cell was titrated with T antigen forming unit (TFU), which was measured as follows: Serial dilutions of the virus were inoculated into HEK on coverslips, and the cultures incubated at 35°C for 48 hours in the presence of cytosine arabinoside. After incubation, cells on the coverslip were stained with anti-T conjugate and examined under a fluorescent microscope.   Since the dose response between the percentage of fluorescent cells and the dilution of the inoculum was observed only in the range where the percentage of fluorescent cells present was below 20%, preparations with 5 to 20% fluorescent cells were selected and the accurate percentage of fluorescent cells present was determined by counting.   TFU was calculated from the percentage of fluorescent cells present, the number of total cells on a coverslip and the volume and dilution of the inoculum.   Estimation of the capacity to induce T antigen from preparations containing more than 20% fluorescent cells, which was adopted in some reports, was not used to avoid the influence of multiplicity reactivation.   Using the technique described above, it

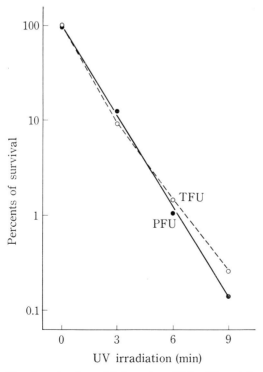

Fig. 42.   Inactivation of Adenovirus 12 by Ultraviolet Irradiation

was found that PFU and TFU were inactivated in the same way (Fig. 42),*
contrary to previous reports.   Since the information necessary for the T antigen
only (T information) must be part of the whole viral genome, the above result
cannot be interpreted as showing target sizes of the T information and the whole
viral genome.   It can be understood by supposing that the T information may be
part of the whole viral genome, but the integrity of the viral genome may be necessary for the expression of the T information.

Irradiated and non-irradiated viruses were inoculated into suckling hamsters,
and their capacities to induce tumors compared.   It was found that the irradiated
virus produced tumors far more efficiently than expected from PFU or TFU.*
The result can be interpreted as showing that the target size of the information
necessary to induce tumors may be smaller than the whole viral genome, and that
information necessary to induce tumors may be part of the viral genome.

The T antigen in hamster tumor cells induced by an irradiated or nonirradiated
virus was then examined through the fluorescent antibody technique in smear
preparations, and no difference was found in the content of T antigen between
tumors induced by irrradiated and non-irradiated viruses ; most tumors contained
cells with distinct FF.*   The result shows that the T information, inactive in
infected cells after irradiation, became active again in tumor cells.   This strange
observation suggests that the T information in infected cells may be in a state
where the integrity of the viral genome may be necessary for its expression, and
that the T information in tumor cells may be in a different stage, where the integrity of the viral genome may be unnecessary for its expression.   This supposition leads further to the possibility that the T information in tumor cells may
be integrated into the cellular genome.   Studies from a different angle are necessary to substantiate these interesting suppositions.

Hiroto Shimojo and Hiroshi Yamamoto

16. TOBACCO MOSAIC VIRUS**

A recent advance in plant virus research, as in other fields of biological science,
is the introduction of immunofluorescent techniques into the study of virus infection, synthesis and localization.   Localization of tobacco mosaic virus (TMV)
in the cells and tissues of infected leaves of tobacco plants (*Nicotiana tabacum*
L.) was investigated by means of a direct immunofluorescent technique, and
information obtained on the biological behavior of the virus within them is reported below.

---

  *   Yamamoto, H. and Shimojo, H.: unpublished observation.
  **   Murayama, D., Yokoyama, T., Kawamura, A., Jr. and Kawashima, H.: Immune
    fluorescence studies on synthesis and distribution of virus antigen in plant.   I. Tobacco
    mosaic virus in the systemically infected young leaves of tobacco plants, *Ann. Phyto-
    path. Soc. Jap.*, **30**, 131–135, 1965.

The antisera used in these experiments were prepared from rabbits by injecting a partially purified virus with Freund's complete adjuvant, and had titers between 1/512 and 1/2048. After routine antibody purification, the γ-globulin fraction obtained was labeled with 10 mg of FITC per gram of protein.

Healthy tobacco plants with 5 to 6 expanded leaves were inoculated with an ordinary strain of TMV. Leaflets about 1 cm square were taken from various parts of these plants after desired incubation periods, then fixed with Carnoy's fixative and embedded in gelatin cakes. Frozen sections were made in a cryostat at $-15°C$.

Microscopic observation under ultraviolet light revealed that sections obtained from healthy tobacco leaves, whether they were stained with fluorescein conjugated antisera or not, had a brilliant red fluorescence. This was apparently due to the autofluorescence of the chlorophyll contained in the chloroplasts. This autofluorescence, however, became weak after a few minutes' treatment of the section from a diseased tobacco plant, with acetone as a fixative.

Treatment of sections from diseased leaves with the conjugates resulted in the appearance of a specific brilliant yellow-green fluorescence in the infected cells. It was noted that the fluorescence of chlorophyll was greatly reduced or disappeared in the cells when the plant began to show external mosaic symptoms. This phenomenon, however, improves the detection of the specific staining of the viral antigen. Specific fluorescence was never observed in sections of diseased plant that were treated with fluorescein conjugated normal serum or in sections of healthy plants stained with labeled antisera.

The first change in the infected cells of uninoculated plants as a result of virus multiplication was the formation of specifically stained antigen in the form of tiny specks (Fig. 43, Color Plate V-7). This was found at first in the cytoplasm, especially along the border of chloroplasts, in the cells of both palisade and spongy parenchyma tissues surrounding the peripheral portion of vascular bundles.

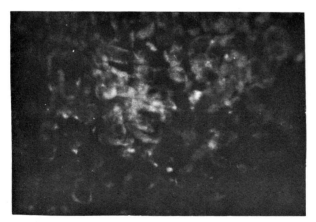

Fig. 43. Early Stage of Virus Multiplication
Specific fluorescence in the form of tiny specks is found within cells of parenchyma tissue surrounding the peripheral portion of vascular bundles.

Color Plate V

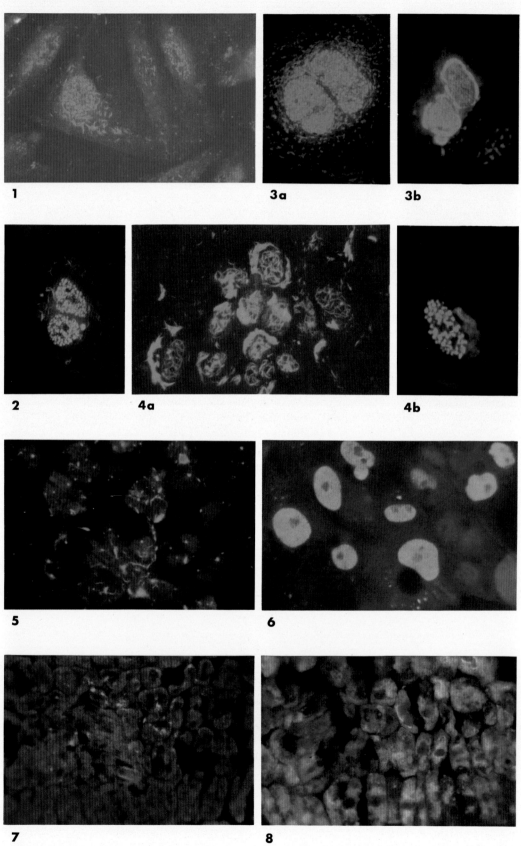

These areas were thought to be the initial infection centers from which the virus spread to adjacent cells.   Border cells of vascular bundles were also susceptible to virus infection.   In some sections, antigen was seen only in isolated cells or in a few cells, whereas in other sections, infected cells were found in groups.   Subsequently, antigens were detected in neighboring and even distant regions of the initial infection foci.

The specific fluorescent granules distributed irregularly in the cell seemed to lie in contact with the chloroplasts but not near the nucleus; then they began to enlarge and were gradually scattered by cytoplasmic streaming into the reticulate pattern of the antigen.   In many cases, the specific fluorescence was observed as a ring around the chloroplasts.

At a later stage of virus multiplication, the virus antigen seemed to be concentrated around the nucleus, where the specific fluorescence was markedly intensified (Fig. 44, Color Plate V-8).   Neither the nucleus nor the chloroplast showed any specific fluorescence.   Hair cells, epidermal cells, guard cells of the stomata, calcium-oxalate containing cells and cells of vascular bundles, except the xylem, also appeared to be infected (Figs. 45, 46).

The tissue sections of the leaves showing mosaic symptoms were found through the immunofluorescent method to be composed of two distinct areas, clearly stained and unstained areas.   It is worthy of note that the border line between both areas is easily distinguishable.   Light green or chlorotic areas of mosaic leaves contained virus antigen in most cells, whereas in the dark green areas only a few or none were stained with conjugate, indicating an uneven dis-

---

⇐

Explanation of Color Plate V

V-1.   Adenovirus 12 tumor antigen in HEK cells, 21 hours p.i., stained with the broad anti-T conjugate.   FF is seen in the nucleus and cytoplasm of each cell.   FD is also seen in the nuclei of two cells.

V-2.   Adenovirus 12 tumor antigen in HEK cells, 20 hours p.i., stained with the broad anti-T conjugate.   FD is marked in the nucleus.

V-3a.   Adenovirus 12 viral C antigen in HEK cells, 20 hours p.i., stained with anti-C conjugate.   Nuclei are filled with fluorescent granules.   There is also migration of fluorescence into cytoplasm.

V-3b.   Adenovirus 12 viral A antigen in HEK cells, 28 hours p.i., stained with anti-A conjugate.   Fluorescence is concentrated in the portion of the halo around the central mass.

V-4a.   Adenovirus 12 tumor antigen in Ham E cells, 30 hours p.i., stained with narrow anti-T conjugate.   FF is seen both in the nucleus and cytoplasm.

V-4b.   Adenovirus 12 tumor antigen in Ham E cells, 30 hours p.i., stained with the broad anti-T conjugate.   FD is seen in the nucleus.

V-5.   Adenovirus 12 tumor antigen in HT 4 cells (in vitro transformed hamster cells by Yamane and Kusano), stained with the narrow anti-T conjugate.   FF is observed in the cytoplasm and nucleus.

V-6. SV_{40} tumor antigen in GMK cells, 47 hours p.i., stained with anti SV_{40}-T conjugate.   T-antigen is observed in the nucleus.

V-7 } See Text Figs. 43 + 44 on pages 147 + 150.
V-8 }

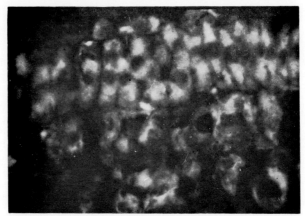

Fig. 44.   Later Stage of Virus Multiplication

Specific fluorescence is observed as a ring around the chloroplast and in the form of a more condensed mass around the nucleus.

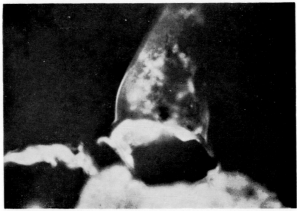

Fig. 45.   Specific Fluorescence Appears Both in the Hair Cells and Epidermal Cells of Tobacco Leaf.

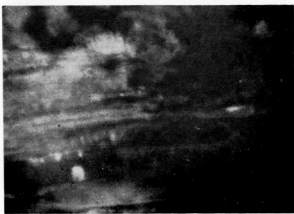

Fig. 46.   Specific Fluorescence Appears in the Border Cells and also in Phloem Parenchyma Cells of Tobacco Leaf

tribution of the virus antigen in the mosaic leaves. Possibly the apparently healthy cells in the dark green areas were resistant to virus infection or synthesis.

Tatsuo Yokoyama

17. TSUTSUGAMUSHI DISEASE RICKETTSIA

——Immunofluorescence for the Sero-Epidemiological
Study of Tsutsugamushi Disease Rickettsia*

The antigenic heterogeneity or strain-specificity of causative rickettsia can be well demonstrated by neutralization and especially by complement fixation tests. With the latter method, many strains from field rodents, trombiculid mites and cases of Tsutsugamushi disease in Japan have been classified into either Gilliam, Karp or Kato types, which are available in Japan as reference strains. This classification is based upon the patterns of complement fixation antibodies in sera of guinea pigs infected with the test strains. However, epidemiological studies, especially on the mode of transmission of rickettsia, could be carried out more easily if a simple, sensitive and rapid method for typing the isolated strains was available. Perhaps such a method could be developed with the use of immunofluorescence.

Table 10. Staining Titers of Fluorescent Antibodies in the Direct Method.

Fluorescent antibodies	Antigenic smears	Dilutions of antibody solution					
		1 : 8	1 : 16	1 : 32	1 : 64	1 : 128	1 : 256
Gilliam	Gilliam	4	4	4	3	2	1
	Karp	1	0	0	0	0	0
	Kato	0	0	0	0	0	0
Karp	Gilliam	2	0	0	0	0	0
	Karp	4	4	3	1	0	0
	Kato	2	0	0	0	0	0
Kato	Gilliam	4	2	0	0	0	0
	Karp	3	2	0	0	0	0
	Kato	4	4	4	3	1	0

Smears of infected yolk sac emulsion were stained with serially diluted fluorescent antibody solution. The intensity of fluorescence is expressed by integers 0 to 4.

---

* Iida, T., Kawashima, H. and Kawamura, A. Jr.: Direct immunofluorescence for typing of Tsutsugamushi disease rickettsia, *J. Immunol.*, **95**, 1129–1133, 1966.

Iida, T., Okubo, K. and Ishimaru, M.: Immunofluorescence for sero-epidemiological study of Tsutsugamushi disease rickettsia, *Japan J. Exp. Med.*, **36**, 435–447, 1966.

Iida, T., Vasuvat, C., Satayapunt, Nipa and Trishnanda, M.: Indirect immunofluorescence in scrub typhus—A preliminary study on antibody pattern, presented at a Laboratory Demonstration Meeting at the Faculty of Tropical Medicine, Bangkok, Thailand, December 16th, 1966.

Table 11. Antigenic Heterogeneity of Reference Rickettsia Strains in Indirect Immunofluorescence.

Reference strains	Immune sera	Dilutions of immune sera				
		1 : 10	1 : 40	1 : 160	1 : 640	1 : 2560
Gilliam	Gilliam	4	4	4	4	1
	Karp	4	3	1	0	0
	Kato	3	1	0	0	0
	Normal	0	0	0	0	0
Karp	Gilliam	4	1	0	0	0
	Karp	4	4	4	1	0
	Kato	3	0	0	0	0
	Normal	0	0	0	0	0
Kato	Gilliam	1	0	0	0	0
	Karp	4	4	0	0	0
	Kato	4	4	4	3	0
	Normal	0	0	0	0	0

Smears of peritoneum of mice infected with reference strains were treated with four-fold diluted guinea pig immune sera to reference strains or normal serum and followed by staining with a 1 : 16 dilution of labeled rabbit antibody against crude guinea pig γ-globulin.

A. Direct Immunofluorescence

For labeling, immune sera against reference strains are obtained from intracerebrally infected guinea pigs or rabbits immunized with rickettsia harvested from rabbit kidney primary cell cultures. As shown in Table 10, the highest titer is obtained in a homologous system, showing that the direct immunofluorescence is also strain-specific (Color Plate VI-1). No fluorescence is manifested with heterologous smears, even at a four-fold higher concentration of fluorescent antibody solution. Thus the use of 2 or 4 units of staining titer is recommended for typing isolated strains by mouse passage.

B. Indirect Immunofluorescence

In direct immunofluorescence, at least three kinds of fluorescent antibodies must be provided. In indirect immunofluorescence, by contrast, only one is necessary. For example, using guinea pig immune sera against the reference strains one needs only a labeled guinea pig γ-globulin antibody, which is commercially available. The strain specificity can be clearly demonstrated by this method, as seen in Table 11. This method might also be useful for typing isolated strains.

In addition, as seen in Table 12, indirect immunofluorescence with guinea pig immune sera against isolated strains shows that their reaction patterns are strain-specific and generally comparable to those in the complement fixation test.

Table 12. Indirect Immunofluorescence and Complement Fixation Tests for Guinea Pig Immune Sera to Newly Isolated Strains.

| New isolates used for immunization | Antibody titers | | | | | | Weil-Felix test |
| | Immunofluorescence* | | | Complement fixation** | | | |
	Gilliam	Karp	Kato	Gilliam	Karp	Kato	
AT–169, No. 12	10	10	640	<20	80	160	20
AT–171, No. 2	160	40	2560	<20	80	320	20
AT–198, No. 4	2560	40	40	640	20	<20	<10
AT–200, No. 10	40	2560	640	<20	640	160	10
AT–202, No. 1	2560	10	40	640	40	40	40
AT–208, No. 1	10	40	40	<20	<20	20	20
AT–212, No. 18	2560	10	10	640	<20	<20	40
KT–9	2560	40	40	640	<20	<20	20
KT–11	2560	10	40	640	80	40	20
KT–15	2560	10	40	640	40	<20	10
AR–104, No. 5	2560	160	640	640	<20	<20	40
AR–104, No. 6	10	40	2560	<20	40	640	40
AR–104, No. 12	2560	160	160	640	40	80	10
AR–104, No. 15	2560	40	10	640	80	80	<10
AR–122, No. 1	2560	160	40	640	40	<20	20
AR–130, No. 6	2560	160	40	640	40	<20	10

* Smears of yolk sac infected with Gilliam, Karp and Kato strains were treated with serially four-fold diluted guinea pig immune sera and followed by staining with a 1 : 16 dilution of labeled antibody against crude guinea pig γ-globulin.

** Guinea pig immune sera against isolates were tested with 4 units of reference rickettsia antigens.

Moreover, a higher antibody titer can be obtained through indirect immunofluorescence.

While treatment of antigenic smears with a 1: 10 or 1: 40 dilution of normal human plasma results in a non-specific fluorescence, the indirect method might provide a promising diagnostic method for a manifest case of Tsutsugamushi fever in which a higher antibody titer would be expected. There is no significant relation between the Weil-Felix reaction with *Proteus* OXK and indirect immuno-fluorescence or complement fixation tests.

Application of indirect immunofluorescence to the serodiagnosis of Tsutsuga-mushi fever was first reported by Bozeman and Elisberg (1963), but the reaction is group-specific in contrast to that in the present animal experiment. However, a preliminary result on the antibody pattern of a Tsutsugamushi disease case which was obtained in 1966 at the Faculty of Tropical Medicine, University of Medical Sciences, Bangkok might be useful in explaining such a discrepancy. Isolation of the organism was made twice by a mouse inoculation method on the

10th and 12th days of illness. Typing of the isolated rickettsia by direct immuno-fluorescence showed that they were both of the Kato type. In indirect immuno-fluorescence, the patient serum specimen on the 12th day showed a highly specific reaction to the Kato strain, i.e. antibody titers of 160, 160 and 2560 against the Gilliam, Karp and Kato strains, respectively. However, antibody titers against all three strains detected on the 30th, 41th and 59th days were at the same level at 1: 2560 dilution. The other two specimens at the convalescent stage were also group-specific. These results agree with those reported by Bozeman and Elisberg, and may be due to the difference in the immune response of the host to the organism. Perhaps the different molecular size of the antibodies produced in the early and convalescent stages of the human case may be responsible for this phenomenon.

Tsuyoshi Iida

18. Staphylococci: An Approach to Analysis of Microbial Structure, Invasion of α-Toxin into Ehrlich Ascites Tumor Cells and Formation of Kidney Abscesses in Mice*

Staphylococci are classified into *S. aureus* and *S. epidermidis*, primarily on the basis of the coagulase reaction and mannitol fermentation. Recently, it was shown that these two species differed in their chemical make-up: the cell wall polysaccharide of *S. aureus* is composed of polyribitol-teicholic acid, while that of *S. epidermidis* is composed of polyglycerol-teicholic acid.

We were able to prepare specific fluorescent antibody, either antibacterial or anti-toxin, and some interesting results were obtained.

Antisera: Anti-bacterial rabbit sera were prepared through immunization with chrome-vaccine of *S. aureus* 226, which was isolated from an infant staphylococcal pneumonia patient, strongly positive in coagulase and α-toxin production. As the antiserum for α-toxin, α-antitoxin commercially manufactured by Well-come Laboratories was used.

Preparation of labeled antisera: Antisera labeled with FITC were prepared according to Kawamura's method.

Determination of staining titer and assay of specificity: Cultures were grown on infusion agar or in broth. In this experiment, the fluorescent antibody reaction seemed to be unaffected by the culture medium used. Inhibition tests were performed by the one-step procedure.

The titer of each labeled globulin was determined by staining smears of homologous organisms with two-fold dilutions of antisera. Anti-bacterial labeled globulin had a staining titer of 1: 128, and α-antitoxin labeled globulin a titer of 1: 256.

---

*   Tadokoro, I. and Tokushige, Y.: unpublished observation.
     Tadokoro, I. and Tawara, T.: unpublished observation.

A. Analysis of the Surface Structure of Organisms

1)   Labeled anti-bacterial globulin was used to stain dried smears made from

Table 13.   Reactivity of Human Strains of *S. aureus* with
Rabbit Anti-Bacterial Fluorescent Antibody.

Specific fluorescent staining	Incidence	Percentage
Positive	440	91.5
Very weak, questionable	41	8.5
Negative	0	0

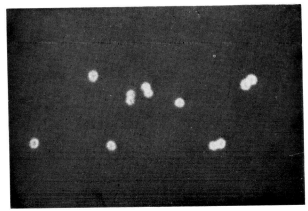

Fig. 47.   Fluorescent staining of *S. aureus* 226 cultured on agar slant with homologous fluorescent antibody. Brilliant, specific fluorescence was observed in ring form.

481 strains of *S. aureus* isolated from human lesions of the skin and middle ear.

The results given in Table 13 indicate that a brilliant, ring-forming fluorescence reaction occurred (Fig. 47) with 440 strains (91.5%), and a very weak, questionable fluorescence reaction occurred with 41 strains (8.5%).   However, the questionable reaction differed from the completely negative reaction found in *S. epidermidis*.

2)   When labeled globulin was used to stain chicken strains of *S. aureus* which were isolated from healthy chicken or Battery lesions, negative results were found more frequently than in human strains; 12 strains showed positive staining and 10 strains often had a strong protease activity, detectable with casein substrate, but this did not occur in human strains. All strains having protease activity gave positive results.

These results indicate that the surface structure of protease-positive strains differs from those of protease-negative strains, particularly in the protein component of the cell wall.

B. Cell Destroying Activity of α-Toxin

Alpha-toxin was demonstrated to be destructive to Ehrlich ascites tumor cells, in vivo or in vitro. The mechanism of destruction was studied by means of the fluorescent antibody technique. An α-toxin preparation purified with ammonium sulfate was brought in contact with Ehrlich tumor cells in test tubes. After 1 hour incubation at 37°C, smears were made and stained with α-antitoxin labeled globulin.

As shown in Color Plate VI-2, specific fluorescence was observed in the cytoplasm of tumor cells but not in the nucleus. When similar smears were stained with labeled anti-bacterial globulin, no specific fluorescence was observed (Color Plate VI-2).

When smears of cultured organisms were stained with α-antitoxin labeled globulin, a brilliant, ring-forming fluorescence, larger than that obtained with antibacterial labeled globulin, was observed.

This suggests that the α-toxin and antitoxin reaction took place on a superficial part of the organisms. In this experiment, it is of interest that the invasion of α-toxin into cells is detectable with the fluorescent antibody technique.

C. Process of Abscess Formation in Mouse Kidney

Intravenous infection in mice of 10^7 organisms of *S. aureus* 226 strain produces multiple abscesses in the kidney cortex in 2 to 3 weeks. Early fixation and multiplication of staphylococci in the kidney were studied by means of the fluorescent antibody technique. Kidney tissues fixed with formalin were used in the tests.

Fluorescent staining mouse tissue from 10 days after inoculation (Color Plate VI-3) shows staphylococci packed in tubuli of the medulla, and the infiltration of inflammatory cells composed of polymorphonuclear leucocytes and macrophages in the surrounding interstitium. Specific fluorescence and Giemsa's staining indicated that staphylococci were present in macrophages but not in polymorphonuclear leucocytes. Subsequently, microabscesses or visible abscesses were formed in the cortex, and after 40 days or more, specific and weak fluorescence was observed in the glomerulus. It could not be determined, however, whether the fluorescence derived from the organism itself or from an antigenic substance.

Ichiro Tadokoro

19. GONORRHEA

The fluorescent antibody method has been used for the detection of gonococci in smears of material obtained from clinical cases (immediate method) as well as in those from cultures (delayed method). Deacon and his colleagues (1959, 1960, 1961) were pioneers in this field of study.

The following is a report of attempts made to test the specificity of the fluorescent antibody,* and to appraise its usefulness in the diagnosis of gonorrhea.**

A. Preparation of Anti-Gonococcus Fluorescent Antibody

Young rabbits were immunized with three randomly chosen strains of gono-coccus freshly isolated from male patients suffering from acute gonorrhea. The rabbits received both one m*l* (2 mg) of alum-precipitated vaccine intravenously and one m*l* subcutaneously in the foot pad on the first and third day, and again one m*l* intravenously three weeks later. Breeding was carried out one week later.

The γ-globulins separated from representative immune sera by ammonium sulfate precipitation were conjugated with FITC, applied to a Sephadex G25 column to be freed of unbound dye and then to a DEAE cellulose column to recover the appropriate fractions. These fractions were then pooled to make a working fluorescent antibody solution.

All fluorescent antibodies prepared stained the stock and freshly isolated gono-coccus strains equally well. The experimental results obtained using a fluores-cent antibody with a staining titer of 1 : 64 follow. The F/P molecular ratio of the conjugate was determined as 2.47. The complement fixation titer of the ori-ginal immune serum was 1 : 64. The strains of gonococcus used for immunization were hypoagglutinable in agglutination tests.

B. The Specificity of the Fluorescent Antibody

The specific staining of the fluorescent antibody was first tested with stock strains of various Neisseriae. The reference strains of *N. meningitidis*, belonging to the serological groups A, B, C and D, were strongly reactive to the anti-gono-coccus fluorescent antibody, while other members of Neisseriae reacted only slight-ly or not at all (Table 14). The presence of common antigen(s) in *N. gonorrhea* and four groups of *N. meningitidis* was demonstrated by cross-absorption tests using both anti-gonoccocal and anti-meningoccocal fluorescent antibody solu-tions.

Secondly, the various stock strains of bacteria, as well as the fresh isolates from urethritis and cystitis patients, were tested for their stainability. Fifteen strains of *Staphylococcus aureus*, 5 of *Staphylococcus epidermidis*, one of *Diplococcus pneumoniae*, 13 of *Escherichia coli*, 3 of *Pseudomonas* sp., 2 of *Citrobacter* sp. and 2 of *Bacterium anitratum* were examined. Appreciable staining was found only in the case of the stock strain of *S. aureus* (209P) at lower dilutions of fluorescent antibody (8 units of staining titer or more). Other strains of *Staphylococcus*, as well as other species of bacteria, were not stained with 16 units of staining titer or more.

---

*   Saito, I.: Detection of Neisseria gonorrhoea by means of fluorescent antibody technique. I. With special reference to the specificity of fluorescent antibody, *Jap. J. Urology*, **55**, 463–472, 1964.
** Saito, I.: Detection of Neisseria gonorrhoea by means of fluorescent antibody technique. II. Clinical appraisal, *Jap. J. Urology*, **58**, 1079–1091, 1967 (English abstract).

Table 14. Staining of Neisseria with Anti-Gonococcus Fluorescent Antibody.

	Dilutions of fluorescent antibody							
	1 : 1	1 : 2	1 : 4	1 : 8	1 : 16	1 : 32	1 : 64	1 : 128
N. gonorrhoea								
Strain NG30	╫	╫	╫	╫	╫	╫	+	±
Strain NG32	╫	╫	╫	╫	╫	╫	+	−
Strain NG34	╫	╫	╫	╫	╫	╫	+	−
N. meningitidis								
Group A	╫	╫	╫	+	+	±	±	−
Group B	╫	╫	╫	+	+	+	±	−
Group C	╫	╫	╫	+	+	±	−	−
Group D	╫	╫	╫	+	+	±	−	−
N. sicca	±	−	−	−	−	−	−	−
N. hemolysans	+	+	+	+	±	−	−	−
N. catarrhalis	±	−	−	−	−	−	−	−
N. flavescens	±	−	−	−	−	−	−	−
N. perflava	+	+	+	±	−	−	−	−
N. subflava	+	±	−	−	−	−	−	−

These results suggest that the use of fluorescent antibody at higher dilutions would give few, if any, misinterpretations in clinical cases. *Neisseria meningitidis* groups stain at these dilutions, but the presence of such agents in the usual material from urethritis patients seems quite unlikely.

C. Clinical Appraisal

The purulent discharges from the urethra contain many leucocytes which are easily stained with lower dilutions of fluorescent antibody. The pretreatment of smears with ethanol, methanol or acetone reduces the non-specific staining of these cells to some extent compared with that after heating or treatment with formol. Absorption of the fluorescent antibody with acetone-dried mouse liver powder was also effective in reducing the background staining. The best results, however, were obtained with the use of higher dilutions of fluorescent antibody (Color Plate VI-4).

Eighty-seven patients, 73 males and 14 females, who were mainly sexual partners of the males, were examined on the first day of their visit to the hospital. Gram staining and fluorescent antibody staining of smears of urethral swabs (or cervical swabs in the cases of the females) were made, as well as cultures on a GC medium (Eiken Co., Tokyo). The pure cultures obtained from suspected colonies were identified through the oxidase reaction and fermentation tests. The results are summarized in Table 15.

Table 15.   Results of Three Tests on 87 Patients.

	Dilutions of fluorescent antibody								
	1 : 1	1 : 2	1 : 4	1 : 8	1 : 16	1 : 32	1 : 64	1 : 128	
Gram staining	+	+	+	−	+	−	−	−	52
FA staining	+	+	−	+	−	+	−	−	51
Culture	+	−	+	+	−	−	+	−	47
	43	4	0	2	5	2	2	29	

Of the 87 patients, 43 cases were positive and 29 negative in all three methods of examination.   Gram staining gave the highest percentage of positive cases. However, of five cases where both fluorescent antibody staining and culture results were negative, 3 had Neisseria other than gonococcus in their discharges.   Of the 6 cases where fluorescent antibody staining was positive and culture results negative, 5 cases were confirmed as gonorrhea, because gonococci were found in a subsequent test performed on the next day.   Thus, the immediate method of fluorescent antibody staining gave results comparable to those of Gram staining and cultures in this test study.

The delayed method of fluorescent antibody staining was also applied to smears from the 14 female patients and about one-fourth of the males.   The smears were cultivated for 16 to 18 hours and samples were then examined by this method. The results were identical to those obtained with the immediate method of fluorescent antibody staining for all cases tested.

The selective medium introduced by Thayer and Martin (1964) facilitates the isolation of gonococci from clinical cases.   We have devised another selective medium using lincomycin and colistin, which similarly suppresses the growth of gram positive cocci and gram negative bacteria.*   It is hoped that the delayed method of fluorescent antibody staining of young cultures on such a selective medium will provide a most rapid and accurate means of detecting gonococci in clinical cases.

Yukimori Tsunematsu

---

*   Shiozawa, F. and Tsunematsu, Y.: On the selective medium of *Neisseria gonorrhoea*, *Jap. J. Bacteriol.*, **22**, 236, 1967 (English abstract).

20. Shigella

——Demonstration of *Shigella* bacilli in intestinal tissues*

A. Materials and Methods

Preparation of labeled anti-Shigella sera: Anti-*Shigella* sera were obtained from rabbits hyperimmunized with *Shigella flexneri* 2a, Strain S-30 and *S. sonnei*, Strain 264–65 killed with formalin and treated with chromalum, respectively. The titer was 1: 8192 by the agglutination test. γ-Globulin fractions prepared from the antisera were conjugated with FITC and the conjugates were purified by Sephadex gel-filtration and by DEAE cellulose column chromatography.   The type-specificity of the labeled antisera was ascertained by blocking and absorption tests, and they showed no staining reaction against *E. coli* isolated from healthy monkeys.

Test samples and staining procedure: Specimens from the large intestine of monkeys infected experimentally with *Shigella* bacilli were fixed with cold ethanol for 24 hours and embedded in paraffin.   Labeled serum was mounted on a section for 5 to 6 hours at room temperature or at 37°C in an incubator.

Observation: A fluorescence microscope (Ortholux, Leitz) with a superwide dark-field condenser (Tiyoda) was used.

B. Results

Healthy cynomolgus monkeys (*Macaca irus*) were orally infected with about 20 mg of *Shigella flexneri* 2a, Strain 5503.   At twenty-four hours postchallenge, fluorescing bacilli were found in the epithelial lining and in desquamated epithelial cells of catarrhic areas of the ascending colon.   The bacilli in these foci were usually short rods or spheres.   They were barely detected in the lamina propria (see Color Plate VI-5).

Three days after oral inoculation with *Shigella flexneri* 2a, Strain 5503, micro-ulcers were found in the descending colon.   Numerous fluorescing bacilli were also found in the lamina propria, in phagocytes and in epithelial cells in the infected area (Fig. 48).   On the other hand, three days after oral inoculation with about 20 mg of *Shigella sonnei*, Strain 264–65, surface epithelial cells of the ascending colon were parasitized.   Desquamated cells in the lumen contained many fluorescing bacilli in their cytoplasm.   *Shigella sonnei* was generally mild in its invasiveness of the mucous membrane, as compared to *Shigella flexneri*;

---

*   Ogawa, H., Takahashi, R., Honjo, S., Takasaka, M., Fujiwara, T., Ando, K., Nakagawa, M., Muto, T. and Imaizumi, K.: *Shigellosis* in cynomolgus monkeys (*Macaca irus*).   III. Histopathological studies on natural and experimental *shigellosis*, *Japan J. Med. Sci. Biol.*, **17**, 321–332, 1964.

Ogawa, H., Honjo, S., Takasaka, M., Fujiwara, T. and Imaizumi, K.: *Shigellosis* in cynomolgus monkeys (*Macaca irus*).   IV. Bacteriological and histopathological observations on the earlier stage of experimental infection with *Shigella flexneri* 2a, *Japan J. Med. Sci. Biol.*, **19**, 23–32, 1966.

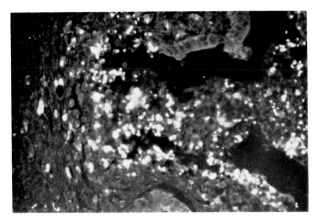

Fig. 48.

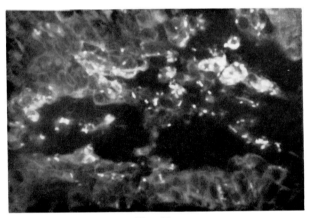

Fig. 49.

i.e. it was found mainly in surface epithelial cells, with a few in those of deeper crypts (Fig. 49).

Hidemasa Ogawa

21. Bordetella Pertussis

——Immunofluorescent Detection of Permeability Changes in Mouse Brains in Pertussal Infection*——

Unimmunized mice are very susceptible to intracerebral infection from *Bordetella pertussis* strain 18–323 since the LD_{50} has a total number of 100 and a sigmoid dose-response curve is obtained when the rate of mortality is plotted against the logarithm of the viable number of organisms injected, which is usually one quarter of the total. The average viable count in brains of moribund mice infected intracerebrally with various doses of strain 18–323 range from 10^8 to 10^9 per brain, and the time until death is dose dependent.

Characteristic features of the infection are bacillary multiplication in close contact with the ciliated layer of the ependymal lining of the ventricle wall, less cellular infiltration in the ventricle cavity at an early stage and meningitis and degeneration of the surrounding tissues secondary to the principal pathogenic process taking place in the ventricle wall. No invasion of the brain parenchyma is observed. Other phase I strains of *B. pertussis* which cause a sublethal infection in the mouse brain act similarly. In strong contrast, *Bordetella bronchiseptica* and *Salmonella typhi* multiply in the ventricle cavity as well as in the brain parenchyma, and cause purulent ventriculitis and brain abscess, respectively. The reason for this characteristic localization of bacillary growth on the ciliated epithelium is not clear. At any rate, a highly virulent strain like 18–323 could settle on and/or within the ciliae even in small numbers, and multiply continuously until it reached the critical number of organisms necessary for death.

Viable counts in brains of mice challenged with 100 LD_{50} of strain 18–323 are not reduced by active or passive immunization until the 3rd or 4th day of infection, but reach a maximum level of approximately 5×10^6 organisms per brain and decrease gradually by the 11th day. In passive immunization, the effect of anti-pertussal horse serum is the same whether it is given before or up to 3 days after infection. This lag appears to be the time necessary for the entry of circulating antibody into the ventricle cavity and is perhaps due to the blood-brain barrier function that is operating normally before the viable count reaches approximately 5×10^6 per brain. This assumption is made valid by the following: If anti-pertussal horse serum is given passively to infected mice on the 4th or 5th day, at which time the viable count is estimated at approximately 10^7 or 10^8 per mouse brain, a rather sharp fall in the number of organisms present in mouse

---

* Konosu, M.: On the healing process of infection with *Hemophilus pertussis* in brain ventricles of mice, *Trans. Soc. Path. Jap.*, **48**, 951–959, 1959 (in Japanese).

Iida, T., Kusano, N., Yamamoto, A. and Shiga, H.: Studies on experimental infection with *Bordetella pertussis*: Bacteriological and pathological studies on the mode of infection in mouse brain, *Japan J. Exp. Med.*, **32**, 471–494, 1962.

Iida, T., Kusano, N., Yamamoto, A. and Konosu, M.: An immunofluorescence of the action of antibody in experimental intracerebral infection of mice with *Bordetella pertussis*, *J. Path. and Bact.*, **92**, 359–367, 1966.

brains is observed.   In the case of *B. bronchiseptica,* which multiplies mainly in the parenchyma, viable counts in brains of mice immunized actively with pertussal vaccine begin to decrease significantly at least 24 hours after infection.   Interestingly, this seems to reflect a different mode of multiplication in mouse brains by two organisms of the same genus.

Under a fluorescent microscope, a further attempt was made to visualize the entry of circulating pertussal antibody into the ventricle cavity and the viable count of 18–233 organisms in mouse brains.   The results obtained follow.

In immunofluorescence, labeled anti-pertussal horse antibody and labeled anti-horse globulin antibody were used to verify the location of the organisms and to detect anti-pertussal horse antibody attached to colonies, respectively (Color Plate VI-6–7).

A. Rate of Appearance in Mouse Brain of Anti-Pertussal Horse Antibody Injected Intravenously 4 days after Intracerebral Infection

Frozen sections were prepared from several mice of the group that was infected intracerebrally with 100 LD_{50} of strain 18–323 and killed at various intervals after the injection of anti-pertussal horse serum.   Viable counts of the

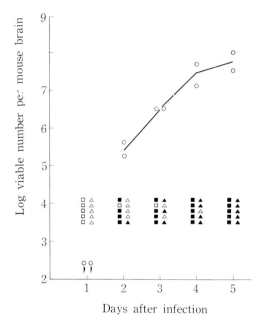

Log viable number per mouse brain

Days after infection

Fig. 50. Viable Counts of *B. Pertusis* and Detection of Antibody in Mouse Brains by Means of the Immunoflorescence Technique
Each of 4 mice of a group intracerebrally infected with 10 LD_{50} (10^3) of 18–323 strain received an intravenous injection of *B. pertussis* immune horse serum; 10 hr. later their brains were excised for staining with FITC-labeled *B. pertussis* horse antibody (□, negative. ■, positive) and FITC labeled rabbit antibody against horse serum globulin (△, negative. ▲, faint. ▲, positive).

organisms in the pooled brain of two mice at the time of the injection of antiserum showed 8.2 log 10 organisms per brain.   Specific fluorescence was first observed in the blood capillaries of the choroid plexus.   Three hours after injection of the antiserum, it was found at the surface and base of the bacterial colonies, and at 6 hours it was seen, with greater intensity, throughout all colonies.

B. Entry of Circulating Antibody into the Brain During the Course of Infection

Each of 5 mice from the group infected intracerebrally with $10 \, LD_{50}$ of strain 18–323 was given intravenous injections of anti-pertussal horse serum 1, 2, 3, 4 and 5 days after infection.   Ten hours later, the mice were killed and their brains taken for frozen sections.   At each time interval, brains of two mice that did not receive the antiserum were processed for counting the number of viable organisms present.   On the first day, the number of viable organisms was so small that a count could not be made by this method, but on the second day it attained about 10^5 per brain and on the 5th day about 10^8.   In association with this increase in the number of viable organisms in the brain, the fluorescence of organisms in the section treated with labeled anti-horse globulin antibody intensified and the number of positive reactions increased (Fig. 50).   It appears that at least approximately 10^6 organisms must be present in the brain before an increase occurs in the permeability of the blood-brain barrier sufficiently great to allow the circulating anti-pertussal horse antibody to leak through.   Cortisone treatment made no difference to the time lapse between injection of antiserum and the appearance of fluorescence due to the presence of labeled anti-horse globulin antibody on the bacterial colonies.   The underlying mechanism involved in this increased permeability is still obscure.

Tsuyoshi Iida

22. MYCOPLASMA
——*Mycoplasma pneumoniae* Infection

One spontaneous pneumonia in mice is caused by PPLO (Color plate VI-8). In the case of human atypical pneumonia, the etiological role of the Eaton agent, now called *Mycoplasma pneumoniae*, was first established through the use of the fluorescent antibody technique.   Since it is difficult to demonstrate the presence of this pathogen in the lungs of hamsters, or to demonstrate the increasing level of antibody to this agent in convalescence from atypical pneumonia, the study of this agent was neglected for almost 17 years.   The indirect fluorescent antibody technique played a decisive role in solving all these difficulties and established the presence of a speculative Eaton agent in experimental animal lungs and the development of antibody during convalescence.

After it was demonstrated that the Eaton agent is a strain of PPLO, and that the organism is readily cultured on agar plates, complement fixation and metabolism inhibition tests became the most generally used means of detecting antibody to this agent. Identification of the organism, which was first made by the fluorescent antibody technique, can now be made by such biological tests as adsorption of guinea pig red cells on the colonies, glucose metabolism, insensitiveness to methylene blue, etc.

The fluorescent antibody technique is still useful in the localization of *M. pneumoniae* in tissues of necropsy material and experimental animals (hamster and chick embryos) and in the identification of freshly isolated or unknown PPLO. It is also useful in the determination of antibody response to *Mycoplasma pneumoniae* in some specific pneumonia patients, for instance in patients with negative conventional serological response to this agent despite isolation of the organism from a throat swab.

The following materials are used in the technique: (1) Specific antiserum against *M. pneumoniae*. Convalescent serum from atypical pneumonia patients with positive serological reaction to the agent is very convenient and useful. Some of these sera may have a CF titer of 1 in 256 to 1024. (2) Antihuman-globulin rabbit serum, conjugated with FITC. (3) Specific serum prepared in animals. To prepare this serum, *M. pneumoniae* must be grown on a glass surface and the colonies harvested, or a liquid medium free of heterologous protein to animals in which the antigen is to be injected can be used. (4) Antigen.* The antigen used in the determination of antibody response includes frozen sections of infected chick embryo lung (Fig. 51) and colonies of the organism grown

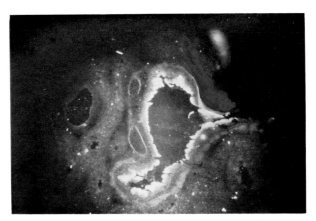

Fig. 51. *Mycoplasma pneumoniae* on the Bronchial Epithelial Surface of an 18–Day-Old Chick Embryo.

---

* 13-day-old chick embryos are inoculated amniotically with the organism and incubated at 35°C for 5 days, and frozen sections of the lungs are made. The PPLO grows on the bronchial surface.

M. pneumoniae is grown on cover slips at the bottom of a Petri dish, in PPLO broth. Colonies of mycoplasma are readily grown on the glass surface after 10 days of incubation.

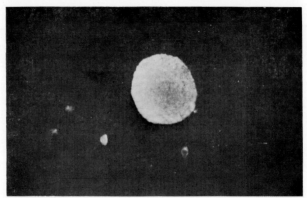

Fig. 52. *Mycoplasma pneumoniae* Grown on a Cover Slip

on an agar surface or on cover slips (Fig. 52). Frozen sections of autopsy or resected materials may be used for etiological study.

Eleven patients with atypical pneumonia were studied both by the complement fixation test and the fluorescent antibody technique. Three of these patients showed significant increases in CF titer and the remaining eight did not show a fourfold or greater increase in titer, although a CF titer of at least 1 in 16 or more was found in one of every patient's paired sera. A significant increase in antibody titer was found in eight of these eleven patients by means of the fluorescent antibody technique (Table 16).

Isao Ebisawa and Shoji Nakamura

23. Syphilis Treponema

Fluorescent Treponemal Antibody Test

The heterogeneity of γ-globulins has been discussed in connection with almost every antigen-antibody system, including that of syphilis. Matsuhashi and Mizuoka reported that antibodies involved in the fluorescent treponemal antibody (FTA) test and the cardiolipin test were found in both the γ-G and γ-M fractions eluted by diethylaminoethyl (DEAE) cellulose column chromatography. The antibody activity in the γ-G fraction was stable, but the antibody activity in the γ-M fraction was labile after mercaptoethanol (ME) treatment. These authors also confirmed the presence of FTA antibodies by employing anti-γG and anti-γM globulin reagents conjugated with fluorescein isothiocyanate (FITC). They further investigated antibodies in the FTA test using fluorescent anti-γG, anti-γA, anti-γM, anti-γD, anti-κ, anti-λ and anti-$\beta_{\text{ICA,E}}$-globulin reagents. The results are briefly described here.*

---

* Matsuhashi, T., Mizuoka, K. and Usui, M.: Studies on the fluorescent treponemal antibody test using fluorescent anti-γ, anti-α, anti-μ, anti-λ, anti-κ chains and anti-$\beta_{\text{ICA, E}}$ globulin reagents, *Bull. Wld. Hlth. Org.*, **34**, 466–472, 1966.

Mizuoka, K., Matsuhashi, T. and Usui, M.: Studies on specificity of antibodies concerning serologic reactions of syphilis, *Dermatologica et Urologica*, **19**, 1225–1229, 1965 (in Japanese).

Table 16. Fluorescent and Complement Fixation Antibody
            Titers in Patients with Atypical Pneumonia.

Case	Days after onset of disease	FA titer	CF titer
1	6	<8	<8
	32	128	1024
2	10	16	8
	25	128	64
3	2	16	16
	39	128	32
4	7	<8	<8
	17	256	1024
5	11	32	32
	30	128	64
6	12	≧64	256
	26	≧64	128
7	9	64	32
	24	64	64
8	8	8	8
	24	32	16
9	12	16	32
	20	32	64
10	12	16	16
	21	64	32
11	14	16	16
	36	128	32

The antigen used in Cases 1 to 6 is from frozen sections of
chick embryos and in Cases 7–11 from colonies grown on cover
slips.

A. Preparation of Antiglobulin Reagents

Anti-γG and anti-γM chain reagents: Antiglobulin fractions 1 and 4 (An-1
and An-4) of syphilitic sera were prepared by Abelson's method, using DEAE
cellulose column chromatography.   It was confirmed, by immunodiffusion
techniques and treatment with 0.2 M mercaptoethanol, that the An-1 fraction
mainly contained γG reagin and that the An-4 fraction included γM reagin.
Venereal Disease Reference Laboratory (VDRL) antigen suspension was mixed
with each fraction in optimal proportions.   The precipitates obtained from each

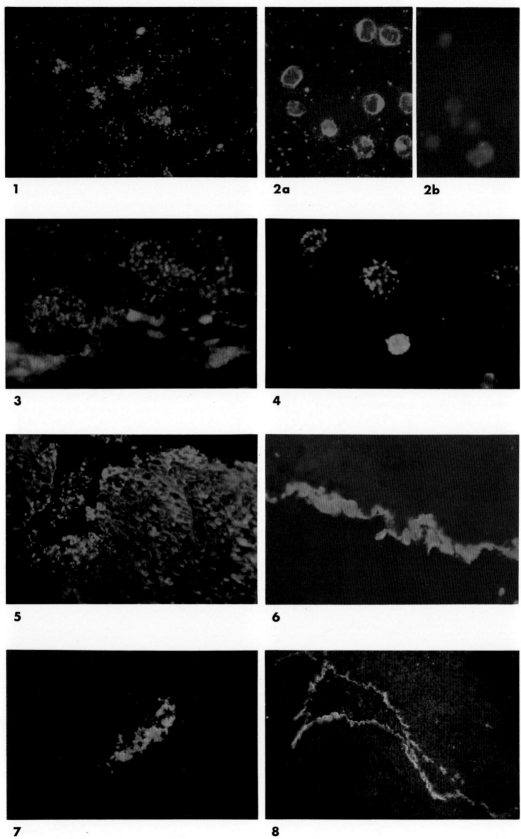

mixture were washed thoroughly and injected, with Freund's complete adjuvant, into the foot-pads of rabbits. Fortunately, nearly half the antisera against γG reagin precipitate contained only antibody corresponding to the γ-chain, which was confirmed by immunoelectrophoresis using papainized γG and reduced γG as antigen. Because most of the antisera against γM reagin precipitate show γM and γG lines in immunoelectrophoresis, the antisera were absorbed with human γG to remove antibodies to light chains and/or γG.

Anti-γA chain reagents: The γA-globulin was separated from the peritoneal fluid of a patient with A-myeloma by salting-out with ammonium sulfate and by DEAE cellulose column chromatography. After purification of the γA-globulin, it was injected, with Freund's complete adjuvant, into the foot-pads of rabbits.

In addition, anti-γA chain antisera were prepared by immunization of rabbits with plasma from human milk. The resultant antisera were adsorbed with cord serum to obtain anti-γA antibody, since they contained not only anti-γA antibody but also antibodies against γG and some components of β-globulins.

Anti-γD reagents: The γD-globulin was purified from the pleural fluid of

---

⇦

Explanation of Color Plate VI

VI–1. Direct immunofluorescence staining of *Rickettsia orientalis* (Ozeki strain) in mesothelial cells of an intraperitoneally infected mouse.

VI–2. Ehrlich ascites tumor cells contacted with α-toxin of staphylococci in vitro (after 1 hour).

    a. Fluorescent stained with α-antitoxin labeled globulin. A brilliant, specific fluorescence is observed in the cell membrane and cytoplasm.

    b. Fluorescent stained with anti-staphylococcal labeled globulin. Only very weak fluorescence is observed.

VI–3. Fluorescent staining of mouse kidney injected intravenously with *S. aureus* 226 with anti-bacterial fluorescent antibody (after 10 days).

VI–4. Smear of pus from an acute gonorrheae patient. Gonococci are found located within and outside of leucocytes. A leucocyte looks like a mass of gonococci. FA staining.

VI–5. 24 hours after oral inoculation of about 20 mg of *Shigella flexneri* 2a, strain 5503. Ascending colon. Fluorescing bacilli are found in the epithelial lining and in desquamated epithelial cells of catarrhalic areas. The bacilli in these foci usually appear as short rods or spheres. They were hardly detected in the lamina propria.

VI–6. Bacterial layer firmly adhering to ependymal cell lining 24 hours after injection of normal horse serum. Labeled *Bordetella pertussis* horse antibody.

VI–7. Detached colonies in ventricular cavity 24 hours after injection of *Bordetella pertussis immune* horse serum. Labeled anti-horse globulin antibody.

VI–8. Murine PPLO (mycoplasma) on " normal " mouse bronchial epithelium stained with FITC-conjugate of " normal " mouse serum. The finding indicates that the normal mouse had antibodies to murine PPLO present on its bronchial epithelium.

patients with D-myeloma by salting-out with ammonium sulfate, DEAE cellulose column chromatography and gel filtration. After purification of the γD-globulin, it was injected with Freund's complete adjuvant into the toes of rabbits. The resultant antisera were absorbed with normal human serum to obtain specific anti-γD reagents, because most of the antisera contained antibodies to some serum components in addition to anti-γD antibody.

Anti-human complement reagents: Antisera against certain components of human complement were prepared by immunizing rabbits with antigen-antibody precipitate-fixing human complement, as reported elsewhere. The antisera contained anti-$\beta_{ICA, E}$ antibodies.

Reagents to anti-κ and anti-λ chains: Type K and type L Bence-Jones proteins, with Freund's complete adjuvant, were injected into the foot-pads of rabbits. Reagents to the anti-κ and anti-λ chains were prepared by mutual absorption by the opposite types of Bence-Jones proteins.

Broad-spectrum antiglobulin reagents: Whole human sera, with Freund's complete adjuvant, were injected repeatedly into rabbits. The antisera were checked

Table 17. FTA Tests with Fluorescent Anti-γG and Anti-γM Reagents

Sera (Patient No.)	Diagnosis*	Treatment**	FTA AB titer against	
			Anti-γG	Anti-γM
474	STS negative	Saline	—	5
		ME	—	—
512	STS negative	Saline	5	5
		ME	5	—
481	STS negative	Saline	20	10
		ME	10	—
496	Primary syphilis	Saline	256	128
		ME	128	8
728	Primary syphilis	Saline	1024	128
		ME	512	64
450	Secondary syphilis	Saline	2048	128
		ME	1024	128
604	Secondary syphilis	Saline	4096	2048
		ME	4096	1024
455	Late syphilis	Saline	2048	128
		ME	1024	128
675	Late syphilis	Saline	4096	1024
		ME	2048	512
718	Congenital syphilis	Saline	4096	512
		ME	1024	512

 * STS: Serologic tests for syphilis.
 ** ME: Mercaptoethanol.

by immunoelectrophoresis, employing fresh and aged human serum. They were also checked by an antiglobulin technique using human erythrocytes coated with incomplete γG-anti-D, γM-anti-Le^a and γM-anti-Le^a or incomplete cold antibody-coated erythrocytes fixed with human complement. Only antisera with a single specificity and high potency against a corresponding antigen were used in the present experiments.

B. Results

Detection of γG and γM syphilitic antibodies by means of anti-γG and anti-γM reagents: The FTA test, using fluorescent anti-γG and anti-γM reagents, was carried out with sera from both syphilitic and non-syphilitic individuals. Most of the sera from syphilitics showed positive reactions to both reagents (Color Plate VII-1). Non-syphilitic sera with positive reactions to the FTA test in 1/5–1/20 dilutions also reacted with both of these reagents. Representative results from these trials are given in Table 17. After ME treatment, a small decrease in the reaction of fluorescent anti-γG antibodies occurred, but all non-syphilitic sera and the serum from one syphilitic individual decreased in antibody titer of fluorescent anti-γM antibodies. A small decrease in titer after ME treatment was observed in the fluorescent anti-γM antibody test in the later stages of syphilis. The reason for this lack of influence of ME treatment is at present being sought.

Complement-binding property of syphilitic antibodies detected by anti-$\beta_{ICA, E}$ reagents: Several experiments were carried out to investigate the complement-binding property of syphilitic antibodies in the FTA test. In tests using fluorescent anti-$\beta_{ICA, E}$ on syphilitic sera inactivated at 56°C for 30 minutes, results were negative for all cases. Some of the sera became reactive, but others did not, after

Table 18. FTA Tests with Fluorescent Anti-Human Complement Reagent

Sera (Patient No.)	Anti-human globulins inactivated (control)	Anti-human complement	
		Inactivated	With fresh human serum added
370	⧺	−	+
383	⧻	−	⧺
439	⧻	−	⧺
440	⧻	−	±
443	⧻	−	±
444	⧼	−	±
448	⧼	−	⧺
452	⧺	−	⧺
456	⧻	−	+
475	⧺	−	⧺
459	−	−	−

Table 19. FTA Tests with Fluorescent Anti-γG, Anti-γM, Anti-γA Reagents

Fluorescent antibody against				Sera	Case Number
Broad	γG	γM	γA*	Diagnosis**	
+	−	±	−	Primary syphilis	1
+	+	+	+	Secondary syphilis	5
				STS positive	1
+	+	+		Secondary syphilis	5
+	+	+	−	Primary syphilis (treated)	1
				Secondary syphilis	3
				Secondary syphilis (latent)	1
				Congenital syphilis	1
				STS positive	1
+	+	−	−	Secondary syphilis (treated)	1
				Late syphilis (latent)	1
				Congenital syphilis	3
				STS positive	1
+	+	−		Congenital syphilis	1
−	−	−	−	Normal	5

* Immunized with A-myeloma protein.

** STS : Serologic tests for syphilis.

they had been mixed in 1/50 dilutions with fresh human sera that were negative in the FTA test. The findings in one such experiment are given in Table 18.

It appears that among the antibodies involved in the FTA test, there are some with a very limited ability to fix complement. Nevertheless, there is no need to inactivate sera for testing by FTA.

Different classes of antibodies in various stages of syphilis, as detected by fluorescent anti-γG, anti-γM and anti-γA reagents: FTA tests on sera from individuals in different clinical stages of syphilis were performed with fluorescent anti-γG, anti-γM and anti-γA reagents; the results are given in Table 19. Serum from one patient with an initial chancre reacted positively with fluorescent anti-γM reagent. Reactivity against anti-γG reagent only was found in five syphilitic sera, three congenital, one late, and one early secondary; the sera of the remaining cases showed positive reactions with both anti-γG and anti-γM reagents. Positive test results with anti-γA reagents were found in some cases of secondary syphilis.

Generally speaking, positive anti-γM and anti-γA FTA test results were found with sera from the early stages of syphilis; FTA tests that were positive only with anti-γG reagents were found in later stages of the disease, such as congenital or late syphilis. Perhaps γM antibodies are produced in the early stages of syphilis, and the γG antibodies gradually become dominant during the course of infection.

Table 20. FTA Tests with Fluorescent Anti-γG, Anti-γM, Anti-κ
and Anti-λ Reagents*

Sera (Patient No.)	Stage of syphilis	Fluorescent antibodies			
		Anti-γG	Anti-γM	Anti-κ	Anti-λ
492–1	Primary	—	±	+	—
663	Primary	++	+	++	+±
492–2**	Primary	+	±	+	+
581	Primary	++	±	+±	±
557	Secondary	++++	++	++++	+++
549	Secondary	++++	++	++++	++++
538	Secondary	+++±	++	++++	+±
527	Secondary	++++	++	++++	+++±
583	Secondary	+++±	+±	+++±	+++
598	Late	+++	±	++	++
628	Late	+±	±	+	+
650	Congenital	+++	+	++	+±
594	Congenital	+++	±	++	+±

* Syphilitic sera in 1/200 dilution.
** Serum 492–2 was taken from the same patient as serum 492–1, but at a later stage.

Table 21. FTA Tests with Fluorescent Anti-γG, Anti-γM, Anti-κ
and Anti-λ Reagents*

Sera (Patient No.)	Fluorescent antibodies			
	Anti-γG	Anti-γM	Anti-κ	Anti-λ
651	—	±	±	—
637	+	+	++	++
636	+++	+±	+++	+++
621	++	—	+	±
610	+++	+	++	+
603	+±	+	++	+++
601	++	+	++	+±
594	+++	+±	++	+±
596	+±	+	+±	+±
572	++	—	++	+++

* Non-syphilitic sera in 1/5 dilution.

Detection of γD syphilitic antibodies by means of anti-γD reagents: The FTA test, using anti-γD reagent, was carried out with sera from both syphilitic and non-syphilitic individuals. No positive reaction was obtained among 20 specimens.

Light chain types of FTA antibodies detected by fluorescent anti-κ and anti-λ reagents: Syphilitic and non-syphilitic sera were checked, without titration, by fluorescent anti-κ and anti-λ reagents to determine whether the antibodies were produced monoclonally, as is known to be the case with multiple myeloma. Representative results of these investigations are given in Tables 20 and 21. No great difference in reactivity was found with these two reagents in sera from any stage of syphilis or in sera from non-syphilitics.   When sera were titrated with fluorescent anti-κ and anti-λ reagents, no significant differences between titers using either of these reagents was observed, either in syphilitic or in non-syphilitic sera.

C. Discussion and Conclusions

The immunological character of syphilitic antibodies active in the FTA test was investigated with various fluorescent anti-globulin reagents.   The results reported above are in some points similar to the observations on blood-group antibody production: that is, in the early stages of syphilitic infection, only γM antibody may be detected, but later γG antibody appears and gradually increases during the course of immunization until finally only γG antibody is produced. There may be a γA FTA antibody present in certain stages of syphilis, since sera from six out of 20 cases of this disease reacted fairly strongly to the fluorescent anti-γA reagents.   However, the antibody belonging to the γA immunoglobulins may appear rather early in the infection, since most positive test results were found in sera from patients with secondary syphilis.   Concerning the character of the FTA antibody, the clinical significance for therapy was investigated, but no close correlation between the class of antibody present and the stage of the disease was observed.

The finding that light chains of both Type K and Type L are usually found in FTA antibodies suggests that the antibodies against complex antigens of *Treponema pallidum* evolved in syphilitic infection are heterogenous not only in specificity but also in the class and/or subclass of immunoglobulins that in the antibodies are produced polyclonally.   However, in the course of the present investigation, one case of early syphilis was encountered in which the FTA antibody could be detected only with anti-Type K light chain reagent, suggesting that in the early stage of syphilis, FTA antibody may be produced monoclonally (Table 20).

T. Matsuhasi, K. Mizuoka, and M. Usui

24. Tyzzer's Disease

Tyzzer's disease is characterized by a strict parasitism of PAS-positive bacillary organisms within the cytoplasm of liver cells, resulting in necrotic hepatitis in different species of laboratory animals.*   After intracerebral inoculation with infected liver material, fatal encephalopathy can be produced in susceptible animals.**   In this case, it is interesting to note that the organisms are found to multiply within neurons and either ependymal or choroidal epithelial cells. Apart from infection with neurotropic viruses, there are no similar findings in other bacterial infections.   It is not easy, however, to identify the organisms in nerve tissues with those in liver tissues, since no culture of the organisms is available for this purpose at present.   Morphological characteristics cannot provide any definite conclusions either, because of the pleomorphic forms of this organism, some of which can be confused with saprophytic bacteria.***

The indirect immune fluorescence technique using rabbit antibody against infected mouse liver has been applied with the hope of solving this problem. As shown in Color Plate VII-2, specific fluorescence was found to be localized within the cytoplasm of nerve cells.   In a smear preparation of the same infected brain, the antigenic specificity of the organisms could be confirmed (Fig. 53), and fluorescein-labeled antibody seemed to combine selectively with the surface

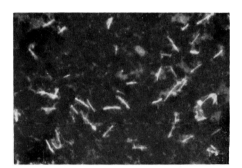

Fig. 53.

* Fujiwara, K., Takagaki, Y., Maejima, K., Kato, K., Naiki, M. and Tajima, Y.: Tyzzer's disease in mice.   Pathologic studies on experimentally infected animals, *Japan J. Exp. Med.*, **33**, 183–202, 1963.

Takagaki, Y., Ito, M., Naiki, M., Fujiwara, K., Okugi, M., Maejima, K. and Tajima, Y.:   Experimental Tyzzer's disease in different species of laboratory animals, *Japan J. Exp. Med.*, **36**, 519–534, 1966.

Tyzzer, E. E.:   A fatal disease of the Japanese waltzing mouse caused by a spore-bearing bacillus (*Bacillus piliformis n. sp.*), *J. Med. Res.*, **38**, 307–338, 1917.

** Fujiwara, K., Maejima, K., Takagaki, Y., Naiki, M., Tajima, Y. and Takanashi, R.:   Multiplication des organismes de Tyzzer dans les tissus cérébraux de la souris expérimentalement inféctée, *C. R. Soc. Biol.*, **158**, 407–413, 1964.

Takagaki, Y., Ito, M., Naiki, M., Fujiwara, K., Okugi, M., Maejima, K. and Tajima, Y.:   ibid.

*** Tyzzer, E. E.:   ibid.

Fig. 54.

antigen and peritrichous flagella (Fig. 54).   Similar findings were also obtained with preparations treated with rabbit antiserum directly labeled with fluorescein, and in this case, the combination of labeled rabbit antibody was inhibited when the preparation was treated previously with unlabeled antiserum.   These results indicate that the organisms in an infected brain are antigenically identical with those in the liver.

The immune fluorescence technique is also applicable to other questions relating to Tyzzer's disease.   For example, titration of immune serum is possible by the indirect method, in which smear preparations of infected tissues are treated with serial dilutions of antiserum, and then with fluorescein-labeled anti-gamma globulin antibody.   This method is much more sensitive than the complement fixation test.*

Kosaku Fujiwara

25. Mycotic Infections**

A. Preparation of Antigens

Candida albicans and *Cryptococcus neoformans* were grown in flasks of Sabouraud dextrose broth at 37°C for 3–4 days.   All cultures were formalinized (1.0%) and, after appropriate sterility tests, were washed twice in physiological saline and subsequently suspended in physiological saline to contain 5×10^7 organisms per m*l*.

Aspergillus fumigatus was inoculated into each of 10 flasks containing 100 m*l*

---

  * Fujiwara, K.: Complement fixation reaction and agar gel double diffusion test in Tyzzer's disease of mice, *Japan J. Microbiol.*, **11**, 103–117, 1967.

** Nasu, T. and Hotchi, M.: Present state of fluorescent antibody techniques in medical mycology, *Shinshu Med. J.*, **14**, 695–701, 1965 (in Japanese).

  Hotchi, M.: The application of fluorescent antibody techniques to the identifica tion of pathogenic fungi in tissue specimens, *Med. J. Shinshu Univ.*, **12**, 123–139, 1967.

of Czapek's broth and *Absidia lichtheimii* in Sabouraud dextrose broth and incubated at 37°C for 4 days on a shaker.   Whole cultures were then formalinized (1.0%) and mycelia and spores harvested by centrifugation.   The mat was washed twice with physiological saline and, after the addition of 10 m*l* of physiological saline to 10 mg of the mat, it was homogenized in a blender (20,000 rpm for 10 min) and ground twice in a French press (450 pounds/cm²).   The homogenate was finally diluted to 1:40 with physiological saline.

B. Immunization Methods

Antisera were obtained from albino rabbits weighing 2.5 to 3.0 kg, which were test bled before immunization for control.   The rabbits received 2–3 m*l* of each antigen intravenously every other day for a period of 3–4 weeks.   Seven days after the final injection the animals were bled.   If the sera tested were found to have a precipitin titer of 1:32 or greater, the animals were exsanguinated.   Disinfectant was added to all antisera and they were stored at −20°C.

Antigens used in the precipitin tests were extracted from each culture by the methods of Westphal et al.   Precipitin tests (ring tests) were carried out according to the beta procedure (antibody dilution method) and each antigen solution was adjusted to contain 100γ crude polysaccharide per m*l*.

C. Preparation of Fluorescent Conjugates and Purification

The preparation of fluorescent conjugates was carried out as described above. As seen in Fig. 55, in order to remove cross-reactions to heterologous fungi, the labeled antibodies were absorbed by the method of Kaufman et al. and diluted. In addition, anti-Candida globulin was conjugated to tetramethylrhodamine isothiocyanate (B. B. L.) for the purpose of double staining.

1. Antigen for absorption
    Candida albicans (JU-401) is harvested, formalinized (1.0%) and washed three times in phosphate-buffered saline (pH 7.2), then centrifuged and packed.
2. Absorption procedure

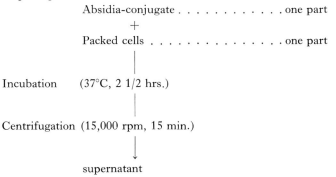

Fig. 55. Absorption Method of Absidia-Conjugate

D. Preparation of Specimens and Staining Procedure

Smears were prepared from culture suspensions of fungus in distilled water and from slide cultures of the same organisms. These smears were fixed by heat, acetone or formalin. After the conjugates were tested on the smears, they were applied to tissue sections from experimentally infected animals and 30 human autopsy cases of mycosis obtained from 1953 to 1962.

Four μ sections from formol fixed paraffin embedded material were deparaffinized as usual. In addition to paraffin sections, organs from sacrificed animals were frozen in n-hexane chilled in a dry ice-acetone bath and three μ sections prepared in a cryostat at $-18°C$. The frozen sections were fixed in acetone at 18°C for 15 minutes. The sections were then thoroughly washed in phosphate-buffered saline (pH 7.0) and stained directly with the conjugates in the usual manner. The double staining method was used for material from mixed infections.

In all cases the second sections were stained by the periodic acid-Schiff (PAS) method to compare the staining properties of the conjugates.

E. Precipitin Reactions of Antisera

The precipitin titers of the antisera are summarized in Table 22. Only a cross-reaction between *Absidia lichtheimii* and *Candida albicans* was observed.

F. Staining Properties of Conjugates to Cultured Materials

Table 23 shows the maximum dilution of each conjugate reacting with homo-

Table 22. Precipitin Titers of Antisera Against Homologous
and Heterologous Polysaccharide Antigens (100 γ/ml)

Antibody \ Antigen	C. albicans	Cr. neoformans	A. fumigatus	Abs. lichtheimii
C. albicans	1 : 256	—	—	—
Cr. neoformans	—	1 : 64	—	—
A. fumigatus	—	—	1 : 64	—
Abs. lichtheimii	1 : 8	—	—	1 : 64

Table 23. Staining Titers of Each Conjugate With Homologous
and Heterologous Fungi

Conjugate \ Antigen	C. albicans	Cr. neoformans	A. fumigatus	Abs. lichtheimii
C. albicans	1 : 256	1 : 1	—	—
Cr. neoformans	1 : 2	1 : 64	—	—
A. fumigatus	1 : 2	—	1 : 64	—
Abs. lichtheimii	1 : 4	—	—	1 : 8

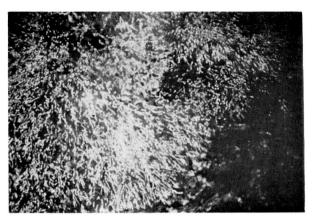

Fig. 56. Specific Fluorescence of *Aspergillus fumigatus* in the Necrotic Area of the Lung (human autopsy case)

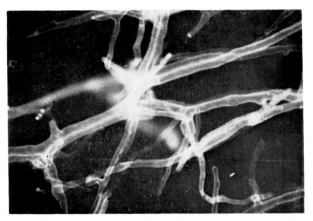

Fig. 57. Smear Preparation of *Absidia lichtheimii* Showing a Brilliant Fluorescence in the Cell Wall

Fig. 58. Smear Preparation of *Absidia lichtheimii*

logous and heterologous fungi. The cross-reactivity was completely eliminated by dilution and absorption.

There were no differences in the intensity of reaction with the four types of fixation. The cells of *Candida albicans* and *Cryptococcus neoformans* exhibited stronger specific fluorescence in the capsular region than in the somatic portion (Color Plate VII-3, 4, 5). The conidia, sterigma and vesicles of *Aspergillus fumigatus* were strongly stained, while specific fluorescence in the mycelia was strongly exhibited in the walls and septa, and sparsely in the somatic portions (Fig. 56). Similarly, the sporangiospores and sporangia of *Absidia lichtheimii* were strongly stained (Figs. 57, 58). The double staining method was applied to mixed smears of *Candida albicans* and *A. fumigatus* (Color Plate VII-6). It was found that the reagents reacted correspondingly to each element of the two organisms. Double staining of mixed smears of *Candida albicans* and other fungi was also successful.

The organisms showed different staining reactions at different stages of growth in culture. Cells cultured for 3–4 days were strongly stained. In cells cultured 5 days or more, however, the fluorescence decreased in intensity, and some of the cells were not stained at all. On the other hand, the fungus agents in the tissues were almost homogeneously stained, and in a large number of cases the intensity of fluorescence corresponded to that of organisms cultured for 3–4 days.

G. Staining Properties of Fungi in Autopsy Materials

The absorbed conjugates were applied to tissue sections. In frozen sections,

Table 24. Comparative Diagnosis of Fungus Infections in 30 Autopsy Cases from 1953 to 1962 at the Department of Pathology, Shinshu University and Niigata University

Diagnosis / Fungus Infections	Histopathological Diagnosis	Diagnosis by means of FA
Candidiasis	13 (3)*	11
Aspergillosis	8	12
Cryptococcosis	1	1
Mucormycosis	3	3
Cand.+Asper.	0	1
Cand.+Mucor.	1	1
Unidentified	4 (3)**	1
Total	30	30

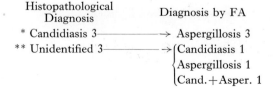

Histopathological Diagnosis   Diagnosis by FA

* Candidiasis 3 ——————→ Aspergillosis 3

** Unidentified 3 ——————→ ⎰Candidiasis 1

Aspergillosis 1

Cand.+Asper. 1

the organisms showed a bright fluorescence on a dark background of tissue elements, while in paraffin sections, the tissue structures were clearly indicated by autofluorescence in addition to the specific fluorescence of the fungal agents.

In experimental cases of mixed infections, double staining of tissue sections made it possible to differentiate between the organisms in the same area.

The staining properties of conjugates on the fungal agents in tissue were the same as with PAS stain. However, in some experimental cases of Aspergillosis, PAS-negative organisms were demonstrated by specific fluorescence.

In Table 24, the diagnosis of mycosis in autopsy materials determined by the fluorescent antibody technique is compared with that from histopathological findings. Three cases of Candidiasis were corrected to Aspergillosis and three unidentified cases were diagnosed as Candidiasis, Aspergillosis and Candidiasis +Aspergillosis by the FA technique.

Masao Hotchi

26. Toxoplasma

Tissue sections were prepared by the paraffin embedding technique of Sainte-Marie. Globulin fractions from pig sera with dye-test titers of 1: 16,000 and 1: 4,000 were labeled with fluorescein by the usual method.

Satisfactory staining was obtained with both labeled globulin solutions without any absorption procedure. The specificity of staining was ascertained by the one-step inhibition test of Goldman and the absorption test with TP cells.

A. Experimental Toxoplasmosis in Mice

Mice were infected with a virulent (RH) strain of Toxoplasma Gondii (TP). Organisms with characteristic shapes were brilliantly stained in the smear preparation of peritoneal exudates. Fluorescence was observed primarily at the obtuse end and in the peripheral area, but the central nuclear area was unstained (Fig. 59).

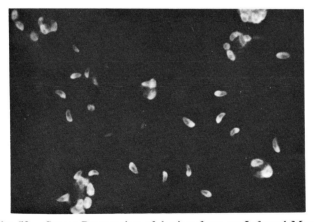

Fig. 59. Smear Preparation of Ascites from an Infected Mouse

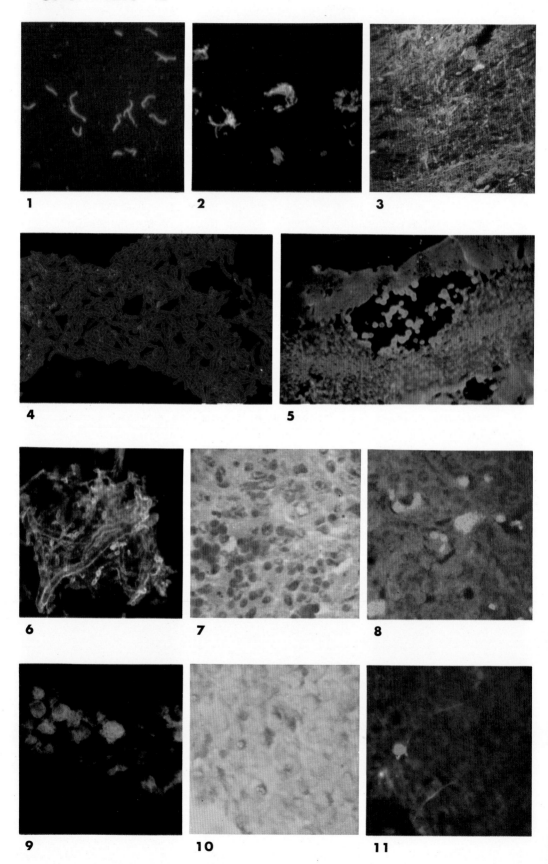

The organs of mice in the parastemic stage were examined. In liver section, organisms were observed mainly in an area surrounding the central vein, where the structure of the liver tissue had disintegrated. Normal structure was maintained in areas where organisms were abscent. The extent of lesion paralleled the number of proliferating organisms. Organisms were present in clusters in Kupffer's stellate cells (Fig. 60), endothelial cells of the central vein and hepatic cells.

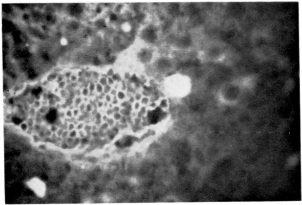

Fig. 60. Liver of an Infected Mouse

A cluster of organisms is found in the sinusoid near the central vein. The cell containing the cluster is a Kupffer stellate cell.

⇐

Explanation of Color Plate VII

VII–1. *Treponema pallidum* (Nicholus strain), stained with FTA positive serum by indirect method.

VII–2. Tyzzer's disease. Mouse brain inoculated intracerebrally. Specific fluorescence is shown to be localized within the cytoplasm of nerve cells.

VII–3. Specific fluorescence of *Candida albicans* in the mucosa of esophagus. Stained with rhodamine conjugate (human autopsy case).

VII–4. Smear preparation of *Candida albicans*. Stained with rhodamine conjugate. Specific fluorescence is found in the cell wall.

VII–5. Specific fluorescence of *Cryptococcus neoformans* in the brain of a mouse. Cellebrum showing typical cyst formation.

VII–6. Double staining of a mixed smear of *Candida albicans* (with rhodamine conjugate) and *Aspergillus fumigatus* (with FITC conjugate).

VII–7. Spleen of mouse infected with *Toxoplasma Gondii* (RH strain). H-E stain.

VII–8. The same field as No. 7. Clusters of organisms are found in a reticulum cell.

VII–9. Many toxoplasmas having a characteristic shape are found in the swollen axillar lymph node (human autopsy case).

VII–10. Human lymph node infected with toxoplasma. H-E stain.

VII–11. The same field as No. 10. The fluorescent round body is shown to correspond to an eosinophilic body residing in the lesion.

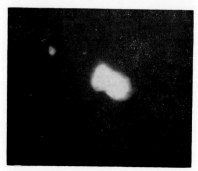

Fig. 61. Kidney of an Infected Mouse

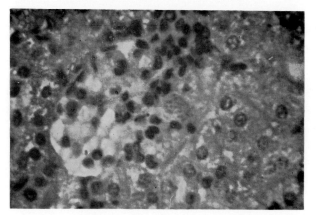

Fig. 62. The same field as in Fig. 61.
Restaining with H-E. A cell containing a cluster of organisms (arrow) exists in a glomerulus.

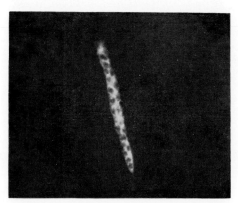

Fig. 63. Brain of a Mouse Infected with a Virulent Strain
A cerebral artery is obstructed by aggregated organisms.

Fig. 64.   Brain of a Mouse Infected with a Low Virulent Strain
Cysts are evenly fluorescent.

Cells containing clusters of organisms were frequently observed in the central vein and sinusoid of affected liver lobules.   In the spleen, organisms were evenly distributed in both red and white pulps.   Clusters of organisms were observed in a reticulum cell (Color Plate VII-7, 8).   In the lungs, many organisms were found in the epithelial cells of the alveoli and in the tissue surrounding the bronchioli.   Organisms were shown to proliferate in cells of the reticulo-endothelial system of the liver, spleen, lymph nodes and lungs.   In the kidney, organisms were not seen even at the end stage of acute infection, although cells containing clusters of organisms were occasionally found in the glomerulus (Figs. 61, 62).   These cells were hematogeneously transferred from other tissues in which proliferation of organisms occurred.   Organisms were not seen in the gray and white matters of the brain, although embolism due to aggregated organisms was found in a cerebral artery (Fig. 63).   In brain obtained from mice infected with a low virulent strain (Beverley strain), cysts were evenly fluorescent and the cyst wall was not distinct in paraffin sections (Fig. 64).

B. Human Lymphadenopathy in Toxoplasmosis

The recovery of TP from swollen lymphonodes is not always distinct evidence for diagnosis.   The detection of parasites in tissue histologically suspected of toxoplasmosis provides conclusive evidence for diagnosis.   In case No. 1,[1] the fluorescent round body was shown to correspond to an eosinophilic body residing in the lesion (Color Plate VII-10, 11).   It resembled closely the form described as " Eosinophiler Körper mit rosettenartiger Kleinkernen " by Roth and Piekarski, who suggested that it originated from clusters of organisms.   A group of scattered fluorescent granules of various sizes and brightness was found in the lesion (Fig. 65).   Most granules were smaller and fainter than TP.   Observation of the disintegrating process of killed organisms in mice proved that degraded organisms, morphologically unrecognizable as TP, remain stainable for some time with FA.*   Serologic tests showed that the rise in titer started three

*   Tsunematsu, Y., Shioiri, K. and Kusano, N.: Three cases of *Lymphadenopathia toxoplasmotica* with special reference to the application of fluorescent antibody technique for detection of toxoplasma in tissue, *Japan J. Exp. Med.*, **34**, 217–000, 1964.

Fig. 65.   Human Lymphnode.   Case No. 1
Fluorescent granular forms (arrow) are found in the lesion.

months before excision. The lymphnode of this case was excised at the convalescent stage when the organisms were disappearing. In case No. 2, many organisms having a characteristic shape were found in the swollen axillar lymphnode (Color Plate VII-9). The hemagglutination test was negative one month before excision and positive at 4,000-fold dilution at the time of excision. This case was examined at the acute stage of infection when the organisms were actively proliferating in lesions.

Kohei Shioiri-Nakano and Yukinori Tsunematsu

27. Systemic Lupus Erythematosus

A. Application of the Fluorescent Antibody Technique (FAT) in the Study of the LE Cell Phenomenon.

1) When the LE cell was stained directly with FITC labeled anti-human γ-globulin rabbit serum, only the inclusion body showed a homogeneous fluorescence, indicating that the inclusion body is bound with the human γ-globulin. The cell nucleus remained unstained (Fig. 66).

When stained directly or indirectly with antinuclear SLE serum, the nuclei of the original leucocytes were clearly fluorescent but the inclusion body showed a much weaker fluorescence (Fig. 67).

With acridine orange the nuclei of LE cells stained bright greenish-yellow and the inclusion bodies dark green (Color Plate VIII-1).

2) Indirect method of LE cell test: One aliquot of FITC labeled SLE serum γ-globulin, instead of unlabeled SLE serum used in the usual test method, was mixed with the same aliquot of normal sieved blood clot, centrifuged, and a blood smear rich in leucocytes was made. Microscopy using ultraviolet light revealed fluorescence of the leucocyte nuclei (Fig. 68). Thus, the antinuclear antibody in the SLE serum γ-globulin reacted specifically with injured nuclei in vitro to produce a free hematoxylin body (free LE inclusion body).

3) The role of complement in the formation of the LE cell is well known. In the procedure of the LE cell test, by the addition of complement inhibitor such

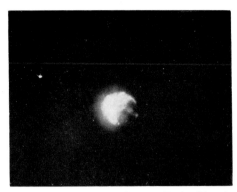

Fig. 66. Fluorescence of LE Cell Inclusion Body Showing Existence of γ-Globulin, Stained with FITC Conjugated Anti-human γ-Globulin Rabbit Serum

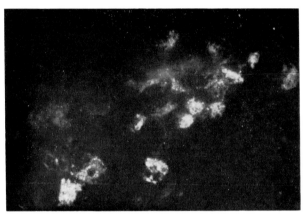

Fig. 67. Fluorescence of Leucocyte Cell Nuclei; Indirect LE Cell Test Using Normal Peripheral Leucocyte Mixed with FITC Conjugated LE Cell Factor

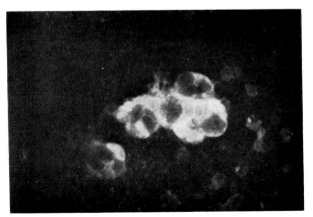

Fig. 68. Fluorescence of LE Cell Stained with Indirect FAT
Original leucocyte nuclei show bright fluorescence, but LE inclusion body remains dark.

as EDTA or heparin to the blood, LE cells decreased markedly in number, and in some cases no LE cell could be detected. However, these inhibitors did not disturb the fluorescent staining of nuclei in blood smear. The complement seems to act by stimulating leucocytes to phagocytize hematoxylin bodies formed extracellularly.

B. Characteristics of the Antinuclear Antibody of SLE

1) The antinuclear antibody has no organ and species specificity. Nuclear materials from all organs of human and animal sources can be used as antigen. The only exception is the head of matured spermatozoa, which shows no fluorescence when stained with anti-DNA-histone antibody (Color Plate VIII-2, Figs. 69, 70).

2) When HeLa cells are stained with anti-DNA-histone antibody, their nuclei stain homogeneously, and the chromosome in the mitotic phase is more brightly fluorescent. The chromosomes of the salivary gland of Drosophila show this even more clearly (Color Plate VIII-3, 4, Fig. 71).

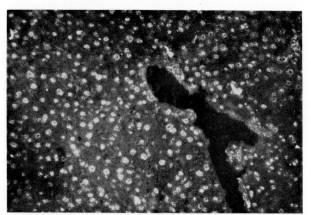

Fig. 69. Rat Liver Stained with Indirect FAT

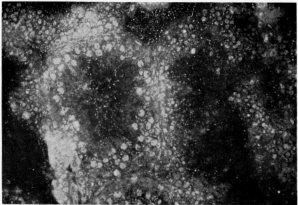

Fig. 70. Rat Testis Stained with Indirect FAT
No fluorescence can be seen at the head of matured spermatozoa.

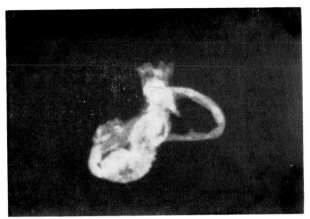

Fig. 71.   Fluorescence of the Chromosome of the Salivary Gland of Drosophila Stained with FITC Conjugated SLE Serum γ-Globulin

3)   After treatment of cell nuclei with some enzymes, e.g. papain, chymotrypsin, hyaluronidase and varidase, or chemicals, e.g. 2-mercaptoethanol, heparin and hydrochloric acid, which destroy the chemical structure of DNA-histone, no fluorescence could be observed.

4)   Using the fluorescent antibody technique, antinuclear antibodies of SLE

Table 25.   Methods for the Detection of Antinuclear Antibodies

1.	LE Cell Test
	Method Zimmer-Hargraves' Blood Clot Method
2.	Test for Antinuclear Factor (ANF) on Leucocytes (indirect fluorescent antibody technique)
	① Substrate Smear of peripheral blood of a normal donor
	② Fixation Fix with 95% ethanol for 5–10 minutes
	③ Conjugate 1 : 40 dilution of FITC conjugated rabbit anti-HGG antibody supplied from the Institute of Medical Science, Univ. of Tokyo
3.	LE Test (Hyland) (Latex-Nucleoprotein Agglutination Slide Test)
	Method : mix one drop of serum and one drop of Latex-nucleoprotein reagent on slide glass
4.	LE Conglutination Test (Latex-Nucleoprotein Conglutination Test)
	Method 0.1 ml of serum or its diluents in pH 7.5 veronal buffer (Ca^{++}, Mg^{++})
	+
	0.01 ml of Latex-nucleoprotein reagent
	+
	0.2 ml of fresh bovine serum
	Mix and keep for one or two hours at 37°C

Table 26.   Results of Serologic Methods for Detection of Antinuclear
Antibodies in SLE Patients

Method	No. tested	Positive	Per cent positive
LE Cell Test	107	70	65.5%
LE Test (Hyland)	107	45	42.0%
Immunofluorescent Technique	102	89	89.3%
LE Conglutination Test	75	40	53.3%

can be classified into several types according to the different components of
the nuclei which react as antigen.   These different types of antibodies all have
a characteristic fluorescence pattern of the nuclei—" homogeneous," " shaggy,"
"speckled" and "nucleolar."   The nucleolar pattern has no relation to antinuclear antibody.   The most characteristic antinuclear antibody of SLE is anti-
nucleoprotein antibody, which is responsible for the LE cell phenomenon, and
shows a homogeneous pattern.   The shaggy pattern corresponds to anti-DNA
antibody, and the speckled one is produced by antibody to the phosphate-
extractable antigen.   The homogeneous pattern is valuable for the detection of
antinuclear antibody, but the most specific one in the diagnosis of SLE is the
shaggy pattern.

C. The Significance of FAT in the Diagnosis of SLE

A comparison of FAT with other methods for the detection of antinuclear
antibody is summarized in Tables 25 and 26.   As shown in Table 26, FAT
revealed 89 positive out of 102 samples of SLE sera (89.3%) and was the most
sensitive of all methods tested.

Yasuo Katsuta

28. NEPHROTOXIC SERUM NEPHRITIS
——Intravenous Injection of FITC Labeled Nephrotoxic Antibody*

Nephrotoxic serum nephritis is induced by the injection of antisera prepared
against kidney tissue.   For example, rats develop renal damage when injected
with serum from rabbits immunized against rat kidney tissue.

Sites of localization, especially in the kidney, of injected nephrotoxic antiserum
have been the subject of many reports since the first report of Masugi in 1933.

---

*   Shibata, S., Nagasawa, T., Takuma, T., Naruse, T. and Miyakawa, Y.: *Japan J. Exp.
Med.*, **36**, 127, 1966.
    Shibata, S., Nagasawa, T., Takuma, T., Naruse, T., and Miyakawa, Y.: ibid., **36**,
143, 1966.
    Shibata, S., Nagasawa, T., Naruse, T., and Miyakawa, Y.:   ibid., **37**, 337, 1967.
    Shibata, S., Naruse, T., Nagasawa, T. and Miyakawa, Y.: *J. Immunol.* **99**, 454,
1967.

Pressman et al. demonstrated the fixation of nephrotoxic antiserum in the glomeruli using radio-iodinated nephrotoxic γ-globulin, but they could not identify
the exact site of the reaction within the glomeruli.   After the introduction by
Mellors and his co-workers of fluorescein-labeled antibodies as histochemical
agents for the detection of tissue localizing antibodies in vivo, this new method
was applied to define the sites of localization of nephrotoxic antiserum.   Ortega
and Mellors have confirmed the selective glomerular localization of nephrotoxic
antiserum in the rat kidney, indicating that it is primarily and perhaps exclusively in the membranes of the glomerular tufts.

The present report is mainly concerned with a new method for the demonstration of nephrotoxic antiserum in the glomeruli using FITC labeled nephrotoxic
γ-globulin, not as a histochemical agent, but as a tracer substance in vivo.

A. Materials and Methods

Preparation of Nephrotoxic Antisera: Male albino rabbits were injected
intraperitoneally with 5 ml of 10–20% saline suspension of rat renal cortical
tissue homogenate, twice a week for 8 weeks.   Ten days after the last injection,
the rabbits were bled from the carotid artery.

Each antiserum was tested for its ability to produce nephrotoxic serum nephritis and antisera which could produce typical changes (massive proteinuria and
characteristic histologic changes) after a single injection of 1.0 ml per rat were
pooled and used for the experiment.

Fluorescein Labeled Nephrotoxic γ-globulin: The nephrotoxic serum thus obtained was conjugated with FITC (Baltimore Biological Laboratories, Baltimore,
U.S.A.) according to the method of Kawamura et al.   Labeled antibody having a
fluorescein to protein molar ratio (F/P) of 1.27 and a γ-globulin content of
3.52 mg/ml was used.

Immunofluorescent Technique: Three different methods were used as shown
in the schema of Fig. 72.

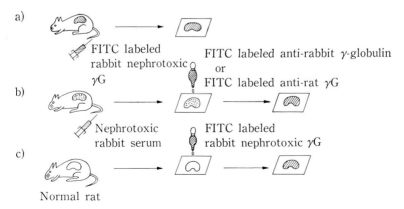

Fig. 72.   Three Different Immunofluorescent Methods for the Study of Rat
Nephrotoxic Serum Nephritis

a) Intravenous injection of FITC labeled nephrotoxic γ-globulin: Kidneys of rats which received an intravenous injection of FITC labeled nephrotoxic γ-globulin were frozen, cut at 4 μ on a cryostat, and examined unstained.
b) The method of Ortega and Mellors: Kidneys of rats which received an intravenous injection of non-labeled nephrotoxic antiserum were cut and stained with labeled anti-rabbit γ-globulin goat serum.
c) The method of Hill and Cruickshank: Acetone-fixed frozen sections of normal rat kidney were stained with FITC labeled nephrotoxic γ-globulin.

B. Results

The Ability of FITC Labeled Nephrotoxic γ-Globulin to Produce Nephrotoxic Serum Nephritis: Male albino rats weighing approximately 150 g. were injected with 1.0 ml of FITC labeled nephrotoxic γ-globulin intravenously. Urinary protein excretions were determined daily after injection and all rats were sacrificed on the 10th day.   As shown in Fig. 73, urinary protein developed within 24 hours after injection and a moderate to massive proteinuria persisted until the time of sacrifice in all rats tested.   Macroscopically, the kidneys were enlarged and their pale surfaces showed scattered petechial hemorrhages.   Histologic examinations of renal tissues showed typical changes of nephrotoxic serum nephritis (Fig. 74).

No toxic effects which might be attributable to the direct influence of FITC injection were observed in the rats injected, even though the amount injected was increased up to 2.0 ml.

Fluorescent Microscopic Findings of Three Different Methods:
a) Injection of labeled nephrotoxic serum—unstained section. In rats killed 20 minutes after injection, FITC labeled nephrotoxic γ-globulin was found as linear deposits on the glomerular basement membrane (Color Plate VIII-5). Nuclear, cytoplasmic or cellular localization was not observed.   No fluorescence was observed in the tubular cytoplasm and lumen.   A similar distribu-

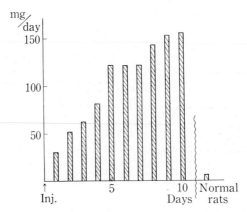

Fig. 73.   Daily Urinary Protein Excretion in Rats Injected with 1.0 ml of FITC Labeled Nephrotoxic γG

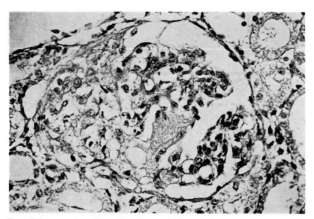

Fig. 74. Rat Glomerulus Sacrificed at 10 Days after the Intravenous Injection of FITC Labeled Nephrotoxic γ-Globulin
The picture shows typical changes of nephrotoxic serum nephritis (PAS stain).

tion of fluorescence was seen in rats killed at 24 hours after injection. Renal tissues from rats killed on the 10th day exhibited fluorescence in the moderately thickened basement membrane which had escaped the extensive destruction (Color Plate VIII-6). Although many protein casts were found in the tubular lumen, the fluorescence was seen neither in these protein casts nor in the tubular cytoplasm.

b) Injection of nephrotoxic serum—fluorescent staining of rabbit γ-globulin. Similar figures to those described above were obtained with this method. Compared to the findings obtained with method (a), however, the intensity of fluorescence was stronger, but the "ribbon-like" distribution of fluorescence along the basement membrane was not so clearly linear (Fig. 75).

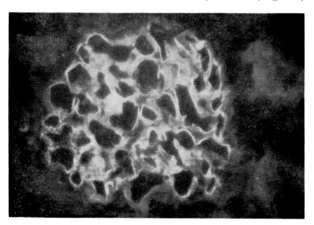

Fig. 75. Rat Glomerulus Sacrificed at 20 Minutes after the Intravenous Injection of Non-Labeled Nephrotoxic Antiserum
It was subjected to immunofluorescent staining with anti-rabbit γ-globulin.
The same distribution as in Fig. 74 is seen, but fluorescence is not so finely ribbonlike.

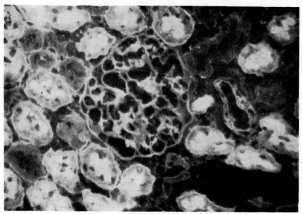

Fig. 76. Normal Rat Kidney Stained with FITC Labeled Nephrotoxic γ-globulin
Specific fluorescence is seen in the basement membrane of both glomerulus and tubule, Bowman's capsule, tubular cytoplasm, and media of small blood vessels.

c) Normal kidney—staining with labeled nephrotoxic serum. FITC labeled nephrotoxic γ-globulin reacted with the basement membrane, both glomerular and tubular, with Bowman's capsule, with cytoplasm of the tubules and with media of small arteries (Fig. 76).

C. Discussion

Fluorescein labeled anti-kidney serum has been used in vitro by Hill and Crickshank as an immunohistochemical reagent for the determination of antigenicity of normal kidney tissue (method c). However, no application has been made of this labeled antibody to the study of in vivo localization of nephrotoxic antiserum. In this paper, studies were undertaken to determine the exact site of localization of injected nephrotoxic antiserum in glomeruli by the use of intravenous injection of labeled γ-globulin of nephrotoxic antiserum (method a), although the site of renal localization of nephrotoxic antibodies has been repeatedly described (method b of immunofluorescence and other techniques). For our purposes; (1) preparation for a potent nephrotoxic antiserum, (2) labeling of γ-globulin of this antiserum with FITC without destroying its specific activity, and (3) an ideal conjugation of fluorescein with protein are essentially required. FITC labeled nephrotoxic γ-globulin thus obtained produced typical nephrotoxic serum nephritis within one day after the injection in all rats used, indicating that this FITC labeled antibody still retains an antibody activity as strong as non-labeled nephrotoxic antiserum. The results obtained from series of experiments using this new method showed that the injected nephrotoxic γ-globulin localizes in a fine linear form on the glomerular basement membrane. Neither localization in the contiguous epithelial and endothelial cells, nor in the tubular cytoplasm and basement membranes were observed.

This result seems to be the first direct evidence that injected nephrotoxic antiserum reacts only with the glomerular basement membrane in vivo. In other words, the proposition of Ortega and Mellors on the basis of their observations with method (b) that glomerular localizing antibodies were found primarily and exclusively in the membranes of capillary loops was for the first time substantiated by our experiment.

Moreover, the detection of nephrotoxic antiserum in the glomerular basement membrane by our method at the fulminant stage of nephritis (10 days after injection) indicates that the antiserum, once it reacts with the native antigen in the glomerular basement membrane, remains for a relatively long time and plays a significant role in the pathogenesis and progression of rat nephrotoxic serum nephritis.

When renal tissue was exposed in vitro to FITC labeled nephrotoxic γ-globulin, specific fluorescence appeared in the basement membrane and cytoplasm of the tubules and in the media of vessels as well as in the glomerulus.

Surprisingly, the same FITC labeled antibodies react with kidney tissue in a quite different way. This in vitro application should be used more widely, for example, for the detection of nephrotoxic antigens in other organs than the kidney.

D. Summary

By labeling the γ-globulin fraction of anti-rat kidney rabbit immune serum with FITC and injecting it into rats, it was found that anti-rat kidney serum localized specifically only on the glomerular basement membrane.

The significance of this fact and differences in three immunofluorescent methods used for the study of nephrotoxic serum nephritis were discussed.

Our new technique appears to be a very sensitive and specific method for detecting the accurate site of immune reaction in vivo and elucidating the pathogenetic mechanism of the disease process.

Toshihiko Nagasawa and Seiichi Shibata

29. Pulseless Disease*

Immunological studies in recent years revealed the following results:

(1) All patients with this disease showed a marked increase in E.S.R. (Erythrocyte Sedimentation Rate).

(2) Electrophoretic patterns of patients' sera showed increases in α_2-and γ-globulin.

(3) The C.R.P. was positive in 70% of the cases.

(4) The ASL-O, Rose-Waaler and serologic tests for syphilis were all negative.

---

* Sano, K. and Saito, I.: Immunological studies of pulseless disease, *Neurologia Medico-chirurgia*, **8**, 29–39, 1966.

(5)   The complement fixation test and various precipitin tests using patients' sera and extract of human aorta were negative.

Studies using FAT were performed to detect specific antigen in affected arteries which might react with the patients' sera.

Gamma globulin fractions from 6 patients and 2 normal adults were labeled with FITC and absorbed with acetone powder of human and mouse liver.

Affected obliterated carotis communis were obtained from 3 operated cases, frozen sectioned in a cryostat, fixed with 100% ethanol and stained at 37°C. for one hour.

Results: Sera from five of six patients showed positive staining of affected arteries.   The staining titer of these sera were almost equal compared to each other and to foreign arteries.   Fluorescent patches or granules were located (1) in the media where elastic fibers were severely fragmented and infiltrated with cells, (2) in the thickened wall of the vasa vasorum in the adventitia (Color Plate VIII-7) and (3) in the adventitia where cell infiltration was found (Color Plate VIII-7, 8).

Thrombosed intima, elastic fibers, and tissues in the unaffected parts of the affected artery showed no specific fluorescence.   The control unaffected arteries were negative.

The nature of these specific antigens remains to be clarified.

Isamu Saito

30. "UNWANTED" SPECIFIC FLUORESCENCE

In the course of studies using FAT, one occasionally encounters unexpected specific fluorescence, even when non-specific fluorescence is practically absent. This fluorescence is limited to definite structures, cells or tissues different from those against which the fluorescent antibody is prepared.   This occurs regardless of whether the source of tissues to be examined and the serum for fluorescent staining are from the same animal species or not.   The fluorescence is inhibited by unlabeled serum of the same origin as the intended specific fluorescence.

In some cases the cause of the "unwanted" fluorescence, i.e. the antigens which reacted with antibodies included in the fluorescent serum together with the intended antigen, could be clarified.   For example, bacterial flora common to several animal species, or pathogens causing spontaneous latent infection in one or all species, such as mycoplasms and HVJ, are known to cause frequently "unwanted" specific fluorescence.   However, in many cases the cause of "unwanted" specific fluorescence remains unclarified.

To differentiate "unwanted" specific fluorescence from the intended specific fluorescence several tests are useful:

a)   Test with control sera: When the sections of the same tissue are stained with control fluorescent sera of different origins containing the same antibody against the intended antigen with negative results, the fluorescence in question can be judged as " unwanted " specific.　In such a case the fluorescence is not inhibited by unlabeled negative serum.

b)　Test with control tissues :　When the same fluorescence appears in the control tissue, which is assumed to contain no intended antigen, it is judged as " unwanted " specific.

c)　Absorption of serum with antigen :　When the fluorescence appears to be stained with serum absorbed with antigen, it is judged as " unwanted " specific.

When the antigen to be detected is known, these tests are effective and the conclusion is certain, but when the antigen is unknown, as in the case, for example, of staining tissues with the patient's serum to detect auto antibody, the differentiation of " unwanted " specific fluorescence is very difficult.

Two examples of " unwanted " specific fluorescence which we encountered are demonstrated in Color Plates VIII-9 and 10.

Nobuo Kusano

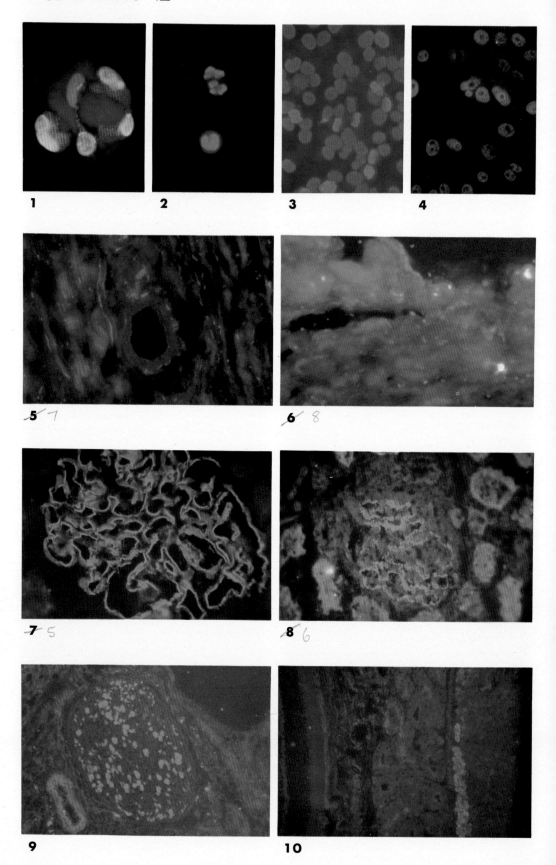

⇐

Explanation of Color Plate VIII

VIII–1. Fluorescence of LE cell stained with acridine orange. LE cell nuclei stain greenish yellow specific to DNA, but LE inclusion body is dark green.

VIII–2. " Homogeneous " fluorescence of human leucocyte nuclei due to DNA-histone antibody. Indirect FAT.

VIII–3. Fluorescence of HeLa cell nuclei. Chromosomes in mitotic phase are stained well. Stained with direct FAT by labeled SLE serum γ-globulin.

VIII–4. Fluorescence of HeLa cell nuclei stained with another type of SLE antinuclear serum. Chromosomes in mitotic phase remain unstained.

VIII–5. Rat glomerulus, 20 minutes after intravenous injection of FITC labeled nephrotoxic γ-globulin. Specific fluorescence is seen in finely linear (ribbon-like) form on the glomerular basement membrane.

VIII–6. Rat glomerulus 10 days after intravenous injection of FITC labeled nephrotoxic γ-globulin. Specific fluorescence is seen in the glomerular basement membrane which has escaped extensive destruction. Autofluorescence is seen in the tubular cytoplasm around the glomerulus.

VIII–7. *Arteria carotis* of patient stained with labeled γ-globulin of patient's own serum. The picture shows a vasa vasorum in adventitia. Several fluorescent spots are seen around thickened wall.

VIII–8. Adventitia of affected *a. carotis* stained with labeled γ-globulin from another patient.

VIII–9. Unwanted specific fluorescence. The cervical ganglion of DD strain of mouse stained with fluorescent anti-influenza chicken sera.

VIII–10. Unwanted specific fluorescence. The eye muscle of DD strain of mouse stained with anti-Japanese encephalitis rabbit sera.

INDEX

A

Abbe's test plate, 84, 85
Absidia lichtheimii, 177
absorption, 50
absorption procedure, 51
acetone-dried powder, 51
  of other organs, 8
achromat, 85
achromatic aplanatic condenser, 84
adeno virus, 94
adenovirus 12T antigen, 137
albumin fraction, 24
alum adjuvant, 18
annular condenser (toric condenser), 82
anti-C' serum, 22
anti-human complement reagents, 170
antinuclear antibody of SLE, 188
antiroller, 56
anti-γA chain reagents, 169
anti-γ chain antibody, 14
anti-γD reagents, 169
anti-γG chain reagents, 167
anti-γM chain reagent, 167
apochromat, 85
Aspergillus fumigatus, 176
autofluorescence, 9

B

Bordetella pertussis, 162
barrier filter, 75, 77
basket-type adaptor, 33
Bence Jones proteins, 21
Biogel, 30
bovine serum albumin (BSA), 16
bright-field microscopy, 75
bright-fluorescence microscopy, 76
broad-spectrum antiglobulin reagents, 170
buffered glycerol, 69, 77
BV barrier filter, 78
BV exciter filter, 78
BV system, 78

C

Candida albicans, 176
canine distemper virus, 119
carbonate-bicarbonate buffer, 38
cardioid condenser, 81, 82
CCl_4, 132
cellulose ion-exchangers, 26
complement, 16
complement method, 72
concentration, 32
condition of fixation, 61
conjugation of fluorescent dye, 23
counterstaining, 72
coxsackie viruses, 126
cryostat, 55
Cryptococcus neoformans, 176
cytomegalovirus, 100

D

DANS (1–dimethylamino-naphthalene-5-sulphonic acid), 34
dark-field condenser, 81
dark-field fluorescence microscopy, 75
DEAE cellulose, 23, 24, 27, 41
DEAE cellulose chromatography, 14
degree of saturation, 12
direct method, 66
double staining, 72, 177
dry-dark-field condenser, 76
dry powder method, 51

E

efficiency of fluorescence, 33
elvanol, 69
euglobulin, 25
excitation system, 77
exciter, 77
exciter filter, 75
exposure time, 86
extraneous specific fluorescence, 9
eyepieces, 85

F

fixation (pretreatment), 60
fluorescein isocyanate (FIC), 34
fluorescein isothiocyanate (FITC), 34, 35
fluorescence-free glass, 77
fluorescence photomicrography, 85
fluorescent dyes, 33
fluorescent treponemal antibody test, (FTA), 166
fluorochrome, 8
fluorochrome-fluorescence, 76
F/P molar ratio, 42, 47, 48, 50
freeze-substitution, 59
Freund's adjuvant, 17

G

gelatin cake, 147
gel filtration, 29
Geon 420, 26
globulin
    A-, 15
    G-, 11
    anti-γA, 21
    anti-γG, 21
    anti-γM, 21
    $\beta_{IA(G)}$-, 16
    β_{IC}-, 16
    β_{IE}-, 16
    γA-, 13
    γG-, 11, 13, 14
    γM-, 13, 15
globulin antiserum
    anti-γA, 14
    anti-γG, 14
    anti-γM, 15
gonorrhoea, 158

H

half-prism system, 86
herpes simplex virus 95
Hill and Cruickshank's method, 192
HJV (Sendai virus), 109
hog cholera virus, 122

I

image intensity, 87
immunizing antigen, 8

immunoelectrophoresis, 20, 21
immunogen, 11
impression preparations, 59
indirect method, 70
influenza virus (A_2, B), 104
interference filter, 75
intravenous injection
    FITC labeled nephrotoxic γ-globulin, 192
iso-pentane, 54

J

Japanese encephalitis virus, 132

L

labeling, 38
lamp housing, 80
liquid nitrogen, 54
lissamine rhodamine B 200, 37

M

measles virus, 115
mercury arc lamp, 77, 78
merthiolate solution, 126
method of fixation (pretreatment), 65
method of immunization, 17
moist chamber, 67
mounting medium, 69
mumps virus, 114
mycoplasma (PPLO), 164
mycotic infections, 176

N

N.A. (numerical aperture), 76, 81
Nephrotoxic serum Nephritis, 190
n-hexane, 54
nonspecific fluorescence, 9
numerical aperture (N.A.), 76, 81

O

objectives, 84
ordinary dark-field illumination, 75
Ortega and Mellor's method, 192

P

paraffin, 178
paraffin sections, 57
Pevikon C–870, 26
pneumococcal capsular polysaccharide, 7

poliomyelitis virus, 129
pox virus, 93
PPLO (mycoplasma), 164
preparation of Freund's adjuvant, 18
preparation of serum globulin, 11
preparation of tissue sections, 55
pretreatment (fixation), 60
pseudoglobulin fraction, 24
pulseless disease, 195
purification of antibody, 22
purification of γG-globulin, 23

Q

quantum efficiency, 76, 77
quantum recovery rate, 33

R

rabies virus, 123
reagents to anti-κ and anti-λ chains, 170
rinderpest virus, 120

S

salting out procedure, 13
saturated ammonium sulfate solution, 11
semi-apochromat, 85
Sendai virus, 9, 109
sensitivity, 7
Sephadex 30, 29, 40
shigella, 160
snap-freezing method, 54
specificity, 6
staining titer, 50
standardization of anti-globulin serum, 20
staphylococci, 154
Stock's law, 33
storage, 52
Sulphorhodamine B, 37
SW condenser, 82
swing-out prism type, 86
syphilis treponema, 166

systemic lupus erythematosus, 186

T

T antigen of polyoma virus, 143
T antigen of SV 40, 143
tetraethyl rhodamine compounds, 37
tetramethyl rhodamine, 36
tetramethylrhodamine isothiocyanate (for double staining), 177
tissue powder, 50
tissue sections, 54
tobacco mosaic virus, 146
toric condenser (annular condenser), 82
toric lens, 76
toxoplasma, 181
tsutsugamushi disease rickettsia, 151
tumor antigen, 137
Tyzzer's disease, 174

U

UG 5 filter, 78
UG 5 system, 78
" unwanted " specific fluorescence, 196
UV auxiliary filter, 77
UV barrier filter, 77
UV exciter filter, 77
UV meter, 80, 87
UV superwide dark-field condenser, 82
UV system, 77

V

varicella-zoster virus, 98

W

wet powder method, 52
Wood's filter, 77

X

xylene red B, 37

Z

zone electrophoresis, 25